Qualitative Methods for
Family Studies
& Human
Development

*This book is dedicated to all of the students who
have taken my Qualitative Methods class—you keep
reminding me of how much there is still to learn.*

Qualitative Methods for
Family Studies
& Human
Development

Kerry J. Daly
University of Guelph, Canada

SAGE Publications
Los Angeles · London · New Delhi · Singapore

For information:

Sage Publications, Inc.
2455 Teller Road
Thousand Oaks, California 91320
E-mail: order@sagepub.com

Sage Publications Ltd.
1 Oliver's Yard
55 City Road
London EC1Y 1SP
United Kingdom

Sage Publications India Pvt. Ltd.
B-42, Panchsheel Enclave
Post Box 4109
New Delhi 110 017 India

Printed in the United States of America

Library of Congress Cataloging-in-Publication Data

Daly, Kerry J.
Qualitative methods for family studies and human development / Kerry J. Daly.
    p. cm.
Includes bibliographical references and index.
ISBN-13: 978-1-4129-1402-4 (cloth)
ISBN-13: 978-1-4129-1403-1 (pbk.)
    1. Family—Research. 2. Family—Research—Methodology. I. Title.

HQ519.D35 2007
306.85072'3—dc22   2006028669

This book is printed on acid-free paper.

07 08 09 10 11 10 9 8 7 6 5 4 3 2 1

Acquiring Editor:	Cheri Dellelo
Editorial Assistant:	Anna Mesick
Production Editor:	Sarah Quesenberry
Marketing Manager:	Amberlyn M. Erzinger
Copy Editor:	Kristin Bergstad
Proofreader:	Kevin Gleason
Indexer:	Maria Sosnowski
Typesetter:	C&M Digitals (P) Ltd.

Contents

Preface

I have resisted writing this book for some time. After the release of the 1992 edited book, *Qualitative Methods in Family Research,* that I worked on with Jane Gilgun and Gerry Handel, there have been a number of opportunities to do a follow-up book. It always seemed like it was too much for one person to tackle. One of the reasons we did an edited book in the first place was to provide exemplars of the many possible ways of doing qualitative family research. Furthermore, as with many types of learning and knowledge acquisition, my confidence in what I knew in relation to qualitative methods seemed to diminish over time. The more I came to know the area, the more I came to an appreciation of the limits of my knowledge. Even though I have been practicing and teaching qualitative research for more than 20 years, I still struggle with whether I am doing it right. Qualitative research methods have always been complicated, but with the increasing variation in the types of methodologies that are emerging across disciplines, it has become even more difficult to keep pace with the proliferation of new epistemologies, methods, and ethical challenges.

My starting point for this book was uncertainty. In my own life, I have come to realize that there is little we can be certain of. In my efforts to study various aspects of this life qualitatively, I have come to the parallel conclusion that there is little I can be certain of when trying to understand complex and changeable human realities. This is never a comfortable state of being, for there is always a tension between the scientific pressure to find certainty and the human reality of unpredictability, contradiction, and complexity. This seems to be especially true when trying to understand developmental change and family dynamics.

As a result, writing a book from a standpoint of uncertainty and awareness of the limits of my knowledge was not a particularly enticing prospect. What I have come to realize in life and in the decision to write this book, however, is that staying with the uncertainty is the most important thing. As soon as I could embrace the idea that this book was primarily about offering choices in a complicated (and uncertain) landscape, I could begin to think about it as possible.

This book is about providing a range of options so that students and researchers can make choices about how to proceed with their own research. Therefore, I invite you, the reader, to join in the uncertainty. The book is not formulaic; it is not a recipe book for how to do it right. It is probably more in keeping with a style of cooking that I learned from my mother, who was raised on a farm in Tompkins, Saskatchewan. Most recipes were in her head, and when she was asked to communicate them, she would use phrases like "make sure it is a good cup of sugar"—meaning a heaping cup somewhat more akin to a cup and a quarter. This is cooking that involves judgment, discretion, and intuitive knowledge but within a tradition and a set of guidelines that ensures that the quality is repeated time and again.

In providing a range of alternatives in the book, I too have had to make choices about what to include and leave out. There are several key decisions that I made about the structure of the book. The first of these was to write from a conviction that qualitative research is part science and part art. While much of qualitative work that is done and published is a form of science, the quality of the product is shaped in large part by the extent to which researchers are able to bring imagination, creativity, and aesthetic practices to the endeavor. Hence, in writing the book, I have emphasized the importance of scientific learning and of following a set of practices agreed upon by the broader community of qualitative researchers. Equally, I have emphasized the importance of cultivating perceptual skills, of self-awareness, and of being creative in both the design and interpretation of our research.

The second choice I made was to try to balance epistemological issues with practical concerns. My decision to place a strong emphasis on paradigms and epistemology is reflective of the belief that how we think about human reality and our relationship as knowers of that reality profoundly influences how we make choices when we conduct our research. I am aware that not everyone shares this view and that there are many who would prefer a more pragmatic approach involving getting right to the design, data collection, and analysis parts of the book. In these parts of the book, I have tried to provide checklists, guiding questions, and examples from the literature in human development, family relations, and family therapy as a way of facilitating the concrete and practical decisions that are made in doing the research. For those who wish to use the book in a more practical way, it is possible to focus on these chapters. At the same time, however, there is no escape from some level of reflexivity and consideration of epistemological positioning, regardless of the methodology chosen. Hence, while questions of ontology and epistemology are concentrated in the early chapters, these issues are carried throughout the book. I have provided examples of how my own epistemological beliefs have changed over time. I think our epistemological beliefs are always somewhat unresolved, and while we may express allegiance to certain beliefs at a particular time, they are subject to review and fluctuation.

The third choice I made had to do with the scope and audience of this book. My intention was to tailor a qualitative methods book for those working in the areas of human development and family relationships. Here my own background and biases influenced the direction of the book. I was trained as a family sociologist with phenomenology and Chicago School symbolic interactionism as my theoretical home and grounded theory as my preferred methodology. Grounded theory thereby receives a lot of attention in this book. While at some level this is a reflection of my playing to my strong suit, I believe it is also a function of the strong presence that grounded theory has in the methodological literature. It has emerged as one of the most clearly articulated and commonly used qualitative approaches across a number of disciplines. Although most of my research has focused on understanding family processes and dynamics, I was deliberate in my efforts to include examples of studies and practices from life course research, couple and family therapy, and the broad domain of family studies.

Finally, I chose to focus the book on what I perceived to be the five methodologies most commonly used in the broad area of human development and family relations research. These include ethnography, phenomenological inquiry, grounded theory methodology, narrative inquiry, and critical inquiry. Again, not all would agree that these were the best choices, and I was aware of the methodologies that I did not include (e.g., discourse analysis, conversation analysis). In the book, I encourage researchers to position themselves within a particular methodology so their work can be assessed according to established practices in that area. That said, I am aware that the boundaries between any of these methodologies are often fuzzy and somewhat fluid, and as a result, researchers are often more comfortable straddling or borrowing from some of these traditions. This is due in part to the compatibilities among various approaches and a practice of "doing qualitative research" as if "qualitative research," at a general level, was the methodology. Because qualitative research methodologies proliferate, I believe there is merit in being clear about the methodological choices we make.

So I invite you now into a world of uncertainty. While we often associate uncertainty with anxiety, it is equally important to learn to embrace uncertainty as a way of staying open to the wonder of our changing world. Families are at the center of this changing world, and it is the stance of openness associated with inductive qualitative inquiry that puts us in a strategic position to understand and communicate about these changes.

Acknowledgments

Sage Publications gratefully acknowledges the contributions of the following reviewers:

Katherine R. Allen
Virginia Polytechnic Institute and State University

David C. Dollahite
Brigham Young University

Jerry Gale
University of Georgia

Jane Gilgun
University of Minnesota

Sandra L. Hofferth
University of Maryland

Kevin Roy
University of Maryland

1

Qualitative Research and the Art of Learning to See

When we do scientific research, we strive for reasoned explanation, representational accuracy, and certainty. When we do art, we strive for arousal, vividness, and interpretive creativity. When we do qualitative research, we do science and art.

Although we uphold a tradition of keeping art and science separate, my starting point for this book is that art and science are inseparable when we do qualitative research. The aim of this book is to open pathways for readers to become good qualitative researchers. In order to get there, I believe it is as important to be creative as it is to be analytical, to be passionate as well as reasoned, to feel as well as to think, and to arouse while offering explanation.

Most of my training as a graduate student, and indeed much of my subsequent reading about qualitative methods, has occurred within the scientific domain. Perhaps the long-standing identity crisis of qualitative research as being on the margins of science has resulted in a more deliberate effort to find legitimacy through the language of science. Learning about qualitative methods in the language of science, however, bypasses the cultivation of what I believe to be some of the most essential skills in being a successful qualitative researcher; skills that have to do with the senses, intuition, and the spirit of a person. Hence, my starting point is qualitative research as an artistic endeavor. It is not until people cultivate an awareness of their own aesthetic capability that they can then take full advantage of the procedures of science.

The focus of this book is on providing a set of systematic guidelines that can be used to conduct qualitative research on individuals and families. However, the effectiveness of these guidelines and methodological procedures is contingent on first learning how to perceive the world that is immediately before us. As a result, this first chapter focuses on perception and the use of our senses as being the most important skills to learn. Although I place an emphasis on the visual aspects of perception through use of the term *seeing* in this chapter, qualitative research must necessarily engage all of the senses. As Allen (2000) reminds us, our challenge as researchers is to come to our senses so that we can fully listen to the voices of individuals and families and expand our repertoires of knowledge generation to include emotional sensitivity, intuitive understanding, and reflective awareness.

Learning to See

The most beautiful thing we can experience is the mysterious. It is the source of all true art and science. He to whom this emotion is a stranger, who can no longer pause to wonder and stand in rapt awe, is as good as dead: his eyes are closed. (Albert Einstein, 1990)

Great poets, artists, and writers stand out because of what they were able to see. Great researchers stand out because of what they are able to see. The most important skill that we can cultivate when doing qualitative work is learning how to see. Learning to see involves the awakening of all our senses so that we become aware of sound, smell, movement, shape, and color.

When Annie Dillard (1974/1985) wrote her Pulitzer prize-winning book called *Pilgrim at Tinker Creek,* she instructed us about what it means to see. This is a book that celebrates the artful craft of rich description, where the smallest details of her colored environment are brought to life in the mind of the reader. She offers this description while sitting on a sycamore log bridge over Tinker Creek with the sunset at her back:

I was watching the shiners the size of minnows who were feeding over the muddy sand in skittery schools. Again and again, one first, then another, turned for a split second across the current and flash! The sun shot out from its silver side. I couldn't watch for it. It was always just happening somewhere else, and it drew my vision just as it disappeared: flash, like a sudden dazzle of the thinnest blade, a sparking over a dun and olive ground at chance intervals from every direction. (pp. 31–32)

When I read a passage like this, I am blissfully bestowed with the eyes of a child crouched on the shore gazing into the pool with an unencumbered awareness of flashing shapes and movements. My other senses also come alive—I feel the sun on my shoulder, the taste of the streamside air, and the sound of the breeze as it brushes the long grass. For me, the success of the writing is in the power of the passage to bring me into that world and out of mine. To be able to see the pond as she saw it, to be in that place without getting my feet muddy, was testimony to the power of the art.

Doris McCarthy has spent a lifetime learning to paint Canadian landscapes. Now in her 80s, she has cultivated the art of seeing her physical world. As she reflected on her career as an artist, seeing was central to her success. In an interview, she had this to say:

> I am very alert visually to what's going on, and I find that's why I am a landscape painter. . . . All I need is to be away from people, and I can sit down and take a look at a rock or a tree or a puddle and start to see it, translate it into paint. (*Globe and Mail,* February 23, 2002, p. R2).

For McCarthy, really being able to see involves capitalizing on her visual alertness followed by the deliberate effort to see her subject matter in a fuller and more focused manner.

James Joyce (1964), in his classic novel *The Portrait of the Artist as a Young Man,* through the voice of Stephen, the protagonist, talks about art as the "human disposition of sensible or intelligible matter for an esthetic end" (p. 211). The challenge, as he goes on to articulate, is to

> try slowly and humbly and constantly to express, to press out again, from the gross earth or what it brings forth, from sound and shape and colour which are prison gates of our soul, an image of the beauty we have come to understand. . . . (p. 211)

The intersection between art and the intellect is captured in the assertion by Stephen that truth and beauty are kin: "Truth is beheld by the intellect which is appeased by the most satisfying relations of the intelligible; beauty is beheld by the imagination which is appeased by the most satisfying relations of the sensible."

Learning to see is the foundation for becoming an effective qualitative researcher. When we "see," we make ourselves present and open fully our senses to the scene at hand. We see, we listen, we feel, and we seek to be attentive to the unfolding moment. As John Berger (1972) says in *Ways of*

Seeing, seeing comes before words and establishes our place in the surrounding world. It is an ongoing process wherein the relation between what we see and what we know is never settled (Berger, 1972).

The Paradox of Learning to See

At the heart of learning to see is a paradox between the deliberate cultivation of "seeing" (or listening) skills and the surrender of all effort to see in a particular manner. This a tension between the use of discipline to get us to a point of attentiveness and the release of mental effort, strategizing, and monitoring in order to see what is actually there. The paradox of learning to see is not unlike the paradox of learning to meditate. In order to be successful at the art of meditating, we must first commit ourselves to practice. Practice involves setting aside time on a regular basis, having a series of disciplined internal conversations about showing up, and then preparing our bodies in the physical space through the staging of sound, light, and the positioning of our body. Once we have prepared ourselves to meditate, the challenge shifts from the deliberate orchestration of conditions to the deliberate state of surrender that is required in order to be in the moment. We shift from controlling the conditions of our meditation to a position of pure observer. The challenge now is not to make the moment happen but to attend to the experience of the present as it unfolds. In meditation, we attend to our breathing and the sensations of our body. As thoughts arise, we watch them pass our horizon like clouds. Meditation is not so much about clearing the mind as it is about attending to the experience of living and breathing in the moment.

As qualitative researchers, we share the fundamental aim of attending to the experience of living. As social scientists, our goal is to serve in the process of understanding how life is. As students of human development and family relationships, we want to know about the fundamental processes of life: processes of change, how we relate to and are affected by our environments, and how we live in relationships. In order to accomplish this task and be able to communicate to others how life is and how it works, our primary challenge becomes how to be attentive to life as we encounter it. Like students of meditation, as researchers we must also commit ourselves to practice. It involves the discipline of learning how to observe, how to situate ourselves in order to see most effectively, and the commitment to return again and again to our observations in order to build confidence in our understandings. In the cradle of that discipline, however, we must learn to clear our minds and attend to the shapes, patterns, sounds, smells, and colors of our participants' worlds.

In the Zen tradition, they speak about the cultivation of the "beginner's mind." There are three important steps in the cultivation of the beginner's mind: attention, attention, and attention. In our everyday lives of making decisions, navigating complex work demands, and negotiating interpersonal relationships, we rely on complex minds that store information, solve problems, and strategize for efficiency of effort. Busy minds are essential for survival in complex social environments and, as a result, we spend most of our energy adapting to increasing complexity. A busy mind is the default setting in a complex culture. Attention in the busy mind is often compromised by preoccupation with plans, expectations, and decisions. To foster a "beginner's mind" is to learn how to see an experience for the first time unencumbered by past experiences or future expectations. It is to see reality as it is presented to us in the present.

In family therapy, therapists may be encouraged take a position of "not-knowing," which provides a useful parallel for how we approach participants in qualitative research settings. "Not knowing," like the beginner's mind, refers to the belief that the therapist does not have access to privileged information, can never fully understand another person, and always needs to learn more about what was, or what was not said (Anderson, 2005). It is about being humble, engaging in respectful listening, and letting the client lead. It does not mean, however, that the therapist (or the researcher!) knows nothing or asks nothing—but rather that the position taken is one of offering questions and speculations but in a manner that "portrays respect for, and openness to the other and to newness" (p. 503).

In order to be a good qualitative researcher, one of our most important challenges is to cultivate the beginner's mind and a stance of "not knowing" so that we can see the reality of the world as it emerges for the first time. Accordingly, there are three steps involved: attention, attention, and attention! Developing our attention is the precondition for the development of all other qualitative skills. If qualitative research finds its strength in discovery, then it is only by allowing ourselves to see reality anew that we can make a contribution to the ongoing discovery of everyday reality. Fortunately, as students of lived experience, we are presented with an endless supply of emerging realities.

To shift from the default setting of a complex mind to a beginner's mind is a significant challenge. Complex minds make it difficult to see for many reasons. Most significant among these is our own embeddedness in the experiential life world. In spite of our best efforts, whether they be preparing to meditate or to enter into a qualitative interview, we bring with us our habits, our learned social skills, and a set of personality characteristics that predispose us to act in certain ways. When we do field work of any kind, we may intend to fully attend to the experience that we are interested in understanding, but we must also accept our position as active agents in the interactive setting. We rely on our complex minds to negotiate these settings while at the same time seeking to attend to the reality of participants' experience as it unfolds. The paradox of learning to see means that we need to manage the tension between our predispositions to act in certain ways and our desire to attend to the newness of the situation.

Complex minds make it difficult to see because of our attachments to preferred ways of seeing the world. In the family therapy literature, for example, narrative approaches direct us to examine the way that dominant stories monopolize our ways of seeing ourselves and our relationships. We are attached to these stories and as a result, it becomes very difficult to see ourselves or others in any other way. Therapy can guide family members to construct new stories that help them to see their experience in a different light. Dominant stories hinder how we see because of our need to fit emerging reality into previously established patterns of perception. Learning to see the "new" means being mindful of the automatic desire to fit experience into our dominant stories. When we do observations as part of our research, we need to be mindful of how our own dominant stories and attachments to certain types of knowledge affect the way we see our participants' stories. As researchers, it is important to be attentive to how participants present the stories of their lives in ways that both fit within and fall outside of the dominant stories.

The familiarity of our social world also hinders our ability to observe the world anew. We carry with us frames of relevancy and familiarity that bring with them expectations for how reality will appear. I once had the experience of going to Northern Ontario in the autumn to see the trees change color. I was particularly keen to see all of the fall colors: bright reds, oranges, and yellows. On the day I arrived, I went for a walk in the forest and was startled by the fact that the dominant color I was seeing was green. We usually look for and see green in the spring. But up there, the wind had blown down most of the maple leaves and what stood out on the brown forest floor were beautiful green ferns. I found myself searching for orange because that's what I wanted to see, but surprisingly, I kept coming back to green. My experience of disappointment in relation to orange was balanced by an experience of surprise at seeing green. When we do qualitative research, surprises such as this are usually contingent on our ability to get beyond what we expect to see. In this light, I have learned to take experiences of surprise very seriously. Surprise serves as a corrective check on our tendency toward habituation. Surprise reminds us to pay attention and look closely.

In phenomenology, terms such as *taken-for-granted reality* and *typification* help us to understand how this works. Through development, we accumulate a stock of knowledge that gives everyday experience a measure of predictability. We begin to assume that experiences we anticipate in the future will be similar in character to experiences we have had in the past. Through this process of recurring and predictable life events, we begin to assume or "take for granted" that there will be continuity in everyday experience. Typification is the means by which we make our entry into the future secure: We are able to enter into the unfolding experience of everyday reality because of our knowledge of typical past events. Although the process of typification serves us as an essential means for "gearing into the everyday life world" (i.e., engaging in the predictability of everyday reality), it can also blind us to experiences that are rooted in very different typifications. bell hooks (1992), for example, talks about the way that whiteness is represented in the black imagination. Although there is a long tradition of white ethnographers describing and making assumptions about black culture, there is little in the written record that focuses on the way that blacks see white culture. As hooks describes these perceptions, it is quickly apparent that these are radically different typifications that are rooted in generational experiences of domination and colonialism and felt through a lingering experience of racist terror and anguish. When we do qualitative research, we want to understand the experience of the other but are caught in our own existential practice of trying to fit that experience into our own schemes of relevancy and typification. We are always limited by our own schemes of relevancy and typification. The key is to be aware of these limitations, to reflect on them as we endeavor to understand the other, and to know when these are of such a radically different nature that they surpass our ability to understand or see clearly.

Paradox of Control and Our Ability to See

Central to the paradox of learning to see is the paradox of control. Like meditation, learning to see in qualitative research means using strategies of deliberate control and strategies that allow for the release of control. Annie Dillard likens this tension to the experience of walking with and without a camera. Walking with a camera involves calculated, controlled measures associated with composition, light, and position. Walking without a camera, there is a submission to the "come what may" contingencies of the experience. In Dillard's (1972) own words, "my shutter opens, and the moment's light prints on my own silver gut" (p. 31). Without the camera, she becomes "above all, an unscrupulous observer" (p. 31). When we do qualitative research, we straddle this tension—at times working the camera to manipulate conditions and compose the shot; at other times, turning off the camera and being fully present to the vignette before us.

This tension of control is often apparent when we seek to conduct observation studies in public spaces. The challenges to the senses become quickly apparent. What family or families should I look at? What am I missing? How do I look at them and are they looking at me? How can I begin to separate sound from noise? These are tensions that straddle the need to control our frame of reference and yet open ourselves to the full complexity and sensual stimulation of the scene at hand.

Perhaps the greatest challenge is learning how to surrender control so that we can see more effectively. As qualitative social scientists striving for a respected methodology, we fill ourselves with anxieties about "doing it right." In contrast to the mathematical principles of statistical research, qualitative research is steeped in a tradition of guidelines rather than prescriptions, reflections on roles rather than rules, and the construction of anecdotes rather than answers. These practices make the accomplishment of certainty difficult and in spite of efforts to do it right, leave us as researchers with an unsettled edginess. In response to this lingering state of uncertainty, there are many strategies we use to try to increase control in our research practices. We have borrowed from the language of positivism to make our procedures "systematic" in order to ensure that our results are "robust." We reference the scientific literature to justify and legitimate what we do; we conduct audit trails (Lincoln & Guba, 1985) and have adopted the principles of reliability and validity in our work. We secretly uphold the model of the scientific researcher who is fully in control: "designing" the study, "manipulating" the data, and "drawing" conclusions. These efforts at increasing control may enhance the credibility of what we do, but they do not necessarily enhance our ability to see clearly the lived experience that lies before us.

> To empty one's mind of all thought and refill the void with a spirit greater than oneself is to extend the mind into a realm not accessible by the conventional processes of reason. (Hill, 1966)

Learning how to relinquish control as a way to enhance our ability to see does not mean that we throw out the social scientific practices that seek to enhance control. Rather, we use those practices of control as the basis upon which we juxtapose our efforts to release control. Like walking with a camera, we calculate when, where, and how we will take the picture; once we arrive, we need to set the camera aside to see more fully the possibilities that are present. Allowing ourselves to let go of control when we are at the active edge of data collection comes with both advantages and disadvantages. On the surface, the disadvantages may be more apparent: We are aware of feeling anxious about lack of structure (e.g., when we conduct interviews without preset questions), we may feel vulnerable as a result of being perceived as unprepared or unprofessional, and we may feel unsure about what we are discovering or what we will find next. On the other hand, there are many advantages to loosening control: We allow our eyes to open wide to unanticipated responses as well as anticipated ones; we leave open the possibility of discovering the right questions to ask, not just the questions we had prepared; and we have a better chance of allowing ourselves to go beyond our preconceived expectations about the nature of their experience.

The advantages of releasing control became apparent to me in research that I carried out on the meaning of providing care. Influenced by the work of Karen Davies (1994), I became aware of how we must think differently about clock time that aims at productivity and efficiency and care time that must be responsive to the unpredictable needs of others. We can control clock time through the use of schedules, calendars, and all manner of time management strategies; it is more difficult to control time when we are asked to respond to the rather sporadic needs of a child who gets sick at inopportune times or the desperate call in the middle of the night from a good friend who suffers from mental illness. Care time involves surrender to the immediate experience of the other and involves a loosening of control over our need to orchestrate our everyday temporal lives. When we do qualitative research, we must contend with this same dialectic between the use of strategies of control and strategies of responsiveness. Like clock time, our research designs provide a structure within which to work; like care time, we are called to pay attention to the unanticipated turns of our participants' stories.

Control is like a toggle switch that becomes part of our practice as qualitative researchers. Like the practice of meditation, or shifting between clock time and care time, maintaining and releasing control is a central dynamic in our effort to understand the experience of life around us. Our success rests in the energy of the paradox itself, not in the negation of one by the other. In keeping with this, it is important to differentiate this approach of toggling control from the emphasis that has been placed on tabula rasa in the qualitative tradition. For example, in some versions of grounded theory methodology, the ideal of approaching social reality with a blank mind is upheld. Specifically, literature reviews, accounts of theoretical influences, and reflections on experience are discouraged as contaminating influences on the clean receipt of our participants' experience. Although the suspension of preconceived ideas and influences is a laudable goal, it may be as impractical as expecting a calm and unfettered mind when we sit ourselves down to meditate. For those of us who have tried meditation, we know to expect trees full of chattering monkeys. The solution is to stay on the edge between control and releasing control: on the one hand, drawing on the principles of discipline to position ourselves by setting the research stage; on the other hand, resting confidently in our efforts to set the frame for our inquiry and loosening our control in order to see clearly. Rather than suspending preconceived ideas, we hold them in tension with our desire to open ourselves to the reality that is presented to us. Managing control in qualitative research involves holding in place the incompatible expectations of orchestration and surrender, discipline and presence.

Lessons From the Art World: Positioning Ourselves to See Fully

> As for art . . . it is an incomplete, never-ending narrative of human pains and disappointments, of the world as man experiences it . . . it unfolds intelligibly the narrative of the secrets of the world and of man. Each time in a different way it creates the world anew, making it accessible to our reason, our senses, our emotions. (Milovan Djilas, 1990)

Learning to be a qualitative researcher parallels very closely the process of learning to draw. When I encounter street artists who do caricatures, I usually pause to observe how effortlessly and quickly the artist is sketching the portrait. For those of us lacking in these skills, there is an appreciation for the competency that is being displayed. Strokes are confident and sure, and the character of the subject emerges in an expected but magical way. Like driving, reading, riding a bicycle, or shaving, there is an unthinking ease that accompanies the careful execution of tasks that are subsumed in each of these activities. In a book about learning how to draw, Edwards (1999) talks about the ability to draw as a "whole" or "global skill." When we get good at "it"—whether it be driving or drawing—all of the component skills become integrated into the smooth and automatic flow of the global skill. The hallmark of a global skill is that once you have integrated the component skills, you have this capability for life. Hence, once we learn to ride a bicycle, we can jump on a bike at any time in our life and the skills are there. With drawing, according to Edwards, once you have integrated the basic skills, you can draw, and you need not go on forever adding additional basic skills. Improving as an artist can involve the refinement of technique, but these are like small architectural details on the sound structure of the building.

Acquiring whole skills such as drawing or doing qualitative research comes with a number of pedagogical challenges. When I first learned to do qualitative research, the emphasis was placed on getting into the field as quickly as possible and then finding my way through readings and class discussions. At the time, I felt like I was being asked to drive on the freeway as a way to learn how to drive. It was anxiety provoking because I had neither the whole skill nor any of the component skills to feel competent or safe in this new endeavor. Pedagogically, it was sink or swim. Upon reflection, I did both. Two decades later, I feel that I have acquired the whole skill as the foundation for the qualitative work that I do. I don't remember when the whole skill came together, but I know it is there now. It wasn't a magical moment, but rather like the sedimentation of many granular moments both in the field and in my office staring down piles of transcripts. I have pondered many times about how I came to have this in order to understand how to teach others the global skill of qualitative research. My conclusion is that it occurs on two levels. First, immersion in the field, on-site puzzle-solving, making mistakes, building confidence by doing, managing research relationships, overcoming anxieties and fears—are all part of the practice of qualitative research. It is the same as learning to parallel park—positioning, going up the curb, and eventually the easy glide into the space like a foot into a sock. There is no shortcut to bringing the component parts together—marinate they must. Second, I believe that there are a number of important component skills that we can learn as a basis for doing qualitative research well. When learning to draw, for example, the global skill of drawing is achieved only when students learn how to perceive edges, perceive spaces, perceive relationships, and perceive lights and shadows. These are learnable and teachable skills that all focus on perception, or, how to see. Like drawing, perceptual skills are at the root of learning how to be a good qualitative researcher.

Drawing Informs Research:
The Cultivation of Perceptual Skills

The world of art provides us with a number of tools for enhancing our perceptual skills as qualitative researchers. These individual skills become important elements in the development of our whole skill as qualitative researchers.

Composition

Any photograph, painting, or sculpture begins with the process of composition. In the art world, the artist begins with a set of parameters determined by the format of the medium: the size of the canvas, the camera viewfinder, or the block out of which a sculpture is to be shaped. Within these parameters, the components of the subject matter must be placed. The artist distributes the shapes and spaces within the boundaries of the chosen medium. There are decisions about focus and emphasis, foregrounding and backgrounding, positive and negative spaces, and viewpoint. Using "L"-shaped fingers, the artist works through a series of critical decisions about the composition of the piece.

In qualitative research, we also begin with decisions about composition. When we set out to understand even the simplest phenomenon having to do with family relationships or human development, we are confronted with a complicated array of possibilities. Early on in my qualitative class, I send students on an assignment to observe families in public places. Using DeVault's observational work about families at the zoo as a template, I ask students to observe families in places where they might naturally be—in the food court, at religious services, or in the park. In our class discussions, there are two themes that students typically bring back for discussion: the first has to do with their feelings about being intrusive and the second has to do with questions about composition. Public spaces are visually complicated spaces when we shift from being in those spaces for our own purpose to being observers of those spaces. Students who have gone to the food court at the mall talk about their uncertainties about where to sit to get the best view, whether to focus on one family in front of them or the three families that are around them. They are unsure about whom to observe—all members of the family at once or one person who is carrying out a role. They are unsure about what to observe—talk, gender activity, physical interactions, or discipline. The challenge in these busy settings is differentiating important sounds from the noise.

These kinds of uncertainties are common when we do qualitative research. The social worlds we are seeking to understand are complex and filled with too much detail. In the same way that we cannot depict 360° panoramas on a flat canvas, we must be selective in what we can frame in our social observations. Stephen, from Joyce's novel, gives this direction for the artist:

In order to see that basket, said Stephen, your mind first of all separates the basket from the rest of the visible universe which is not the basket. The first phase of apprehension is a bounding line drawn about the object to be apprehended. An esthetic image is presented to us either in space or in time. What is audible is presented in time; what is visible is presented in space. But temporal or spatial, the esthetic image is first luminously apprehended as self-bounded *(sic)* and selfcontained *(sic)* upon the immeasurable background of space or time which is not it. You apprehend it as one thing. You see it as one whole. You apprehend its wholeness. (p. 216)

In phenomenology, *bracketing* is a term used to bring attention to a particular aspect of our conscious awareness. In our research, it is always necessary for us to be selective in our subject matter and to bracket a manageable subset of reality for our inquiry. Allowing the edges of our format to be too broad, we risk losing ourselves in the complexity; too narrow and we lose important information about context. Making decisions about where we draw the edge for our compositions is often accompanied by an anxiety about what we have excluded. If I focus my gaze here, I will miss what happens over there, which may be more interesting or more revealing to me in my inquiry. This is unavoidable, but rather than allowing that anxiety to steal energy from our attention, it is important to commit to a composition that holds promise for our inquiry.

There are many ways that we construct the composition of our work when doing qualitative research. Articulating a clear research question, giving a rationale for the focus we have chosen, locating our inquiry in existing knowledge and literature, and formulating questions to be asked are ways that we as researchers begin to compose edges, spaces, and shadows in our work. In photography, "depth of field" describes choices about the range of focus. When we focus a camera on an object to take a picture, the underlying optical phenomenon is called the circle of least confusion. The object of focus is the circle of least confusion, whereas objects that are out of focus on the film plane become increasingly large "circles of confusion." Depth of field is the term used to describe those circles of least confusion that appear to the human eye to be in focus. When we do qualitative research, finding the appropriate depth of field or range of focus is one of our first challenges. When faced with complex family realities and a wide range of compositional possibilities, we must compose the picture in order to locate on our film plane the circle of least confusion—a range of objects in focus that provides a basis for close scrutiny. Finding the appropriate depth of field is an important compositional strategy in qualitative research. In qualitative research, focus is often narrowed to understand the details of everyday living: how decisions are made, how relationships are managed, and how identities are constructed.

When we compose our research, it is important to be mindful of how we allow our attention to be drawn to certain kinds of experiences. We are drawn to experiences that we find interesting or important. Equally, we are likely to shift our attention away from topics that appear boring or mundane. Yet there are times when a focus on the mundane aspects may offer more insight into family dynamics than the features that "stand out." For example, in video analyses of family socialization practices, Kreppner (2005) talks about encountering the analytic barrier of "triviality": "during our earliest discussions of what we had observed in the families, we found ourselves trapped by our focus on exceptional events and our neglect of those behaviors we believed were self-evident and not interesting enough" (p. 80). It wasn't until they started focusing on the "trivial" that they began to see more fully the patterns of family interaction and communication.

Composition is a matter of selection that involves not only technical decisions about framing edges and spaces, but moral and aesthetic decisions that reflect values, interests, and preferences. In the Introduction to his book *Frame Analysis*, Goffman (1974) argues that in our effort to understand the organization of everyday experience, we need to concern ourselves not so much with what it is that a camera takes pictures of, but rather with the camera itself. In other words, it is not the nature of reality itself that is important, but the conditions under which we perceive reality. These are matters of selective attention, focus, and engagement with the subject matter.

Attending to the Subject Matter

One of the difficulties in learning to draw is that we bring a host of prior expectations to our subject matter. As a result, when we are asked to draw a picture of ourselves from memory, we usually produce a cartoon-like stick person with exaggerated ears and pokey hair. When we are asked to draw a picture of a farm scene without looking at one, we tend to produce a picture that reminds us of our Grade 3 efforts. Even when we are asked to reproduce a picture from an image, our drawings are confounded by prior frames of reference about how big heads should be or what hands look like. In order to understand how these prior frames of reference can actually interfere with our artistic abilities, one of the exercises that you can do is to draw a face from an upside down picture (Edwards, 1999). Remarkably, our reproductions are much more sophisticated. Instead of trying to reproduce a mouth, we are only trying to reproduce a series of lines and shadows. By drawing the face upside down, we are better able to get past our preconceived notions about what the face should look like. By making the familiar image unfamiliar by turning it upside down, we can see it more clearly.

When we do qualitative research, one of our biggest challenges is to position ourselves in a way that allows us to get beyond what we expect to see. For example, when I first started researching the meaning of family time, my way of seeing was strongly influenced by the dominant and now familiar story. It goes something like this: Women moved into the paid labor force in unprecedented numbers; men continued to work full-time; patterns of consumption grew, accompanied by a pattern of overwork to sustain these consumer needs; levels of work—family conflict grew; "time famine" in families was the result. My inquiry was thereby shaped by this preoccupation with the need for family members to have more time with each other. Family time was the Holy Grail in the work—family literature. With two young children at home, I was feeling the time crunch in my own family. Accordingly, my goal was to try to understand how this was experienced and with what kinds of consequences. Throughout, my underlying orientation was to understand families as victimized in some way by these powerful forces. Along the way, several sources of information arose that made me sit up and pay more attention to what people were saying. The first of these was the release of Arlie Hochschild's (1997) book *The Time Bind* where she reported that a significant number of women in her sample sought refuge from the work—family stress not at home having more family time, but by having time with calm and reasonable colleagues at work. The second piece of information that reminded me that I needed to pay more attention was the emerging finding from international time diary studies that parents were actually increasing the amount of time they were spending with their children over the previous decade, not decreasing. Both of these results run counter to the dominant story. As I tried to make sense of my data about family time, I had to reorient myself to a different attentiveness to the participants' stories. One of the strongest themes to emerge in my own data was the degree to which children shaped and controlled the experience of family time. Although the dominant story focused on the problems of family time for parents, the descriptions that I was hearing were focused on this as a problem for children. Family time was in the service of children, often in response to the wishes of children and usually involving child centered activities (for more on this see Daly, 2001). In light of these discoveries, it made sense that parents were spending more time with their children, and it also made sense that they might wish to escape from under the weight of responsibilities of their children by spending more time at work.

In order to see clearly the stories that are being presented to us (as opposed to the stories we expect to hear), it is sometimes necessary to turn them upside down so that we might see the story lines more clearly. Learning that parents were spending more time with their children turned the dominant story on its head. With it upside down, the lines become more apparent and the path of discovery opens up.

Representation

In both art and science, representation is the symbolic means by which we portray aspects of reality. Poets use verse, sculptors use marble or clay, and scientists use papers and monographs to communicate symbolically their interpretations of physical and social reality. Representation is the means by which we make sense of the world and communicate those understandings to our audiences.

In qualitative research, representation is ultimately a matter of verbalization of what we see. When we seek to represent reality to others, we must provide commentary on that which we are seeing. Although our first responsibility is to attend to the reality at hand in order to see it clearly, it must be followed by a description in words. We use words to articulate where our attention has been drawn. We use words to be selective in the aspects of reality that we can fully attend to. We verbalize what we see in order to construct a plausible explanation of what is going on.

Generating substantive theory or creating an ethnographic account is a verbalization of what we see. It is a commentary designed to communicate with our audiences the way we have seen reality. Representation in art can take many forms. There are those who strive for accuracy and seek to provide detailed and realistic images of reality; those who wish to provide impressionistic portrayals of reality through the use of color, mood, and light; and those who portray what they have seen through abstract representations of reality. Similarly, in qualitative research there are those who strive to be true to the reality at hand and offer precise ethnographic accounts; those who are deliberate about offering interpretative accounts of that reality by offering their own impressions and responses to the reality they have seen; and those who through their creative commentaries of reality seek to provoke, challenge, and arouse in a more abstract way. The forms of representation are many, and we will examine these in more detail in Chapter 2 where we discuss the ways that different paradigm assumptions influence the forms of representation.

It was Lord Alfred Korzybski, one of the originators of the discipline of General Semantics, who first warned about the dangers of confusing the map and the territory. When we do provide representation as artists or social scientists, we are cartographers who seek to provide guides to reality.

Even when our aim is to represent that reality as accurately as possible, we are still offering symbolic constructions of that reality. Our explanations are second-order stories—our created stories of the stories that we see and hear—once removed from the lived experience of our participants.

Learning to see and being successful in communicating what we see are foundational skills for both artists and social scientists. While we may have gifts in our personal abilities, our success is more likely contingent on our effort to cultivate these skills over time. Furthermore, perception and seeing are never "neutral" acts that result in some kind of straightforward representation. Rather, seeing and perception are always shaped by past experience, current values and beliefs, and future goals and expectations. In this regard, it is important, too, to recognize that both art and science are not activities that occur only within the individual, but rather are shaped by cultural preferences, priorities, and meanings.

In the next chapter, I turn attention to the importance of our beliefs about the acquisition of knowledge as the basis for moving forward with our research inquiry. Beliefs about what constitutes "good art" or beliefs about the "right way" to do science are embedded in cultural values and community practices. Although there is no one right way to do qualitative research, it is important to pay attention to the broader context of values and practices that can shape the way we design our research studies.

Science, like art, takes many forms, and in thinking about qualitative research as a scientific endeavor, it is important to begin with the diversity of science. These are uncertain times for science! Where once we may have thought of science as having only one form that included theoretical propositions, hypothesis testing, and the rigorous gathering of evidence, it now takes a variety of forms that are shaped by a variety of beliefs and practices. Epistemology is at the root of these different scientific practices and it is to this concern that attention now turns.

2

Epistemological Considerations in Qualitative Research

"Don't bog me down with this philosophy of
science stuff! I just want to get on with the project!"

Reflexive note: One of the tensions I am experiencing in writing this book is trying to pay attention to broad philosophical issues about knowledge acquisition and, on the other hand, being very practical and offering readers some ideas about how to do the nitty-gritty work of qualitative research. I imagine that what many people in my audience most want from a textbook like this is to see a set of steps that would allow them to get the work done, and to be able to reference an authoritative text that offers a sound rationale for various methodological procedures. I myself have sought out such texts with the idea that I could carry out the empirical project unambiguously and somewhat formulaically. My experience of doing qualitative research tells me that this is not really possible. What routinely sabotages this quest for simplicity (as in life itself) is the unavoidable emergence of a set of more complex questions about how I have come to see the research question as being important, how to reconcile any number of perspectives on the issue, my own beliefs about the issue, and an awareness that there are many ways that I could proceed in trying to find out more about the issue.

(Continued)

(Continued)

> Given these tensions, I think that learning to do qualitative research is like walking over a bridge with no railings. There is a pathway forward but there is also a feeling that, given some of the complex epistemological challenges, one could easily lose balance and fall over the side. Staying on the path means finding a balance that involves learning from the methodological literature how to do it while at the same time being vigilant to the broader questions about scientific beliefs and epistemological positioning.[1]
>
> I believe very strongly that to be an effective qualitative researcher, you need to be able to find your own sense of balance as you walk the bridge, and this can come only from reflexive scrutiny of your own scientific beliefs and preferences. I am aware—prompted in large part by one of the reviewers of an unpublished version of this book—that this belief in the importance of epistemology is in itself reflective of my own epistemological positioning. In other words, my belief that ongoing subjective reflection on epistemology is necessary to the qualitative enterprise is indicative of my own values and preferences about how to do science. Furthermore, I put epistemology first because I believe that it is important to make choices and to gain some clarity about positioning oneself epistemologically before developing a research strategy. Not all would agree and some would argue (as another reviewer did) that it is only by doing the research that we can come to an understanding of our epistemological positioning. As I reflect on my own experience of doing research, I agree with this as another path because my epistemological thoughts are often shifting and I do see my position differently as I encounter different research situations. Nevertheless, I remain committed to the idea that it is important to struggle with these complex epistemological options at the outset of our research.
>
> Accordingly, the next few chapters do not offer simple strategies for how to carry out a qualitative research project but, rather, are intended to serve as a means to find your own sense of balance and focus as you make your way across the bridge.

When we set our sights on learning how to do qualitative research, we are usually guided by a pragmatic motive. We have a thesis or dissertation to do, a question we want answered, or a funded research project to carry out. Accordingly, we articulate a set of learning objectives that will give us the skills, procedures, and guidelines for successfully carrying out our project. Our primary concern is with learning "the method" so we can systematically move our way through the processes of design, data collection, and analysis. Indeed, this book is designed to accomplish such a task.

Before attending to the practical features of our research design, however, it is first necessary to consider at a more foundational level how we think about the process of manufacturing knowledge. These are matters of epistemology that have to do with our assumptions about the nature of knowledge itself. When we ask about epistemology, we raise questions about what is knowable, how we can come to have knowledge, and what relationship we have (as researchers) with that which we are trying to grasp. I think of epistemological considerations as the first principles that underlie the research process. These principles are matters of belief and values that shape the claims we seek to make in carrying out the practical aspects of our research. If we can start by being clear about our first principles, or our assumptions about what is knowable, there is a better probability that we can be clear about the character, strengths, and limitations of our research products.

There are a number of reasons why it is important to pay attention to epistemology before we carry out the practical aspects of our research. The first of these has to do with carrying out our work with a sense of integrity. Integrity is characterized by the qualities of soundness and consistency among values, beliefs, and methodological strategies. To strive for integrity is not only a matter of upholding the character of the researcher, but also a matter of ensuring the quality of the research product. The second is a practical concern that has to do with defending the integrity of our work. Qualitative researchers seeking to publish their work often encounter epistemological crossovers in the evaluations of their work (e.g., references are made that the research is "soft" or "impressionistic"; see Ambert, Adler, Adler, & Detzner, 1995). Even though the research may have been rooted in a set of social constructionist epistemological assumptions, it is critiqued on the basis of a set of objectivist assumptions rooted in a more positivist orientation to science. Being able to articulate and defend the relationship between our epistemological assumptions and our research strategies is critical to the defense and, ultimately, the sharing of our acquired knowledge through the publication of our work. The third reason epistemology is important is that it serves as a catalyst to bring values to the foreground of the scientific endeavor. One of the beneficial by-products of the postmodern science wars is that we have come to understand that science, like all other cultural endeavors, involves specific values, political agendas, and competition for resources. Taking time to reflect on epistemology serves to clarify how we are thinking about fundamental scientific terms like data, objectivity, and rigor.

If epistemology is about values, beliefs, and first principles, then procedures we develop in any scientific project cascade from this source. We can think about the process of shaping a research project like a cascading stream.

As indicated in Figure 2.1, epistemology is the source that ultimately gives direction to the path of inquiry. The second level of the cascade is to consider the way that scientific paradigms steer the course of the flow. Third, assumptions and concepts from theories give direction to the movement of ideas. At the fourth level, methodology outlines the procedural assumptions as they are determined by epistemology, paradigms, and theory. Methods are the most specific and tangible level of the cascade and refer to the techniques we use in data collection. The stream ultimately spills into a collected pool that we can think of as the data that come together as a result of this process.

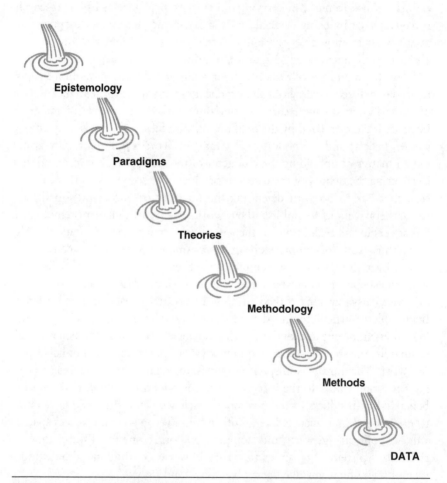

Figure 2.1   The Cascade of Knowing: From Epistemology to the
Collection of Data

Source: From Crotty, Michael, *The Foundations of Social Research: Meaning and Perspective in the Research*, copyright © 1998. Adapted with permission of Sage Publications, Inc.

This cascading process is one of making a series of successive decisions that starts with the articulation of broad philosophical assumptions about the nature of knowledge to a set of specific decisions about data-gathering techniques and procedures. As a result there are many paths that are possible, depending on choice of epistemological positioning, paradigm assumptions, preferred theories, methodological approaches, and specific methods techniques. Cascading our research process from the broad philosophical assumptions about knowing to the specific findings rooted in data segments is a way of achieving integrity in our research. Here are some of the questions and considerations that would come into play in this process.

Epistemology

Epistemology raises the fundamental question of science, which is how do we, as inquirers, come to know the realities that we are trying to apprehend? Essentially there are two positions here with many variants on each. The first position is objectivist which is rooted in the belief that there is a concrete, knowable reality that exists independently of our thought processes. According to this view, the task of science is to explain how this external reality works. This is not a process of creating knowledge as much as it is a process of discovering the patterned reality that exists in the world. There is a belief that with a sustained, replicative, and accumulative scientific effort, we can come to understand that reality according to a set of law-like predictions. We generate facts about this reality as a reflection of our belief in certainty and the pursuit of truth. An objectivist epistemology thereby rests on the separation between the knower and the known: the scientist is expected to explain reality without influencing it. As Guba and Lincoln (1994) have phrased it, this is science through a one-way mirror where the values and biases of the inquiry are prevented from influencing the outcomes of the research.

The second epistemological position is subjectivism. According to this position, there can be no separation between the knower and the known because all knowledge is constructed through a meaning making process in the mind of the knower. Accordingly, there can be no objectivity as the inquirer is always shaping the direction and outcome of the inquiry. In the subjectivist epistemology, "bias" is a meaningless term as all products of inquiry necessarily include the values, preferences and understandings of the inquirer. Rather than seeing the products of this work as enduring, predictive facts, there is an understanding that our explanations of social reality are created in the minds of the observer. A subjectivist epistemology does not necessarily imply the impossibility of knowledge. However, the nature of knowledge takes on a decidedly different character: rather than pursuing the ideals of accuracy and certainty, it accepts that knowledge is subject to differing viewpoints and explanations, subject to the interpretations of different value standpoints and subject to revision as a result of changing conditions and circumstances.

These two epistemological positions have given rise to many philosophical debates with the result being that there are many ways to conceptualize the relationship between the two. The first is to think of these two positions as separate categories that are incommensurable. Hence, to take an objectivist standpoint is to assert a commitment to seeing reality as it is that does not allow for any recognition of subjectivity. Conversely, to uphold a subjectivist viewpoint is to give precedence to the construction of meaning as it occurs in the mind of the inquirer. According to the incommensurability argument, these are incompatible positions that cannot logically be held simultaneously: either you believe that knowledge is created in the mind (subjectivism) or instrumentally discovered in the world out there (objectivism).

Another way to conceptualize this relationship, however, is to consider these two positions on a continuum. At one end of the continuum, subjectivism can be thought of as highly individualized, idiosyncratic perceptions of reality. At this pole, individual constructions of meaning need not have any correspondence with an objective reality. The only reality that does exist is the self, and the only knowable reality is the one that we carry in our minds. At the other end of the continuum, objectivism holds to the position that it is entirely possible to apprehend reality without the contaminating effects of perspective or interpretation. It is rooted in a belief that observation can be pure: that reality can and does present itself to us and, as inquirers, our role is to "re-present" that reality in a way that maintains its natural integrity without interference from us.

Between these two ends of the continuum, there are many possibilities that allow for gradients of subjectivity and objectivity. Indeed, few social scientists hold to these extreme positions. For example, some researchers might see themselves as being committed to an objectivist standpoint by maintaining their efforts to understand a patterned reality, but they acknowledge that their chosen focus, theoretical perspectives, and interpretations play a role in determining how that reality is explained and represented. We have used the term *postpositivist* to describe this position. Social constructionists would likely see themselves as having more of a subjectivist epistemology but by virtue of their belief that there are shared meanings that can be understood and known, they also hold to aspects of an objectivist epistemology (i.e., shared meanings are a form of objective reality). Other social constructionists would put the emphasis on knowledge as a coconstructed endeavor whereby the subjective meanings and experiences of the participants are brought into a dialogical process involving an interplay between the researcher's subjectivity and the participants' subjectivity. The constructed outcome thereby includes multiple subjective experiences (including the researcher's) and the presentation of a patterned reality consisting of shared meanings that at least hints at the presence of an objectively available external reality. Whereas the incommensurability argument emphasizes the incompatibility of objectivism and subjectivism, a continuum model emphasizes these positions as matters of degree.

Greer (1969) articulates a pragmatic epistemology that falls somewhere in the middle of this continuum. He argues that social science research rests upon three fundamental assumptions: (1) that there is a world that exists beyond our senses that is knowable and that we do not fully control (objectivist but subject to our selective inquiry); (2) that this world beyond our senses is knowable through a process of communication (interactive and constructed through subjective standpoints); and (3) that we value knowing the results of our interaction (subjective) with that world (objective), and thus the value of accumulating knowledge about that world.

Subsumed under the question of how we come to know reality is a question about the nature of the reality that we seek to understand. Questions about the nature of reality itself are questions of ontology. Although ontological issues are addressed directly in Chapter 4, it is necessary to clarify briefly their meaning and importance in relation to epistemology. The distinction between ontology and epistemology is most apparent in the objectivist standpoint. Given the separation between the knower and the known, we uphold a dualistic viewpoint that makes and maintains a distinction between what goes on in the mind and external reality. That which is to be known is always outside of the inquirer's mind, and as a result, we can differentiate what is externally real (ontology) from the relationship the scientist has with that reality (epistemology). Conversely, ontology and epistemology collapse in on one another when reality is constructed in the mind of the knower. Without an external knowable reality, there is no ontology separate from epistemology because reality is in the mind of the knower. Epistemology becomes paramount when the relationship between the knower and the known is embodied in the scientist.

Although we tend to think of qualitative research corresponding with a subjectivist epistemology and quantitative research corresponding with an objectivist epistemology, it is evident that both quantitative and qualitative approaches can span this full spectrum of epistemologies (for an example of how quantitative research spans these epistemologies, see Alan Acock's discussion of myths in quantitative research in Bengston, Acock, Allen, Dilworth-Anderson, & Klein, 2005, p. 10). In qualitative research, auto-ethnography takes the experience of the inquirer's self as the subject matter and presents this as the product of inquiry. Ellis and Bochner (2003), for example, provide an overview of approaches in qualitative inquiry that place a strong emphasis on the subjectivist voice of the researcher. They begin the article by presenting their own reflexive dialogue about writing the article and go on to describe a variety of approaches used in the literature including personal stories and narrative accounts, reflexive ethnographies and experiential accounts. Other qualitative researchers use a variety of objectivist practices that are designed to capture the essence of objective reality without unnecessarily influencing it. For example, many qualitative researchers uphold the credo "letting the data speak." This implies many things: that data are real outside of the lived experience of their originators; that data have agency; and that data have an independent reality that can be understood if we listen closely enough. These are essentially objectivist assumptions. As qualitative researchers, we also uphold an objectivist position when we use strategies such as interrater reliability. Having several researchers interpret the data according to a constructed coding scheme puts an emphasis on arriving at the "correct" or accurate interpretation of data. Underlying this practice is a belief that the reality we are trying to understand is knowable, separate from us and governed by "real" patterns and principles. This is qualitative research using an objectivist epistemology.

Reflecting on our epistemological positioning is an ongoing project. As the source for our model of cascading inquiry, questions of epistemology provide a means for examining our foundational beliefs about what we can know and how we can know it. Paradigms, the next level in our cascade, provide more specific information that allows us to situate ourselves in a set of scientific belief systems.

Paradigms

Paradigms serve as a means to understand different types of scientific activity and belief. Thomas Kuhn, a historian and a philosopher of science, popularized the term *paradigm* in his landmark work of 1962—*The Structure of Scientific Revolutions*. Kuhn was interested in the process of change in science and was particularly concerned with examining moments of dramatic turn in beliefs, practices, and results. In an examination of Kuhn's work, Masterman (1970) offered insight into the complex meanings of the term paradigm. Although she identifies 21 separate definitions of paradigm in the book, she argued that Kuhn uses the term in at least three different ways: (1) beliefs, (2) habits, and (3) tools. Most important, paradigm refers to a set of beliefs. These are shared beliefs within a community of scientists about what science is and what it is not (e.g., between science and superstition); beliefs about what constitutes appropriate and legitimate scientific procedures; standards of achievement; and most simply, a collective way of seeing based on shared organizing principles governing perception itself. A second meaning of paradigm is that it refers to a set of scientific habits and recognized achievements. In the course of carrying out "normal puzzle-solving activity," scientists operate within a common, taken-for-granted frame of reference. They work with inherited concepts, theories, and methods—prior scientific achievements—that keep their focus on addressing puzzles and away from challenging these habitual patterns. The third and final meaning of paradigms is that they are "tools." Within any paradigm, there are instruments and tools that are commonly used in the puzzle-solving activity. These include specialized language and concepts, conventions about analysis and interpretation, and most tangibly, books about theory and methods that offer concrete guidelines for the work that is to be done. Beliefs, habits, and tools are all important for understanding how paradigms guide scientific inquiry.

One of the most important contributions of Kuhn's work was the emphasis he placed on shared beliefs as the basis for holding together a community of scientists. Kuhn saw science as a puzzle-solving activity that was guided by a set of taken-for-granted beliefs and practices. These beliefs and practices come under scrutiny when scientists encounter the unexpected or an anomaly that can no longer be accounted for by previous or existing beliefs and practices. These crises bring into sharp relief former beliefs, habits, and practices and precipitate the creation of new ones. It is through the process of crisis that we become aware of how collective beliefs can and must change within the activities of science.

Recognition that scientific belief systems change opened up the realization that there can be many types of scientific belief systems and practices that exist at any time. These systems of belief can coexist and compete. Kuhn's work sparked discussion of many different kinds of paradigms: there were paradigm shifts within specific disciplines as dominant theoretical or methodological approaches were found wanting and were replaced by others. For example, structural functionalism, which was a dominant force in family studies in the 1950s, 1960s, and early 1970s, was found wanting when it could not offer adequate explanations of power, conflict, and inequities in families. Feminism and conflict perspectives brought forward different belief systems and introduced new scientific habits and practices. At another level, however, the paradigm debates introduced new communities of scientists—communities that were shaped not by discipline but by a set of foundational beliefs about what it means to do science.

It is with this latter definition in mind that we will explore the different kinds of scientific paradigms operating within the social sciences. Paradigms are based on different epistemological assumptions. Whereas epistemology specifically refers to the philosophical assumptions about knowledge and the relationship between the researcher and that which is to be known, paradigms refer to the collective beliefs within a community of scientists about how science should proceed. Each of these paradigms has implications for how we carry out qualitative research with families.

Paradigms, according to Kuhn (1962), are a "prerequisite to perception itself" (p. 113) because what people see depends both upon what they look at and what their previous experience has taught them to see. Five main paradigms have emerged in the social sciences: positivism, postpositivism, social constructionism, the critical paradigm, and postmodernism. Each of these paradigms is itself constructed, each representing a constellation of beliefs and practices. Although each of these paradigms has defining characteristics, the boundaries between paradigms can often be blurred. Each of the paradigms discussed below is a prerequisite to perception itself because each directs perception based on different beliefs, habits, and tools.

Positivism

Beliefs. Positivism is built on the epistemology of objectivism. There is a belief that the world beyond ourselves—both natural and social—can be understood and explained. This is known as realism—the belief that the world outside of our minds is patterned, measurable, and ultimately predictable. The root *posit* indicates a belief in the systematic observation of direct experience in order to posit, or put forth, an explanation of that reality. In the same way that a photograph serves as a positive image of observed experience, research reports and theoretical explanations are viewed as positive representations of reality. These are the rudiments of traditional scientific belief where the patterns of an observable social world are given to scientific explanation. In order for this to be possible, there is a belief that reality itself is systematically organized and characterized by regularities, uniformities, and coherent logic. In contrast to religious, philosophical, or metaphysical ways of knowing, positivist science opened the road to certainty. At the heart of the positivist belief is the correspondence theory of truth. Scientific observation and explanation, when conducted with rigorous adherence to the rules of methodology, are able to provide an accurate map of reality. The goal of science is to achieve the correspondence between what is true in reality and what is true in explanation.

Habits. Traditional positivist science has as its primary purpose the production of facts. Given the belief in the possibility of generating precise and law-like explanations of reality, positivists seek to measure that reality with precision. Empiricism is the habitual practice and refers to the activity of verifying propositions by means of sense data. Accordingly, providing explanation is a matter of generating unmediated explanations of reality. In order to accomplish this, it is necessary for the researcher to abide by the practices of objectivity. In the process of representation, this involves keeping separate the processes of researcher's perception from the realities that we seek to understand. Minimizing bias, perfecting the precision of measurement, and refining the accuracy of explanation are the main habits of the positivist community.

Tools. Positivism rests on an accumulation model of science. Through a process of refinement, testing, and retesting, there is an expectation that knowledge accumulates, becomes more complete and more accurate. The tools of positivism are designed to support this effort. For example, there are respected theories, rigid methodological rules, and established bodies of knowledge that guide the scientific practices of positivism. Methodologically, hypotheses are generated, corresponding measures constructed, conditions controlled, and data collected in order to test empirically the propositions put forward. These procedures are part of a process of theory verification that accumulates in a growing body of knowledge. Given the emphasis on precision and certainty, quantitative research is typically the preferred approach. A variety of tools are used to support the principle of objectivism in quantitative research, including standardized measurement, reliability and validity, tests of significance, and formal theory. Given the importance of measurement as a tool, the variable is the primary means for explaining social reality.

Implications for Doing Qualitative Family Research. There are many examples of qualitative research that start with an objectivist epistemological assumption. As Charmaz (2002) has pointed out, some versions of grounded theory methodology assume that there is an objective reality that can be understood, accurately represented, and theorized about. Positivist qualitative research seeks to preserve empirical practices and standards. As a result, there is an emphasis on following methodological rules in order to ensure rigorous results. This research would be concerned with the representativeness of the sample, would use methods to assess reliability and validity of the data, and might use coding schemes of the data as a way to quantify the patterns in the data. Through all of these practices, one of the main goals is to minimize the biasing effects of the researcher on the data. This is a process of manufacturing distance in order to bring forward as accurately as possible the experiences being observed. Hypotheses or propositions may be put forward, and the qualitative data are used to test their plausibility. Some qualitative research designs within this tradition may also be concerned with replicating prior theory or empirical discoveries as a form of verification.

Postpositivism/Critical Realism

Beliefs. In the social sciences, "positivism" has taken on a negative valence. The recognition that there are limitations to certainty of knowledge and perfection of measures has resulted in a tendency for researchers to distance themselves from the ideals of the traditional scientific approach. In its place is a set of modified beliefs that uphold many of the practices of empirical science while at the same time acknowledging the limitations on achieving a fully positive representation of that reality. Accordingly, the foundational belief is known as critical realism: the idea that an objective reality exists out there but that this is a reality that is imprecisely apprehendable.

Sir Karl Popper's introduction of "falsification" served as an important demarcation between positivism and postpositivism. Whereas positivism emphasizes the practices of verification, postpositivism accepts the precept of falsification. The positivist process of verification is designed to bring about a conclusion of certainty about the nature of reality. Falsification, by contrast, introduces the idea that any explanation or theory about the nature of reality, regardless of empirical support, is subject to falsification in any subsequent empirical test. The importance of falsification for understanding the postpositivist belief system is that it replaced absolute certainty with the tentativeness of falsifiable knowledge.

Habits. Postpositivism proceeds with many of the same habits as positivism. Although it is acknowledged that measurement efforts are always somewhat imprecise and that theoretical conclusions must always be held tentatively, rigor is upheld as a primary value. Accordingly, there is a concern with measurement, objectivity, tests of significance, and statistical procedure.

Tools. In the postpositivist tradition, experiments, surveys, and even some kinds of observational studies are used to create explanations of social reality.

Theorizing activity often occurs in the form of constructing models based on tests of relationships among variables. Statistical significance between variables is the primary means for focusing explanations of family reality.

Implications for Doing Qualitative Family Research. Like positivism, a post-positivist approach would also adhere closely to methodological rules in order to give an accurate portrayal of the experiential reality of those being interviewed or observed. Although the emphasis is still on representing the experience of participants as accurately as possible, there is recognition that researchers can never remove themselves fully from this process. As a result, researchers are likely to acknowledge the potential for bias in the research and may indicate in their work the ways they tried to minimize the effects of this bias. This may include reflexive statements about personal experience. Once these are explicitly examined, they are set aside in order to minimize their impact on the presentation of the data. In this regard, there is an effort to create distance while at the same time recognizing the interpretive influence of the researcher.

Many of the early ethnographies that we have of various cultures in the anthropological tradition would fall under this paradigm. In these ethnographies, the emphasis was on the representation of these cultural realities from the perspective of an outside objective observer. One of the golden rules within this tradition was to protect against "going native" in order to maintain an objective standpoint and to see the cultural reality from the outside. This was in the service of the goal of portraying these cultures as they "really" are. Of course many of these ethnographies were fraught with the faulty interpretations of Western eyes that assigned interpretations to activities and rituals that were infused with all kinds of moral judgments and values. Although these researchers often acknowledged their position as outsiders to the indigenous meanings, there was, nevertheless, a tendency to overlook the important distinction between their representations of these cultures and the cultures as they "really" were.

Qualitative articles written within this paradigm are likely to follow the organizational format of a traditional social science article with sections on design, methods, findings, and discussion. Although the interpretive influence of the researcher is acknowledged, the voice of the researcher is generally not apparent in the final written account.

Social Constructionism/Interpretivism

Beliefs. This paradigm is rooted in a belief that all reality is a constructed reality. According to this view, reality is that which is created in the liminal zone between a perceived external reality and a subjective meaning-making process. Interpretation is that which occurs between the internal processes of the mind and the externally available processes of the social world. At an epistemological level, social constructionism lies between the subjectivist and objectivist polar extremes. It accepts the presence of an external reality that is subjectively perceived and understood from the perspective of the observer.

In a way that is consistent with an interpretivist paradigm, but with the idea historically preceding the creation of this paradigm, John Dewey, the pragmatist philosopher, argued that "facts" exist in a useful way but that they are always contingent on prior frames of reference. For Dewey, a fact is a complex of sense data organized with respect to a prior frame of reference (Greer, 1969). The meaning of prior experience is necessary and instrumental for shaping the intellectual formulation of any social event. From this perspective, all facts are constructed facts that are as variable as the frames of reference that social scientists bring to their inquiry. In this regard, "facts" are fully socially constructed.

A key belief in the interpretive paradigm that is often overlooked is the importance of the social aspects of the constructionist effort. This can be understood in a couple of ways. First, interpretive processes are deeply embedded in, and shaped by, the shared meanings that we have about activity, language, and cultural symbols. As a result, we don't simply create idiosyncratic meanings of behavior, but we construct meanings on the basis of socially available, shared understandings of reality. It is in this regard that we can view culture as not simply a symbolic representation of who we are, but as a source of social information that we draw on in the process of constructing meaning. Second, social constructionism is based on a belief that we construct meanings in the course of interaction. Whether this is an informal conversation at the family dinner table or a formal conversation between a researcher and a participant, the way we come to understand the other is through a social process where meanings are interactively built. In the research process, there is acknowledgment that the way we come to understand the reality of participants involves a process of coconstruction insofar as there is an interplay between the meanings of the researcher and the meanings of the participant. Social constructionism is different from constructivism, which has its roots in Piagetian cognitive psychology (Gergen, 1985). Whereas social constructionism emphasizes meaning-making as an interactive process, constructivism places emphasis on the cognitive processes of meaning-making in the individual.

Given the importance of meaning-making and the interpretive process, social constructionism acknowledges the potential for reality to be represented in multiple ways. Rather than seeking to represent the facts of a singular reality accurately, social constructionism would hold to the belief that there are many interpretive possibilities that can be brought to an understanding of social reality. Hence, there are multiple realities that can be articulated based on the values, standpoints, and positions of the author.

Habits. In order to understand the meaning of experience, social constructionists rely heavily on talk as the primary medium for research activity. Whether the format of the research involves observation, interview, or focus group, talk is the basis for discerning how participants are making sense of their own experiential reality. In contrast with the positivist emphasis on causal explanation, social constructionism is more likely preoccupied with the question of how participants have experienced a particular phenomenon. One of the guiding mantras in qualitative research has been to arrive at a "thick description" (Geertz, 1973) of a phenomenon that brings forward the detail and nuance of the experience.

Tools. Social constructionists rely heavily on the practices of qualitative research that focus on the meanings of words and experiences. Descriptions of how individuals experience infertility or divorce are more important than rates of infertility or divorce. In carrying out research with participants, there is an assumption that the researcher is engaged with them in a process that includes conversation, observation, and interpretation. The primary tools in this paradigm are interviews, requests that participants tell their stories in the spirit of the narrative tradition, and observations of activities and practices.

Implications for Doing Qualitative Family Research. The emphasis in the social constructionist paradigm is on the way meanings are constructed in the situation. The primary focus of the research within this paradigm is on the way that participants construct the meaning of their own everyday realities. There is a recognition that this reality is changing and subject to interpretation by the participants themselves. As a result, there is less concern here with what "really happened" and more concern with how people are making sense of events at this point in time. Epistemologically, there is an acceptance that the researcher plays a very significant role in the way these meanings are created. Meaning-making occurs at many different levels when research is conducted within this paradigm. First, researchers create the parameters within which participants talk about their realities. By virtue of the topics chosen, the questions asked, and the responses given, researchers play a powerful role in shaping how these realities are brought forward by participants. It is in this regard that we can think of these resultant data as "contrived" (Speer, 2002) insofar as the definition of the research situation profoundly shapes the way participants choose to describe the meanings of their experience. In an interview setting, researchers are participants in the construction of meaning and would acknowledge their role in the coconstruction of the reality that is brought forward in the interview setting. Not only do researchers within this paradigm elicit a version of participants' reality, but they then subject that reality to further interpretation in the process of data analysis. At this level, researchers are interested in understanding the broader patterns of meaning construction that exist within the project sample. This involves a shift from individual meanings of experience to the generic patterns of meaning that contribute to an understanding of the research phenomenon.

Qualitative articles written within this paradigm would typically maintain a focus on the way participants have constructed their reality in relation to the research topic. At the same time, the voice of the researcher, as a participant in the construction of this reality, would be apparent. This would typically include in the Methods section of the paper a detailed description of the researcher's values, experience, and interests in relation to the topic at hand. It would include a discussion of how the research question was framed as well as a justification in relation to the researcher's background and interests. There would typically be a detailed discussion of the procedures within the research with special attention to who conducted the interviews and the ways they may have shaped the direction and outcome of the research.

Although many qualitative researchers position their work within this paradigm, there is a tendency when reporting results to fall into a more positivist mode of presentation. In other words, there is a tendency for the researcher's self to disappear in the Results section, and the data be represented "as if" they represented participants' reality. In order to maintain epistemological integrity here, it is important to keep the interpretive voice alive in the Results section. This may include reflexive excerpts about how categories or themes were generated; discussion of the interpretive meaning-making process; or comments and questions by the researcher about the unresolved nature of reality such as conflicting values, contradictions, or incomplete understandings. In addition, it is important, when including data excerpts, to have the questions or comments that either precede or follow participants' comments in order to maintain the presence of the researcher's voice in the coconstruction of data.

Critical Paradigm

Beliefs. The foundational belief of the critical paradigm is that the world is structured on the basis of unequal relations and consists of competing interests. Conflict, power, and injustice are endemic to our culture.

Accordingly, the hallmark of the critical paradigm is that it views science as a political endeavor whose aim shifts from simply seeking to understand reality to taking a values stance that endeavors to change reality. Scientific activity does not occur outside of the cultural politics in neutral, disengaged fashion, but rather, it is seen as a power-based discourse that also reflects a set of interests and has the capacity to bring privilege to certain kinds of positions. For example, Marxian theory is focused on the nature of oppression in social class relations. The goal of this theorizing activity is not simply to explain the nature of this oppression, but to change the fundamental relations of power. Similarly, feminist theorizing activity and research that is part of the critical paradigm offers explanations of unequal power relations between women and men in families as a basis for bringing about more equitable relations in families (Osmond & Thorne, 1993). Feminist research has been instrumental in shaping the fundamental beliefs of the critical paradigm and these have been summarized as including an action orientation, attention to power, attention to history and context, emphasis on inclusivity and social justice, and an emphasis on self-critique and reflexivity (Avis & Turner, 1996).

Habits. In the critical tradition, research focuses on three key themes: race or ethnicity, class, and gender. These are the primary dimensions along which the structures of power and inequality are manifested in our culture. Research in the critical paradigm is attentive to the historical and material conditions of power relations. History is important to the critical lens for understanding how inequality has emerged over time in relation to a variety of social and political conditions. For example, an analysis of the historical roots of patriarchy can serve as an important frame for the analysis of the division of household labor in the home. Rooted in the Marxist emphasis on the economic relations of productive activity, material conditions place the focus on the economic underpinnings of power relations. In this research, conditions of work, income, and social class play an important role in analyzing the dynamics of power in family relationships.

Tools. Given the focus on social change, researchers in this paradigm put an emphasis on reflexive practices that bring values issues to the foreground. Clarity about values and beliefs is necessary for the articulation of the research agenda, which involves not only the formulation of a research design, but the assertion of a possible solution to the oppressive relations that have been identified. One of the primary tools within this paradigm is more collaborative work with participants toward a shared goal. As a result, there is a deliberate effort to address the traditional hierarchical relationship between researchers and participants. Action research or participatory action research provide a means for researchers and participants to work together on a more equal power basis to articulate with greater clarity the nature of the injustice and its ramifications, to bring evidence to the concern at hand, and to work interactively to create viable strategies for change.

Implications for Doing Qualitative Family Research. Qualitative research that is conducted within this paradigm is attentive to the political nature of all aspects of the research process. Qualitative methods have been embraced by many feminist family scholars who see a necessary link between patriarchal practices within families and the patriarchal tradition of positivist science (Harding, 1987, 1991). In order to bring about political change within families, it is necessary to adopt a form of research scholarship that brings to the foreground women's concerns, values, and experiences (Thompson & Walker, 1995). In qualitative studies with a critical orientation, injustice and inequality are articulated as the catalyst for the research; women's perspectives, interpretations, and strategies for change are solicited; and the researcher brings forward the data as a way to foreground women's experience and the possibilities for change.

Reflexivity plays an important role in this work. There is a strong emphasis on how researchers position themselves in relation to participants. Transparency about personal and professional experience as well as political agendas is an important element in this work. Allen (2000), for example, argues for the importance of "consciously reflecting on how our personal life history and values are relevant to the particular inquiry in which we are engaged as a way to improve our ability to critically analyze the knowledge we produce" (p. 5).

Although feminist work has dominated critical qualitative research in the field of family relations and human development, there have been other excellent examples of qualitative work done in the areas of social class and race/ethnicity. For example, Rosenblatt's qualitative work on interracial/intercultural couples brings to the foreground issues of living with intercultural differences and racist responses (Rosenblatt, 1995b; Rosenblatt & Stewart, 2004). In an examination of parenting practices, Lareau (2002) has identified important social class differences in the culture of parenting. Based on extensive ethnographic work with families from many economic and racial backgrounds, she has identified the emergence of "concerted cultivation" among middle-class families and the emergence of the "accomplishment of natural growth" in working-class families. For middle-class families, the concern was with cultivating in their children the skills and qualities that would position them for success; in working-class families, parents were less concerned with optimizing children's talents and were more likely to see children as subordinate to adults, maintain distinctions between adult's and children's entitlements, and emphasize discipline over the expression of ideas.

Although articles written within this tradition are explicit about cultural values, political agendas, and strategies for change, they also appear in many formats ranging from traditional scientific papers to the presentation of narratives and position papers that include women's voices.

Postmodernism

Beliefs. In the spirit of Kuhn's (1962) idea of scientific revolution, the paradigm of postmodernism was spawned out of the crisis of modernism. Modernism itself was rooted in the early seventeenth-century belief that the newly emerging practices of science held the key to the well-being of human kind. Francis Bacon (1561–1626), for example, articulated the spirit of modernism when he called for a utilitarian commitment to invest time, energy, and resources to master nature through systematic experiment (Roberts, 1997). This was the promise of progress through science that was at the core of the modernist spirit. Nature was to be tamed, harnessed, and controlled and the way to do it was through systematic observation, induction, and explanation. This was an ambitious project that, in his own words, sought to restore the power of "man" since the fall:

> The true and lawful end of the sciences, is that human life be enriched by new discoveries and powers . . . [the goal of which is] the reinvigorating of man to the sovereignty and power . . . which he had in his first state of creation. (cited in Roberts, 1997, p. 655)

Modernism gradually took hold over the course of the seventeenth century, and with the emergence of an increasingly critical attitude toward metaphysics and the authority of the Church, science found a place of new authority. As science unlocked the mysteries of nature, it gained prestige by virtue of its ability to reveal the rational foundations of the world through the discovered laws of physics and chemistry. The modernist promise of knowledge through systematic inquiry gave rise to a spirit of optimism—not only for what could be understood, but for how it could serve the betterment of humankind through the control of nature. Reason, systematic inquiry, control, the authority of science, and the belief in progress were central to the modernist belief.

In the same way that modernism emerged out of a process of supplanting Church authority with the authority of science, postmodernism arose out of a fundamental challenge to the unquestioned prestige and authority of the scientific community. Although the crisis of modernism is difficult to identify with any precision, it was constituted by a confluence of late 20th-century forces, including globalization, recognition of diversity, and an environmental movement that arose from the control and destruction of nature. The optimism of industrial progress had come to an end amid an environment that was choking to death on the unwanted byproducts of progress. The crisis of postmodernism spawned a new critical attitude: one that was skeptical of progress, one that challenged the dominant assumptions of scientific certainty and opened up the possibilities of competing forms of knowledge that reflected different interests and standpoints.

Postmodernism is different from positivism/postpositivism in a number of important respects. Whereas positivism and postpositivism are concerned with the practices of science, modernism and postmodernism are more general and are concerned with changes in many spheres of life including not only science, but art, architecture, and literature. Postmodernism is generally considered to be a rupture in the modernist movement toward progress whereas postpositivism upholds in a modified form many of the underlying beliefs of positivism. Positivism and to some extent postpositivism are subsumed by the modernist beliefs in certainty, refinement, and accumulation of knowledge.

Habits. Postmodern researchers accept the fluidity and changeability of social knowledge. There is a move away from traditional dominant discourses to a recognition that there are many possible perspectives on any single issue. For postmodern researchers, transparency of values and standpoints becomes paramount. In keeping with this, it is important to elicit multiple viewpoints and to represent these according to both consistencies and contradictions. Postmodern researchers put an emphasis on voice and work to ensure that many voices are brought forward in the research. There is also a fundamental questioning of the authority of the researcher to interpret or represent the meanings communicated by participants. This is known as the "crisis of representation" (Marcus & Fischer, 1986) within postmodern thinking. In contrast with the certainty of positivist science, postmodernism is willing to accept inconclusive and relative positions.

The crisis of representation calls into question the procedures of traditional empirical science. Given the belief that there is no singular objective reality that can be represented, there is an underlying skepticism about what we can know with any certainty. As a result, "traditional scientific inquiry" is incompatible with postmodern assumptions. Rosenau (1992) makes the distinction between "extreme" and "moderate" postmodernists, with the extreme position reflecting a skeptical stance toward science with an emphasis on relativism, uncertainty, and living without explanation. The moderate position, however, offers another path, which is to keep elements of social science in play but with modifications. Rather than seeking to "discover" meanings, the challenge is to pay attention to how we locate meanings in multiple expressions and texts—while acknowledging that these meanings are tentative and changeable. For the moderate postmodernist working as a social scientist, research is not rejected but is viewed as necessary for making underlying assumptions explicit, and the search for certain and conclusive evidence is replaced with the effort to understand and interpret diverse and complex phenomena that are tentative and changeable (Rosenau, 1992).

Tools. Keeping inquiry alive within postmodernism involves a fundamental shift from the substance and constitution of experience to the representational devices used by individuals and researchers to convey the image of objective or subjective reality (Gubrium & Holstein, 2003c). The emphasis is on how individuals construe their reality rather than on what that reality is. This approach is rooted in an understanding of language as constitutive of reality insofar as the words and discourse we use do not reflect some other reality but are a form of action that is reality. Postmodern researchers are concerned with the texts or the rhetoric that is produced in the course of an interview. There is a concern for the way these texts are produced; what they say about voice, authorship, and audience; and the types of discursive practices that are used to convey the story. The key tool for the postmodern inquirer is to pay systematic attention to the way texts of all kinds—from media images to methodological writing and ethnographies—construct the realities they otherwise presume to merely represent (Gubrium & Holstein, 2003a). The content of the interview is thereby taken as a coconstructed reality and not simply a reflection of participants' experience of some other kind of reality outside the interview.

Implications for Doing Qualitative Family Research. Postmodern research typically calls into question traditional scientific formats, methodological rules, and disciplinary conventions. Accordingly, qualitative research is guided by a set of paradigmatic assumptions about the necessity of questioning dominant discourses and opening space for the expression of multiple voices, but is not bound by any preordained set of methodological rules or practices.

Nevertheless, texts have now been developed (e.g., Gubrium & Holstein, 2003b) that outline the pitfalls and challenges of doing postmodern research. Within this paradigm, there is considerable latitude in terms of how the research is conducted, but it is conducted with different "sensibilities." Postmodern sensibilities include a recognition that interviewers and respondents collaborate together in constructing their narrative(s) and that the authority of the researcher to interpret or represent the respondent's reality is called into question; moreover, the forms used to report findings have expanded dramatically to include poetry, drama, use of the media, the Internet, and film (Fontana, 2003).

Researchers working within a postmodern paradigm continue to publish their work in some scholarly journals—sometimes using fairly traditional scientific categories. The key is the reflexive monitoring that occurs throughout this work that is deliberately attentive to the processes used in the production of the research products. Caution is exercised in making any definitive claims, and the focus is on bringing forward a variety of voices and viewpoints that offer a view of a reality that may be fraught with contradiction and competing interests. In light of the interest in moving away from dominant discourses or definitive representations, these reports are typically cast as being illustrative but unresolved.

Interpretation is central to the work of postmodern research but has a different goal when working within a postmodern frame of reference. In a positivist or postpositivist approach (i.e., modernist science), interpretation is oriented toward sifting through the data in order to identify patterns in experience that most accurately reflect that experience. In postmodernist interpretation, the goal is not to resolve conflicting interpretations but to bring forward multiple meanings and divergent interpretations (Rosenau, 1992).

How Do I Decide? Where Do I Stand?

How we position ourselves in relation to epistemological and paradigmatic considerations is challenging. These are abstract ways of thinking, and it is often difficult to know at the outset of a project where we stand in relation to these positions. What is critical, however, is that we open ourselves to reflect on these possibilities in order to come to a better appreciation of our values and preferences when conducting research. Reflexive memos, like personal journaling, can serve as an important vehicle for understanding our researcher identity—how we think about our own values and interests, how we position ourselves in relation to participants, and the degree to which we present our voice in the reports of our research. This is an ongoing activity, one that can involve shifting positions and preferences as we work our way through the research process.

Accordingly, it is important to think about our relationship to paradigms as being changeable. For example, we might start off with a social constructionist positioning and move to a critical paradigm as we come to terms with moral or political concerns that emerge in the course of the project. A postpositivist starting point may shift to a social constructionist position as we gain confidence in our own research abilities and are willing to risk being more subjectively present in the research. In this regard, I tend to think of paradigms as a form of costume that we put on that serves as a means for understanding who we are and how we act.

The following questions may serve to help situate yourself:

A. Is my primary concern to meet the standards of rigor that are part of the scientific tradition? Do I want my sample to be large and representative so that I can generalize the results? Am I concerned about reliability and validity? Is my goal to minimize the amount of biasing effect that I might have on the respondent? If yes to these, then you are likely positioning yourself as a positivist or postpositivist.

B. Is my primary concern to understand how participants make meaning about aspects of their family lives in a way that is changing and involves multiple perspectives? Do I see myself as having an influence on the way participants tell the story of their lives? Am I interested in presenting these multiple viewpoints (including my own) in ways that reflect the emergent nature of reality? If yes to these questions, then you are likely situating yourself as a social constructionist.

C. Am I primarily concerned with issues of social justice and think about research as a means to bring about social change? Does my research focus on competing interests, systems of oppression and injustice, and political strategies used in the process of change? Do I see myself as having partisan interests and as working on behalf of oppressed groups? If yes to these questions, then you are likely positioning yourself as a user of the critical paradigm.

D. Am I primarily concerned with understanding a variety of voices and viewpoints and the way they come together to constitute a version of reality? Am I primarily concerned with how the interview itself is a means to construct reality? Am I aware of the ways in which my own authorship of analytic texts is not so much about the representation of another reality but is a construction of reality? If yes to these questions, then you are likely positioning yourself as a postmodernist.

In the next chapter, we explore another aspect of the research process: the way we think about the relationship between the social world that we are trying to understand and the activities and procedures associated with scientific explanation.

Note

1. I use the term *positioning* in relation to epistemology as a way of describing how researchers define their own beliefs about what it means to know and their relationship to knowledge-generating activities. This is not to be confused with the more specific use of the term in *positioning theory* where it is used as a metaphor in discourse analysis to determine how persons are "located" within conversations or jointly produced storylines (Van Langenhove & Harré, 1993).

3

Paths of Inquiry for Qualitative Research

The epistemological assumptions associated with each of the paradigms have implications for how qualitative researchers conduct their inquiry. Of particular importance here are how we begin the process of inquiry, how we develop explanation through this process, and how we formulate outcomes for this process. In the tradition of scientific inquiry, this process has been described in several different forms: deduction, induction, and abduction. Although qualitative research is often most closely aligned with induction, I would argue that all three approaches influence the paths of inquiry.

How we think about theory is central to a discussion of paths of inquiry. In deductive approaches, theory is usually the starting point, whereas in inductive approaches, theory is typically the product. Abduction, which is concerned with finding the "best explanation," is shaped by both the presence and inadequacies of existing theory and the need to generate new theoretical explanation. At the outset of this discussion, it is important to acknowledge that not all forms of qualitative inquiry are concerned with theory—either as a starting point or an outcome of inquiry. Some approaches, such as phenomenology or narrative, may be more interested in upholding the integrity of the description of the lived experience than in either the testing or generation of theory through deduction and induction.

Deduction

In his articulation of the logico-deductive model, Sir Karl Popper (1959) argued that the origin of a theoretical idea is not of particular importance to the scientific enterprise. The magic of how ideas come into the minds of scientists is for psychologists to figure out. What is of critical importance is how these ideas are transformed into testable hypotheses that then can be examined through a controlled methodological process to see the extent to which the ideas were supported by the observation of reality. In deductive paths of inquiry, evidence, in the form of data, is gathered in an effort to either support or refute the theoretical idea put forward.

The original emphasis in a deductive path of inquiry was on verification. This was rooted in the positivist idea of "a correspondence theory of truth" that put emphasis on the degree to which data collected from the sensory world mapped onto the theory being proposed. In instances where there was a close mirroring between theoretical ideas and observed reality, especially through repeated testing, scientists were in a position to make claims that theories could be verified. Theory, in the positivist tradition of verification, came to be associated with certainty, truth, and predictability.

However, in the process of examining the nature of "truth claims" in positivist science, Popper argued that truth claims in science should always be treated as tentative and subject to disproof. He argued that nothing can ever be proved in absolute terms because there are always potential instances of reality that can be at odds with the proposed theory. Accordingly, he argued that the emphasis in the scientific method must shift from verification to falsification. A theory is always a proposal or conjecture as to the nature of reality, and as a result the emphasis must always be on the potential of the theory for refutation or disproof. Hence, although a theory can withstand many empirical tests, for Popper, it must always be held as a provisional explanation of reality. The shift from verification (and a focus on truth) to falsification (provisional explanation) represented a key shift from positivist to postpositivist beliefs in the paths of scientific inquiry.

In the social sciences, deductive approaches have typically been associated with the use of hypothesis testing and quantitative data collection methods. Glaser and Strauss (1967), in their original articulation of grounded theory methods, argued the need for a systematic means for generating, rather than verifying theory. Their book was created in reaction to the dominant emphasis in sociology in the first half of the 20th century on the verification of "great man" theories. In their view, this had a limiting effect on the creative generation of new knowledge, and as a result they turned their energies to the processes of theory generation. As I will discuss later, this did not mean that verification strategies became irrelevant. Rather, the emphasis shifted to how to generate new theory while at the same time holding the need to verify knowledge as both possible and necessary.

Although it is less common, some qualitative researchers do begin with specific theoretical ideas for which they then set out to gather evidence. For example, in the tradition of attachment theory in parent–child relationships, researchers will propose hypotheses about issues of separation anxiety and observe interactions to assess the strength of their theoretical propositions. In a study of dying, Wright (2003), began the research with a concern and a frustration about the dominance of Kübler-Ross's stage theory, and as a result, set out to explore how dying individuals and their family members experienced the dying process. While not testing hypotheses from the theory, she was nevertheless interested in understanding the degree to which prior existing theory like this had permeated the dying experience.

Gilgun (2005a, 2005b) writes about the potential uses of deductive strategies in qualitative research. The starting point is an existing conceptual or theoretical model followed by an active search for evidence that undermines the current conceptual model. These starting theories or models range from those that are "tightly defined" in existing theory to a set of roughly formulated ideas and hunches that may be rooted in personal or professional experience (Gilgun, 2005b). This is consistent with Popper's postpositivist principles of falsification and involves the identification of negative, disconfirming cases that in turn leads to a reformulation of the model to fit the cases. The resulting models that are produced through this process must always be put forward with a tentativeness. As Gilgun explains, these new models are also incomplete and subject to new evidence that will precipitate a further reformulation.

Induction

In contrast with Popper's notion that theoretical ideas simply "appear" in the minds of great theoreticians (and which are then tested), induction is built on the principle that theoretical explanation is developed on the basis of observation of the world as it exists out there. In its purest form, induction involves suspending any preconceived ideas about the nature of the reality being observed. The goal of induction is to come to an understanding of a phenomenon through observation and inquiry. In its most simple terms, induction is the scientific process of building theoretical explanation on the basis of repeated observation of particular circumstances. Hence, if we want to understand the nature of step relationships, the division of labor in gay and lesbian households, or the meaning of unemployment for fathers, we need to ask questions, observe behaviors, and listen to stories that provide a basis for constructing an understanding and explanation of their experience in each of those situations.

The inductive path of inquiry is perhaps most apparent in grounded theory approaches. A grounded theory is one that emerges out of repeated observations of a particular reality. At the root of this process is the creation of theoretical concepts and hypotheses that emerge in the process of comparing empirical observations. As one experience is compared with another, common elements are identified and conceptual categories are created. As additional evidence is gathered and compared, these conceptual categories are refined and eventually form the basis of relevant theoretical abstractions. Through these procedures, a theory is inductively derived. It provides a generic form of explanation that is rooted in, and shaped by, the experience of those being observed.

In phenomenological research, Moustakis (1990) has outlined a more detailed process by which the inductive analysis occurs. At the outset, the researcher immerses him- or herself in the setting that is of interest. This is followed by a period of reflection and incubation and an awareness of how participants assign meaning to their own experience. There is then a process of intuition, illumination, and expanding awareness. As this awareness broadens, the researcher begins the process of description and explanation. In the final phase of induction, the researcher synthesizes and brings together the individual stories and the meaning of the lived experience.

Most qualitative methodologies follow some form of inductive reasoning. Although not all approaches have theory as their desired product, most approaches are concerned with providing some form of description or explanation that moves from the particular to the general. Prus (1987), for example, has argued that one of the valued outcomes of inductive modes of inquiry is the creation of generic concepts. Through the process of qualitatively examining and understanding specific human behaviors, we can be in a position to understand better some of the fundamental principles of social action and human behavior. One example of a "generic concept" in the family field is Pauline Boss's concept of ambiguous loss. Through observation of a variety of human experiences like soldiers missing in action, abducted and missing children, people with Alzheimer's disease, or people experiencing infertility, ambiguous loss emerges as a generic term for helping to understand the common elements associated with each of these human experiences. Although each is different in its situational conditions, they share a core of common properties, including some combination of physical absence and psychological presence, or conversely psychological absence and physical presence. As a generic concept, it helps us to understand these complex experiences of loss that are typically accompanied by conditions of uncertainty and lack of resolution.

As our sensitivities about various paradigm positions have grown, there has been an effort to articulate more clearly some of the different ways that inductive inquiry is conducted in relation to paradigm assumptions and values. Kathy Charmaz (2003b), for example, has made the distinction between objectivist and constructivist[1] grounded theory methods as a way to outline more clearly the manner in which paradigm beliefs shape both the process and the product of inductive inquiry. In other writings that I have done, these ideas formed the basis for a distinction between objectivist and interpretive induction (Kuczynski & Daly, 2003).

Objectivist Induction: Positivist/Postpositivist Roots

Objectivist induction is rooted in a positivist orientation. For Charmaz, many variants of grounded theory rooted in the work of Glaser, of Strauss, and of Corbin are built on positivist underpinnings with a belief in the presence of an external, objective reality that is apprehended by a somewhat neutral observer who then presents the data as an accurate representation of that reality. Hence, in its most mechanical form, induction involves a direct relationship between "objective" observations of social reality and theories arising from this reality that provide explanation.

This form of induction is consistent with the most traditional ways of thinking about scientific induction. For example, the earliest forms of "Baconian" induction emphasized the importance of the "purity" of observations (Haig, 1996). Barney Glaser (1992) was most insistent on maintaining this purity of observation by adopting a tabula rasa starting position. For Glaser, theory emerges directly from data through the process of comparison, and it is essential to keep out preconceptions and predisposing sensitivities from other theories. As a result, Glaser warned against the dangers of conducting a literature review prior to going into the field because of the distorting effects it would have on the natural inquiry. In his own words, "Categories emerge upon comparison and properties emerge upon more comparison. And that is all there is to it" (Glaser, 1992, p. 43). As part of this, it is important for the researcher to work deliberately at maintaining an objective stance that involves putting to the side any preconceived ideas about the reality at hand. For Glaser, these preconceptions reflect personal interests and bias that eventually "force" the data and ultimately "derail" the inductive process (Glaser, 1992, p. 123).

Later works by Strauss and Corbin (1990, 1998) are categorized by Charmaz (2003b) as being consistent with the postpositivist paradigm. Although there is a strong emphasis on representing the reality of participants through the development of emerging theory, there is acknowledgment of the role of theoretical sensitivity in shaping the inquiry, recognition that participants bring a variety of perspectives about the same reality, and awareness that there is always the potential for conflict between the researcher's understandings and the participants' points of view.

Objectivist practices of induction have also played an important role in the ethnographic tradition. When ethnographers traveled to strange and exotic lands, they often had the goal of writing "objective" accounts that were expected to be reliable and valid representations of these cultures. Representation was the goal and care was taken to maintain their objective stance with an ongoing vigilance to the dangers of "going native" (Wax, 1971). The resulting ethnographies were intended to be timeless, objective monuments of the cultures studied but in hindsight were often riddled with the assumptions and colonizing objectives of the researcher's culture (Rosaldo, 1989).

Objectivist induction has been called "naive" because of the inadequate explanation of what data are and how they are transformed into theory. Data can never be "raw" or "theory free" because they cannot exist without the perspectives that define them (Lincoln & Guba, 1985) or the methods that select them. In the same way that there are questions about "how data speak" for themselves, there are questions about how theory emerges from data. There are few practical methodological guidelines for how to make "emergence" happen. Theories do not emerge on their own, but rather involve a more complicated process of layering webs of meaning over data. This complex layering of meaning is central to an understanding of "constructivist" or interpretive induction.

Constructivist Induction: Interpretivist and Social Constructionist Roots

Constructivist approaches offer a moderate position between the emphasis on objectivity in positivism and the relativism of postmodernism. For Charmaz (2003b), a constructivist approach is built on the assumptions that there are multiple social realities, that there is shared construction of knowledge that occurs between the researcher and participants, and that there is a goal of achieving an interpretive understanding of participants' subjective meanings. From this perspective, the creation of an explanation is coconstructed insofar as there is no pretense about the researcher's not having a profound influence on how the data are created, managed, interpreted, and brought forward in the process of analysis. Both the researcher and the participants are engaged in the research and confer meaning upon it (Charmaz, 2003b).

The methodological principle of theoretical sensitivity is key to an understanding of constructivist induction. In contrast with an objectivist position that insists on a tabula rasa approach, the researcher approaches a problem from the perspective of theoretical sensitivity to existing concepts, ideas, and theory. Furthermore, in the process of conducting analysis on the data, the researcher, with these prior understandings in mind, plays an active and deliberate role in organizing and assigning meaning to the data as a way of constructing higher order categories and theory. In contrast with objectivist induction that emphasizes the importance of accurately representing external reality while minimizing researcher influence, interpretive induction is concerned with the interpretive process by which theory is meaningfully constructed.

When the object of discovery is human action in social contexts, interpretive induction is concerned with two layers of meaning: the meanings that are held and communicated to researchers by their subjects concerning their everyday lives, experiences, and perceptions, and the meanings that researchers bring to these meanings as they endeavor to understand, explain, and theorize about these everyday realities. The process of layering meaning is part of the "irreducible conflict" between the scientific perspective and the experience of everyday life (Becker, 1964). Whereas everyday reality tends to be specific and localizing, scientific reality tends to be abstract and generalizing. As a consequence, when scientists develop theories, there will always be a conflict between the meaning structures brought to the endeavor by the scientist and the meaning structures that exist as part of the commonsense world they are seeking to understand. This is a kind of "double hermeneutic" whereby social scientists observe and interpret the experiences of individuals who are themselves interpreting the worlds they experience (Prus, 1994, p. 20). Schutz (1971) articulated this tension between scientific and everyday language in the distinction between first- and second-order constructs. The constructs that the social scientist develops are constructs of the second degree—they are "constructs of the constructs made by the actors on the social scene, whose behavior the scientist observes and tries to explain in accordance with the procedural rules of his science" (Schutz, 1971, p. 6). The double hermeneutic involves the "dialectical interplay" between the subjective meaning of people's specific and general experiences described using everyday language and the objectifying reality of the researcher's reconstructions of that reality using concepts and theory (Rothe, 1993).

The reconciliation of these two layers of meaning has been articulated as the "crisis of representation" that arises from uncertainty about adequate means of describing social reality (Marcus & Fischer, 1986). Questions regarding researcher position and authority, use of language, and a skepticism about scientific metanarratives and legitimating practices raise concerns for theory construction because "problems of description become problems of representation" (Marcus & Fischer, 1986, p. 9).

One of the paths through the crisis of representation is a position that argues that there is no division between the layers of meaning held by researchers and participants, but that the meanings that are articulated as theory represent a hybrid of meanings consisting of a researcher's observations and related experiences and participants' expressions of their perceived reality. Of importance here is the recognition that researchers are also everyday participants in the culture under study. As a result, researchers are always straddling first- and second-order meanings by virtue of having to reconcile their dual citizenship as members of the culture that they seek to understand and as members of a scientific discipline. Social scientists cannot detach themselves from participating in their own experiential world.

Inductive Inquiry: Postmodernist Influences

Postmodern ways of thinking reject the idea that there can be an objective or singular truth and instead emphasize the importance of understanding multiple perspectives, conflicting values, and different versions of the same reality. In the study of families, this means that we not only seek to understand families in their diverse forms, but that we seek to understand how members of families have different experiences of the same family.

One of the ways postmodernism departs from other forms of induction is in the insistence that the many voices in the research process be brought forward and acknowledged in the products of the research. One of the ways of achieving this is to engage participants in the process of presenting their own reality to the world. These are "dialectical practices" that involve interactive research that invites reciprocal reflexivity and critique between researchers and research participants (Lather, 1986). This approach is intended to guard against excessive imposition and reification on the part of the researcher, and instead to allow for the interplay of both researcher and participant selves. This process of inductively creating understanding is a collaborative process where the aim is to work intersubjectively with participants in order to present a variety of perspectives on their lived experience.

In postmodern approaches, there is an emphasis on including the researcher's subjective self. This is in distinction to objectivist approaches that try to keep the self out entirely, or interpretivist approaches that emphasize the interpreting role of the researcher in the process of analysis. In postmodern forms of induction, the researcher's subjectivity must be understood as its own form of experiencing the reality in question. This approach is in sharp contrast to the traditional objectivist approach that tends to treat the self of the social scientific observer as a "contaminant" that should be separated out, neutralized, minimized, standardized, and controlled (Krieger, 1991).

Postmodern thought directs us to drop the pretense of intellectual, objective accounts and, instead, formulate texts that keep all the voices in play. At the most fundamental level, it is imperative to maintain continuous reference to the subjective meaning that the actions had for the actors. At another level, it is necessary for researchers/observers to comment on the subjective meanings of those actions in the context of all other observed actions. In doing this, however, social scientists cannot detach themselves from their own participation in this experiential world. It is in this regard that representation always involves self-representation (Denzin, 1994). Social scientists are both members and nonmembers of the world they are investigating. In the process of inductive construction, social scientists are both the subject of the study and the narrators (Hertz, 1996). The researcher is fully "partisan" (Altheide & Johnson, 1994, p. 487). The result is that the products of a postmodern inductive account include the subjectivity of both the theorist/researcher and the participants.

A "moderate" postmodern position is one that rejects an anything-goes relativism. Rather, it seeks to portray complex social realities in complex ways by keeping alive multiple perspectives on the same reality (including the researcher's own viewpoint), acknowledging the dynamic and changeable nature of that reality, and recognizing the presence of contradictory and conflicting viewpoints as a natural outcome of inquiry.

Abduction

Although induction and deduction have dominated our thinking about the relationship between explanation and data, the notion of abduction, as a different form of reasoning, has become increasingly important for how we understand what occurs within qualitative analysis (Dey, 2004; Kuczynski & Daly, 2003). Abduction was introduced by the American semiotician and pragmatist philosopher Charles Peirce. Whereas induction and deduction point to a process of inquiry that either moves from data to theory or from theory to data, abduction involves a process of inference that involves consideration of both, but goes beyond what is immediately available. Abduction is often precipitated by an awareness that there are deficits in the explanation that is available in existing theory or in the immediate interpretation of the data. As a result, abduction involves moving beyond the available data and theory in order to generate a number of possible and plausible explanations or reconceptualizations (Dey, 2004). It means engaging in a form of reasoning that involves connecting findings to different kinds of theory (outside of the theory that you started with) that might help to see the data in a new light. Bengston, Acock, Allen, Dilworth-Anderson, and Klein (2005) refer to this as a process of "borrowing" from other theories, disciplines, or substantive domains in order to envision new possibilities for theoretical explanation.

One of the contributions abduction makes to qualitative analysis is that it places a greater emphasis on what actually occurs in the process of "inference." How theory and explanation are constructed is often an obscure and mystifying process. Abduction makes apparent the process by which an initial conception of an idea comes about and how it gets into the system of explanations of phenomena.

Abduction is concerned with producing plausible interpretations of data in relation to theory. As a result, abduction is consistent with Kuhn's (1962) idea that normal science is concerned with puzzle-solving activity that involves an interplay among the tools of existing theory, the formulation of hypotheses, and the construction of plausible explanations that are shaped by observation. Like Kuhn's idea that anomalies in normal puzzle-solving activity give rise to more revolutionary forms of explanation, abduction is often triggered by the incongruity between current explanations and a set of observations that do not quite fit with those explanations.

In contrast with the rather mechanical relationship between theory and data in both induction and deduction, abduction is more likely to generate explanation based on a process of imagination, metaphor, and analogy. In this regard, abduction highlights the way reason and creativity come together in the process of "inference to the best explanation" that goes beyond the determining influence of inherited theories and unexplained data. The interaction of reason and creativity come together in the abductive process through an initial imaginative stage (using words like *impressions, musing, recognition*) and an evidencing process (observations, clues, formation of rules) where the focus shifts to understanding how well the new ideas illuminate the surprising or unexplained phenomenon (Shank & Cunningham, 1996).

As indicated in Figure 3.1, abduction involves a wandering search for the best explanation that moves beyond the direct linear relationship between theory and data that occurs in either induction or deduction. In abduction, the reasoning process shifts to a search in unfamiliar or different terrain in order to generate novel possibilities for explanation. Like any puzzle-solving activity, it is rooted in an exploration of external clues, parallel processes, and new information—all within the context of immediate evidence and preexisting explanation. Abduction is a process designed to generate new insights into the subject of our investigation. Abduction is dynamic and progressive insofar as it is responsive to the discovery of new evidence. As such, it involves searches for the best explanation at a moment in time that is followed in turn by the posing of new questions and a deepening exploration. The result is that we may generate a number of possible explanations that may both complement and contradict one another. In the end, the aim is not so much to determine which explanation is "true" but to decide which interpretation is the most meaningful way of managing the data (Dey, 2004).

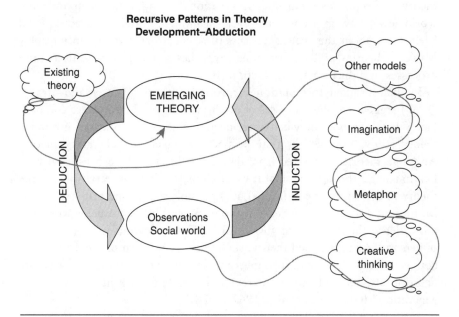

Figure 3.1   Induction, Deduction, and Abduction

Induction, Deduction, and Abduction in Practice: Cycles of Inquiry

Although induction and deduction may appear to be polarized as different and incompatible paths of inquiry, they typically work together as compatible processes in practice. Moreover, abduction introduces opportunities for thinking more broadly about how explanation is generated. When conducting a qualitative study, there is an interplay between what we already understand through our reading of theory and the empirical research (deduction), what we fail to understand but come to understand through observation and analysis (induction), and what we can bring to an understanding of the process by virtue of borrowing or searching for explanation from other domains (abduction). Prior understandings shape the direction of our inquiry—sometimes at the very specific level of hypotheses or propositions, at other times at a more general level of steering our curiosity into general domains for exploration. At the root of this process is a dynamic, iterative interplay between that which we know (which directs us deductively to certain aspects of reality) and that which we wish to discover through the exploratory paths of inductive inquiry. Overton (1991) has described this process of inquiry as the recursive cycle of knowing where theory, concepts, experiments, observations, along with metaphors and worldviews, flow in a continual cycle of induction and deduction. David Klein talks about the cyclical process of science that involves an interplay between theories and observations, hypotheses and generalizations, and processes of induction and deduction (Bengston et al., 2005).

In their original formulation of grounded theory, Glaser and Strauss (1967) argued that the processes of discovery and verification were compatible. What is important when carrying out a discovery-oriented grounded theory study, however, is that primacy be given to generating theory. Although theories generated from data are subject to the processes of verification (e.g., through comparative analysis, testing for variations in the theory under different conditions), it is possible that giving primacy to verification and testing, if carried out too soon, can block the generation of a more dense theory. It is in this regard that verification is in the service of generation in grounded theory, such that "generation of theory through comparative analysis both subsumes and assumes verifications and accurate descriptions, but only to the extent that the latter are in the service of generation" (Glaser & Strauss, 1967, p. 28).

Strauss and Corbin (1998) take an explicit position on this and argue that grounded theory analysis involves a necessary interplay between induction and deduction. Although they maintain an emphasis on inductive processes that involve moving from the specific case to the general explanation, they acknowledge the importance of prior knowledge in the creation of theoretical explanation. For them, interpretation of data is a form of deduction because it involves using our prior understandings of reality that we carry in our heads. In this regard, emerging explanation always involves the interplay between what we already know (i.e., basis for deduction) and what we are discovering in the field (basis for induction). Theoretical sampling, which is sampling on the basis of emerging theoretical concepts, is also a form of deduction that involves some level of testing emerging ideas in relation to the available observations.

In recognition that analytic insights are often to be found in the realms of imagination and metaphor that lie outside of the direct link between theory and data, abduction plays an important role in the practice of creating explanation through qualitative inquiry. Hence, although there is an emphasis on inductively "making sense of the data"—directly from the data—it is necessary as part of this process to step periodically to the side and search for ways to understand the data in the context of other meaning systems. This involves a search for analogy, metaphor, and parallel processes that help to illuminate, and offer explanation for, the unexplained phenomenon at hand.

In the practice of conducting any particular study, these cycles of inquiry may also have a developmental thrust to them. Although there are a number of pathways for how this might unfold—depending on paradigm assumptions and methodology—there are also a number of phases that would mark the process. In the following section, I use the example of trying to understand the division of domestic labor in same-sex relationships. The example is based on a postpositivist grounded theory model.

Phase I: Design and Orienting to the Issues (Deductive Beginnings)

Any inquiry begins with some decisions about the issue to be explored and the questions to be asked. In the process of putting parameters on our inquiry, we must necessarily position our research into a broader body of knowledge. This is essentially a deductive endeavor. In order to determine what we need to know, we must assess what we already know about the broad topic to be examined. To identify a "gap in the research literature" as a springboard for inquiry is to use existing thought and explanation deductively as a way of shaping inquiry. Taking stock of current knowledge through an engagement of theoretical sensitivity is a way of using existing theory and empirical research to chart the course of inquiry. Starting with these existing a priori ideas puts an emphasis on deduction as a way of shaping the direction of our qualitative study. Thesis work and research grant proposals must typically include a review of existing theory and literature and, as a result, put an emphasis on deductive processes at the early stages of research development.

Understanding Same-Sex Couples: The Deductive Stage. The division of labor in same-sex couples is one of those areas of empirical research where there is little existing literature. As a result, one of the first steps would be to examine related bodies of literature that provide some direction for the shaping of the research study. This might involve having a critical look at the division of household labor literature generally in order to identify the kinds of social conditions that affect contributions to childcare and housework. In this literature, there would be indications that education and employment status would be relevant and important factors in shaping the amount of domestic work contributed by women and men. Although this information is not directly applicable to gay and lesbian relationships, it is information that serves as a means to sensitize the researcher to the ways such factors might influence contributions to domestic work in these relationships. Other empirical literature on gay and lesbian parenting or relationship formation and maintenance may serve to provide additional clues about how the division of labor is constructed in these families. In addition to consulting the empirical literature, various theoretical perspectives can serve to construct the deductive orientation to the project. Theories about negotiation in relationships or theories about the gendered nature of care could also play an important role in shaping the direction of the inquiry. Drawing on these existing empirical and theoretical literatures, although not directly related to the research question at hand, is an important deductive strategy that gives some direction to the inductive inquiry that follows. Specifically, this deductive activity gives rise to questions about how the negotiation of the division of labor is different from the heterosexual literature; it gives rise to questions about how care is provided in gay and lesbian relationships and how this is similar to or different from other gender dynamics associated with care; or it alerts us to be mindful of the possible importance of education and employment status when trying to understand this division of labor. Furthermore, the theoretical literature on negotiation might sharpen the focus on what actually gets negotiated in the relationship beyond the specific tasks of who does what activity. Specifically, I would be curious about how identities are being negotiated, how cultural expectations are being interpreted and brought into the discussions, and how expectations and standards of housework and childcare are being discussed and worked out in the relationship.

Phase II: Articulating Questions and Opening Pathways (Inductive Explorations)

As the activities of Phase I would suggest, many of our research questions are deductively arrived at from a review of the existing literature. A review of the existing literature, however, especially in areas that have not received much attention (such as this one), serves the important function of highlighting areas of knowledge where explanation is lacking. Induction is the means by which we begin to ask tentative questions about areas we know little about. For example, when we carry out an emergent research design, we begin with general questions that open the conversation with participants and then refine that exploration with more-specific questions as our understanding unfolds. This is a process of discovering the right questions to ask. In my own experience of conducting interviews in the various studies I have done, I usually begin with a small set of questions that arise from the research design. I usually discover that some of these questions are effective and open up important areas for discussion. I also realize, fairly quickly, that some of the questions are not effective or even relevant for coming to an understanding of participants' experience. Encountering a "dud" question usually sparks the search for a better question. Hence, in the process of engaging in the conversation, I discover new questions that are critically important for getting at salient aspects of their own experience. These are questions that are inductively derived, and they lead me deeper into aspects of their experience that are important for the emerging explanation.

Understanding Same-Sex Couples: The Inductive Stage. At this stage of the research, I want to be quite careful about how I use the information I have gathered in the deductive stage. My aim is not so much to specifically test hypotheses that I may have formed in that first stage, but it is to use the ideas as a means to orient my exploration of the division-of-labor issues. I want to use this information as a way to sensitize my inquiry. Hence, at this stage, I would want to begin my exploration with some general and deliberately naïve kinds of questions. For example, following along the path of thinking about negotiation, I would want to ask these couples some preliminary questions about whether they make different contributions to work in the home. If they perceive that they do, I might then ask questions about how they make decisions about who does what in the relationship. As they talk about their experience of this, I might hold lightly in the back of

(Continued)

(Continued)

my mind a question derived from theory about how these negotiations lead to different perceptions of identity. So I might ask at some point a question like, "So how do these different contributions and activities that you make to the household lead you to see yourself differently from your partner?" This kind of question, while derived from deductive reasoning in relation to prior negotiation theory, is not intended to test a particular assertion about identity, but rather is intended to open an exploration of the way their experience of a division of labor is related to their perception of self. In this respect, my focus is on asking questions that have an inductive orientation. My goal is to have them describe to me, in ways that are meaningful to them, the activities and strategies that they use in working out a distribution of labor in their household.

Phase III: Recursive Patterns Involving Exploration, Analysis, Interpretation, and the Search for Explanation (Induction↔Deduction↔Abduction)

In many qualitative approaches, the processes of collection, analysis, and interpretation occur in a concurrent fashion. It is at this stage that induction, deduction, and abduction come together in dynamic cycles and patterns. For example, after we cast our exploratory, inductive questions and pay attention to what participants say about their experience, we compare and contrast their experience with that of others. Through this comparative process, we seek to inductively describe their common experiences— moving from the particular to the general. As we begin to see the patterns emerging in the data, we also seek to interpret and offer explanation of the phenomenon. In this search for the best explanation, abduction may be used as a way to introduce new ways of thinking about the data by going beyond the data to compare to other kinds of phenomena that are different but parallel. As we begin to formulate more general explanations across cases, we can then deductively "test" these explanations against the data collected in subsequent cases.

Understanding Same-Sex Couples: The Recursive Stage. As I get deeper into the research with gay and lesbian couples, I begin to formulate some ideas about the kinds of influences that affect how they decide who does what in the relationship. For example (keep in mind that this is a hypothetical example!), one of the patterns I begin to see through my inductive questioning is that they make decisions less on cultural expectations (such as perceived gender prescriptions) for what they should do, and more based on what they see to be their strengths and interests. At the same time, I might

observe that in many cases their agreed-upon arrangements mirror heterosexual rela-
tionships, where one person takes more control over scheduling in the home or being
the primary parent to the child. As I continue with these interviews, and these patterns
persist, my reasoning shifts from inductive exploration to a kind of deductive assessment
about whether my emerging hypothesis about how they distribute their tasks follows
along the same track. As I am doing this research, I might also open up the question
about why they are choosing a complementary form of division of labor (i.e., clearly dif-
ferentiated roles that complement each other) rather than an interchangeable model
where they share the same tasks and move in and out of the same roles. To this end, I
might abductively explore how roles and responsibilities are negotiated in other kinds of
relationships where gender may not be the primary concern. For example, I might look
at how responsibilities are negotiated in organizational management teams, support
groups, or coaching teams. I might also pay close attention to a "negative case" in my
data—one that is somewhat anomalous—and really look at how and why it is differ-
ent. Through this kind of scrutiny, I may gain a better appreciation of the hows and whys
of the dominant group.

Phase IV: Final Analysis and Drawing Conclusions (Induction↔Deduction↔Abduction)

At the latter stages of data collection and analysis, theory begins to take form (inductively) and the researcher begins to hold a sense of confidence about the emerging explanation. At this stage, the practices of verification and deduction may be used again to see if the emerging theory is a good fit for the data being collected. Although the theory continues to be modified at this stage, the emphasis is on ensuring that there is a good fit between the emerging explanation and the data themselves. Negative cases that emerge at this stage may call for additional data collection and model refinement. The continued search for the best explanation involves examination of similar processes and practices (abduction).

Understanding Same-Sex Couples: Having Confidence in the Inductively Arrived-At Theory.
As my explanations about the ways they arrived at a complementary division of labor
begin to "harden" in the latter stages of analysis, I may wish to look back through my data,
as a form of verification, to see that my emerging explanation still makes sense with the
data. I might also do this as a "member check" where I go back to some of the couples
and present some of my ideas to see whether they make sense to them. At this stage of
refining my theory, I am still straddling induction and deduction—verifying and yet modi-
fying when I perceive that I don't have it "quite right." Abduction provides a pathway for
trying to work through remaining puzzles.

These paths of inquiry provide a basis for thinking about the logic of our analytic procedures. When we embrace induction, deduction, and abduction as concurrent and reinforcing processes, we can shift easily between theory construction and refutation and the creative exploration of ideas and a concern for evidence. In an examination of children's family labor in low-income households across a decade of qualitative research, Lisa Dodson provides an example of how induction and deduction can work together in a series of grounded theory studies (Dodson & Dickert, 2004). In the early 1990s, Dodson conducted a number of studies that focused on the inductive process of discovery using a constructivist grounded theory methodology. Life history interviews, ethnography, and focus groups (mostly with young teenaged girls) were used to generate an emergent theory about their labor contributions. In subsequent studies between 1998 and 2002 on the same topic, the analysis shifted to a focus on verification through a process of theoretical sampling where previously identified themes were examined directly in subsequent interviews and focus groups.

In the next chapter, our attention shifts to the nature of the reality we seek to understand when we use qualitative methods in family and human development research.

Note

1. Although Charmaz uses the term *constructivist* here, I see it as more consistent with the term "constructionist" according to Gergen's (1985) differentiation of the two terms (see Chapter 2).

4

Ontology of the Human Realm

Theoretical Foundations
for Qualitative Inquiry

Ontology and the Nature of Human Reality

As a metaphysical term, *ontology* is concerned with the philosophical assumptions that we create about the nature of "being." In qualitative research, the way we go about our inquiry about what human beings do is influenced by our assumptions about the nature of being.

All forms of social scientific inquiry are rooted in a set of assumptions about the fundamental nature of human beings. How we construct this fundamental "nature" shapes the ways we go about inquiring into the patterns of human behavior. Although scholars have argued that the distinction between quantitative and qualitative methods is false because they both seek to understand the same human reality, I would argue that they do make different assumptions about how that human reality is conceptualized. As a result of holding different assumptions about human beings, quantitative and qualitative approaches create very different research products.

Shweder (1996) argues that qualitative and quantitative approaches are fundamentally different because they rest on different ontological assumptions about the nature of human reality. He argues that quantitative research, with its emphasis on pointing, sampling, counting, measuring, calculating, and abstracting, is premised on the notion that there is an objective conception of a "really real" world that can be accurately understood and portrayed in a "quanta" form (p. 178). It means getting beyond subjective accounts of that reality that involve "illusions that should be rejected" (p. 177). Through the rigorous application of methodological and statistical techniques, the goal is accurate representation and certainty of explanation. Ontologically, there is an assumption of a human reality that is doggedly persistent and patterned, a reality that can be measured with standardized questions and variables, and a reality that can thereby be understood and counted on (the pun is intended!).

Qualitative research, by contrast, with its emphasis on interpretation, empathy, narration, and contextualization, is premised on a different set of ontological assumptions. In the tradition of qualia, human reality can be understood only by reference to how reality is made meaningful or by reference to what it is like to experience that reality. Engaging a qualitative approach is contingent upon "respecting" the nature of human subject matter (Prus, 1994). Ontologically, there is an assumption that people meaningfully, actively, and interactively engage in the world in which they find themselves. Studying human beings is different from the study of physical objects because human beings have the capacity to use language, assign meaning, and take themselves and others into account in the way they create relationships and act in the world. Accordingly, human reality is emergent, situational, changeable, and subject to ongoing definition and redefinition. For Prus, these ontological assumptions mean developing methodology that is attentive first and foremost to the "human essence" (Prus, 1998, p. 25). Methodologically, this means going directly to the empirical social world, which is the "actual group life of human beings," for this is the place to form and examine root images, concepts, and interpretations (Blumer, 1969, p. 32). This group life can be understood through language since this is the medium through which social life is created and maintained.

As Acock, van Dulmen, Allen, and Piercy (2005) have argued, however, there are many opportunities to use mixed methods where the information gleaned through both quantitative measures and qualitative explorations can provide perspectives on family experience. Although our research questions will lead us to follow the assumptions of quanta or qualia, it is important to recognize that both can provide different but complementary perspectives that can enhance our knowledge of family reality.

When we think about the ontology of the social world that we seek to understand, it is important to make the distinction between data and phenomena. Whereas phenomena are the undifferentiated, naturally occurring experiences of being in the world, data are empirically selected, recorded representations of that world. As Charmaz (2003b) has argued, data are always reconstructions because they involve researcher narration and recall. Hence, when we use the term *gather data,* we engage in a scientific process with several components. First, through a process of selection, guided by our research questions, we choose to focus on certain aspects of experiential phenomena, thereby excluding other aspects. As Oakley (1974) has said, "a way of seeing is a way of not seeing" (p. 27). In this regard, data collection is always premised on the idea of framing phenomenological reality. Second, to speak of gathering data is to acknowledge the instrumental role of the researcher in recording the phenomena of interest. To *gather* is defined as the act of "bringing together," "assembling," "harvesting," or "amassing." Every spring, I head out into the bush wearing my rubber boots to gather fiddleheads (the tightly coiled, edible heads of the wild ostrich fern). This is a process of locating, assessing the quality of the field, selecting plants, and picking individual heads. Similarly, when gathering data, the researcher locates, selects, observes, and records the phenomena of interest. Data, therefore, come into being only through the agency of the researcher. Finally, data are constructed into a different form from the phenomena of interest. In qualitative research, data are often in the form of audio or video recordings that are then converted into transcriptions of conversation. An audiotape of an interview, a videotape of a meeting, or the transcription of an interview is data, not the phenomena themselves. Although there is a correspondence between data and phenomena, data involve a type of "reformatting" of the reality at hand.

Ontology is therefore concerned with the phenomena that we are seeking to understand. In general terms, there are a number of ontological assumptions about the nature of human reality that shape the direction of qualitative inquiry:

Meaningful Reality

There is an assumption that human beings are involved in intentional activity. Humans have minds that allow for self-reflection, assessments of situational conditions, and the ability to anticipate future events. Minding behavior is the means by which individuals assign meaning to their own actions and the actions of others. This interpretive process is central to the human condition. Although there are continuities in the way meanings are assigned to situations and activities, these meanings are part of an ongoing process of constructing and reconstructing reality.

The Meaning of Meaning

Meaning is a central if not hackneyed term in the qualitative tradition. As Bruner (1990) has so thoughtfully articulated, the construction of individual, psychological meanings is fully contingent on participation in the symbolic systems of culture. In his words:

> The very shape of our lives—the rough and perpetually changing draft of our auto-biography that we carry in our minds—is understandable to ourselves and to others only by virtue of those cultural systems of interpretation. But culture is also consti-tutive of mind. By virtue of this actualization in culture, meaning achieves a form that is public and communal rather than private and autistic. (p. 33)

Social Reality

Our humanness is made possible only through interaction with others. We are born into a social world, and it is as participants in that world that we meaningfully construct our own realities. The way we construct meaning is always "borrowed" insofar as it is our observations of meaning-making in others that provides the basis for our own minding and meaning-making behavior. Although we can talk in principle about subjectivity as an individual process, it is always confounded by the influence of the other. Our ability to live meaningfully in this social world is contingent on interactions with, and interpretations of others. In this regard, individual subjectivity can only be understood as it is embedded in a network of intersubjectivity. Identity and perceptions of the self are essentially social in nature insofar as the self is a product of reflected appraisals from others. Negotiation and alignment of action in any situation are contingent on this intersubjectivity where a shared, commonly available set of meanings and expectations serves as a basis for aligning action. Bruner (1990) carries this one step farther by acknowledging that living in a social reality also involves mechanisms for accommodating difference. He argues that living within a shared cultural community is not just about shared beliefs or common values, but rather must also include a "set of interpretive procedures for adjudicating the different construals of reality that are inevitable in any diverse society" (p. 95).

Symbolic Reality

To live in a meaningful social world is to use language as a means for communicating and aligning action. Language is a set of learned symbols that provides the medium for meaningful interaction with others. This symbolic reality is made possible by the shared meanings that are given to a word, an utterance, a gesture. Social life is made possible by this shared symbolic reality, for it provides a basis upon which to make indications to another in interaction that can be interpreted in a way that is consistent with the intention.

Words are the currency of qualitative inquiry. It is through words that people bring to life the experience that they have. We can think of language taking several forms. Most commonly, we think of language as being referential or representational whereby the words are seen to stand for lived experience. Ontologically, this is a realist position that involves understanding the correspondence between what was said and what was experienced. Accordingly, researchers would be interested in whether participants were telling the truth about their experience and whether they were being accurate in their descriptions of experience. Language can also be thought of as being constitutive of reality. In this view, words do not stand for some other experience, but rather they constitute and create reality. It is through words and conversation that we live our lives, and these words are the reality of interest. Ontologically, this is a relativist position that focuses on the use of language in constructing reality. Finally, we can also think of language as relational insofar as words provide the interpersonal tools with which we create and engage in relationships. We use language to "do" relationships in and outside of families and with research participants. Language used in the service of those relationships is the means by which we come to understand socially meaningful, interactive reality.

Temporal, Emergent Reality

Meaning-making activity is an ongoing project that involves continuities with the past and the production of new meanings in relation to the future. As Elias (1992) argues, time is a construction that people create and learn through symbols that arises out of a need for synchronized activity. In order for any synchronized interaction to proceed, the situation must be defined along many temporal dimensions including pace, turn taking, the interpretation of past events, and projections about the future. Mead's (1932) theory of action focuses on activity that is seen as the emergence of events that constitute a present with a past and future horizon. In contrast to a linear view of time, past, present, and future are not points on a line but are contingencies that are always fluctuating in accordance with lived experience in the present moment. For Mead, this is the "specious present." In this regard, social reality is an emergent experience of defining situations with the shared symbolic tools acquired in the past while at the same time navigating the contingencies of an uncertain future. Definitions of time in a situation serve to shape the meaning of situated identities that are "activated in a present, informed through the use of the past, and structured by anticipating and sharing futures" (Katovich, 1987, p. 188). According to this ontological assumption, human reality must be understood as an unfolding process of constructed meanings.

Mundane Reality

Reality, as it is lived on a day-to-day basis, is often experienced as mundane and unremarkable. When experienced in this way, meaning-making activity is concerned with strategically getting through the day in a way that may be guided by the practical considerations of efficiency, avoiding embarrassment, or seeking attention. This is, as phenomenologists would suggest, the "taken-for-granted reality" that is part of "gearing into" the everyday life world. It is not special or even particularly reflective—but rather is part of living pragmatically. For example, in an observation study of couple interaction, Driver and Gottman (2004) talk about the importance of paying attention to the "unremarkable" aspects of marriage relationships such as eating, responses to family phone calls, and making decisions as a way of understanding major emotional components of marriage, including conflict and romance.

Mundane reality is even more apparent when unusual or unexpected events occur. These events have been referred to as "epiphanies" (Denzin, 1989) or "problematics" (Schutz, 1971); they serve to punctuate the taken-for-granted flow of experience. By their unusual nature, these events draw attention to the prevalence of mundane reality.

Contradictions in Social Reality

The presence of paired opposites or contradictions are a normal part of social relationships and are essential to change and growth in a relationship (Baxter, 1990). Central to any relationship is the contradiction of identity: sustaining a distinct "I" at the same time the "we" identity is being constructed (Baxter & Montgomery, 1996). Consistent with these ideas, Bakhtin (1981) talked about the way dialogue in a relationship involves simultaneous differentiation from, yet fusion with, another. Specifically, there is a constant interplay between the forces of unity (centripetal) and the forces of difference (centrifugal). The tension between autonomy and connection, identified as one of the most central contradictions in relationships, is a key ontological assumption about human nature. Contradictions are inherent in social life and not evidence of failure or inadequacy in a person or in a social system (Baxter & Montgomery, 1996).

Ontological Assumptions About Human Development

When we shift our focus specifically to human *development* research, there are a number of other ontological assumptions that warrant attention. Time is a central ontological principle in human development research. Individuals tell the story of their past from the standpoint of the present. We seek to understand how individuals perceive change over time—including both patterned, stage-related transitions (e.g., Erikson, 1963) and those event-related experiences of significant transition and change. Context is also critical for understanding human development, with Bronfenbrenner's (1979) model of ecological context identifying the various social and cultural layers within which development is embedded. The family itself is one of those critical ecological contexts within which development occurs. According to Pratt and Fiese (2004), the family is an intermediary between the individual and the wider cultural context that provides a place for children to learn about the complexities of value acquisition, expression of human emotion, and socialization to appropriate behavior. Accordingly, when we seek to understand individual development, it is important to pay attention to the relationship between individual biography and the collective family history (Miller, 2000).

In the study of both individual and family development, transition has been a central area of focus. With its emphasis on the processes of change, qualitative research has been particularly interested in understanding the way individuals and groups make transitions from one stage to another or from one set of roles and identities to another. This focus provides a means for understanding both normative and expected transitions in the course of individual and family development (e.g., the transition to parenthood) and unexpected, nonnormative events such as "problematics" (Schutz, 1971), critical incidents or events (Strauss, 1959) or "epiphanies" (Denzin, 1989). Sassler (2004) for example, using a grounded theory approach, has examined the process by which young people enter into cohabitating unions and identified a number of different meanings they bring to their experience (e.g., accelerated cohabitators vs. purposeful delayers). Although less common, qualitative research has also taken a longitudinal approach to examine the ways families change over time. For example, a study of women in deep poverty in a rural area of one American state examined how these women experienced different forms of economic vulnerability at three points in time over a 6-year period: first when they were engaged in the process mandated by the state to get off welfare, a period where they tried to find work, and a year following the termination of welfare benefits (Blalock, Tiller, & Monroe, 2004). This kind of research is effective in illustrating the strategies that families use in adapting to change as well as highlighting systemic barriers to change.

Although there are many theoretical approaches for understanding human development, the concepts of a life course approach provide a basis upon which to delineate key ontological assumptions in human development. According to Giele and Elder (1998), the life course approach refers to the "sequence of socially defined events and roles that an individual enacts over time" (p. 22). It involves an interplay between the age-related states of individuals as they grow biologically and adapt psychologically, and the external events and activities that occur outside of the individual but that shape the course of that person's development. This includes being part of a cohort or a generation and involves the effects of historical events, cultural norms, and social structures.

Specifically, there are a number of components of developmental reality rooted in a life course perspective that have implications for how we carry out qualitative research (Giele & Elder, 1998).

Human Agency

Although human development can be understood by identifying patterns of physical growth and social-psychological development, it is important to understand the agency of individuals as they actively seek to adapt their behavior to the environment. As a result, the qualitative study of human development is concerned with understanding the *motives* of individuals as they seek to meet their *needs*, their *decision-making strategies* as they navigate complex environments, and the way they *organize* their lives around *goals* such as being economically secure or having satisfying relationships. Gender plays an important role in understanding how individuals subjectively navigate these environments.

Timing of Lives

Although agency places the emphasis on the way individuals actively navigate the course of their own lives, it is also critical to understand the way individuals *respond* to the timing of external events in their lives. Here the focus is on adaptation to changing conditions and the way individuals draw on resources as a way of coping with these changes. This includes changing economies and the conditions of work, proliferation of technology, globalization, increased consumption, and changing norms and practices in families.

To examine the timing of lives is to look at the intersection of the subjective experience of age and the social roles that one takes on in relation to changing social structural conditions. For example, in order to understand the timing of marriage or parenthood in people's lives, it is important to consider the way historical conditions associated with education and work have influenced this transition. The focus here is on the interplay between the construction of individual biographies and the historical events of which they are a part.

Location in Time and Place

Individual development must be understood within social and physical contexts. Development occurs within physical contexts such as houses, neighborhoods, and countries that come with their own cultural meanings. Individual development is also shaped by the temporal context of being part of a generation (e.g., the depression or baby boom) and being influenced by key historical events (the fall of the Berlin Wall or 9/11 terror attacks). When examining human development in time and place, we can understand both the "general and unique aspects of individual location," which provide a means for understanding the way personal experience is "socially and individually *patterned* in ways that carry through time" (Giele & Elder, 1998, p. 9).

Linked Lives

Individual development is embedded in a milieu of social action where individuals interact and mutually influence each other. This happens at many levels (interpersonal, institutional, cultural) and involves the interplay between individual motives and social and cultural expectations. As a result, it is concerned with the way relationships in families or with friends or coworkers affect the course of one's own development. It is also concerned with the way individuals are shaped by neighborhoods, religious affiliations, and ethnic practices. There is always variation in the degree to which individuals integrate cultural norms and expectations and the degree to which there is discontinuity between these expectations and chosen pathways of experience.

In summary, the study of human development involves being attentive to the subjective aspects of meaning and satisfaction associated with various roles and activities (agency), being responsive to key events (timing), monitoring the effects of geographical location and historical events (time and place), and examining the experience of social relationships in families, communities, and other social institutions (linked lives). Drawing on the principles of life course analysis, Palkovitz (2002) provides an excellent example of the ways in which a qualitative study can bring these domains together. Based on 40 interviews with a diverse sample of fathers, he examined the subjectivity of age, timing of the transition to fatherhood, location in time and place (neighborhood, social class, etc.), and social linkages (relationships to partners, parents, and other children). Through an analysis of the ways that involved fathering affects men's adult development, Palkovitz explored the meaning of father involvement in relation to the self (emotions, values, and health), in the context of relationships (i.e., intimate partners, relatives), in relation to friends and community involvement, and in relation to work and career development (including the effects of work-related policies).

Ontological Assumptions About Families

In the same way that our assumptions about human development provide direction for inquiry, so too do our assumptions about the nature of family reality open pathways for how we do our research. The way we define families has become problematic in an era when diversity is the norm. Families can no longer be seen as monolithic structures with a uniformity of experience and a universality of structure and functions (Eichler, 1988; Thompson & Walker, 1995; Thorne, 1982). A variety of forces have contributed to the dethroning of "the family" (Coontz, 1992). Increased labor-force participation by women, divorce, violence, the women's movement, changes in the economy, and individualism have been identified as major forces in changing traditional family structures. In the face of these changes, efforts to define the family as a unique domain with rigid boundaries have met with strong resistance. As a consequence, any effort to study families qualitatively must in some way attend to these diffuse definitions and elusive boundaries.

The ways families have changed in recent years, and how we study them, have become an important focus in the modernist-postmodernist debate. While the modernist position holds to the family as a uniform and monolithic structure, a postmodernist view sees families as varied and diverse (Cheal, 1991). Postmodernism, with its focus on "pluralism, disorder and fragmentation" (Cheal, 1993, p. 9) not only sees the structure of families as diverse, but the ways that families are defined and interpreted as pluralistic. The diverse empirical reality of families is now generally accepted among researchers. This diversity, however, finds expression in many other forms in families, including family structure, language usage, power relationships, and expectations (Gubrium, 1993).

Postmodern ideas play an important role in dereifying "the family." To speak of a reified family is to make reference to family as some kind of unchanging, identifiable family form. From this perspective, the family can no longer be seen as a thing or an ideological representation, but must be viewed as a diverse and changing set of everyday practices (Gubrium & Holstein, 1990). The challenge for qualitative researchers who study families is to confront, represent, or accommodate diverse family realities. Rather than artificially dividing the social world into heuristically convenient categories like the family, it is important to examine the complex unity of people's lives (Bernardes, 1986) as they are experienced across a variety of categories including work, media, education, commerce, class, race, and gender.

One of the ways researchers contend with this is to shift the question from a preoccupation with "What is a family?" (a structural question) to "What do families do?" (a process question). By focusing on the question of how individuals within different kinds of families live as family we can understand what family is through an understanding of family as activities, experiences, beliefs, and practices. Qualitative studies of family time, for example, provide an opportunity to understand how families make choices about eating, talking, and playing; they provide insight into the ways culture and social class influence the experience of family time; and they provide a window on the kinds of values and beliefs that families express in the process of finding time to be with each other (Daly, 2001; Tubbs, Roy, & Burton, 2005).

Qualitative research is well positioned to understand family processes (Daly, 1992a). Burgess's (1926) time-honored definition of the family as "a unit of interacting personalities" opens many possibilities for how we can come to understand families in their many forms and in their variety of practices. Hess and Handel's (1959) *Family Worlds* is a classic qualitative study of families that focuses on what families "do" from each member's perspective. In a retrospective of this work, Handel (1996) conceptualizes families as "complex active agents in constructing their own family life, and we conceptualize each family member, each child as well as each adult, as an agent whose actions contribute to shaping that family's interdependent life together—and apart" (p. 344). Qualitative methods facilitate the study of process in families from the perspective of family members: through interviews, observations, and case studies we can examine patterns of interaction, dynamics, negotiations, transitions, change, and the meanings of spatial and temporal contexts.

With qualitative methods, the focus is not on identifying structural or demographic trends in families but rather on the processes by which families create, sustain, and discuss their own family realities. What are the individual and collective phenomenological experiences of family members? Families are groups that construct individual and shared meanings. There is a concordance between families as a primary locus for the construction of meaning and the assumptions of qualitative research that focus on capturing that meaning. What we seek to do with qualitative research on families is not to understand how many exhibit a set of characteristics, but how some families provide descriptive accounts of the meanings of their experience.

Ontologically, families are a distinctive focus of study. Although it is difficult to identify what these unique features are without falling into a definition of *family*, there are a number of characteristics of "family" that make this a unique social group for inquiry.

"Family" as a Province of Meaning

In an era of diversity, what is critical in understanding family as a social group is the way members define who they are as a family. Using a variation on the theme of W. I. Thomas's dictum, we can say that, "When family members define their family situation as real, it is real in its consequences." Embedded in this idea is the capacity of a family and its members to be self-reflexive about who they are as a group. In order to take into account the competing and myriad meanings of family in contemporary life, it is necessary to conceptualize family as a socially constructed, situationally contingent cluster of meanings that present family activity as a constellation of ideas, images, and terminology (Holstein & Gubrium, 1995).

Within phenomenology, a "province of meaning" is a way to talk about a boundaried, shared reality among a unique collective. In the same way that we can think about "science" or "religion" as unique provinces of meaning, we can think about "family" as a unique province of meaning. Understanding family in this way moves beyond concerns with the "necessary conditions" of family such as blood ties, conjugal relationships, sexual orientation, or coresidency. Family members participate in and ongoingly reconstruct a meaning system that is part of their collective identity as a family. This involves the construction of spatial and social-psychological boundaries that serve to maintain private family meanings. It involves participation in collective activities that produce shared meanings and a collective bank of memories. Family members engage in productive activities in order to provide material support for one another. Through the process of material acquisition, they symbolically display to others who they are. Furthermore, there is usually an investment on the part of family members to work toward a goal of permanency in relationships. As qualitative researchers, we have an interest in understanding how this unique meaning structure is created, managed, and sometimes dissolved. In keeping with Weber's *verstehen* tradition, qualitative methods are well suited to understanding these unique meanings, definitions, and subjective experiences of family members (see Daly, 1992a).

To suggest that families are a unique province of meaning is not to imply in any way that the family is perceived as a monolithic structure. Rather, it is important to examine the ways all family members bring meaning to this collective "province." In the history of family research, we have encountered different challenges to understanding this collective meaning. Several decades ago, there was a concern about the overrepresentation of women's perspectives on family experience, leading Saffilios-Rothschild (1969) to suggest that the field was more aptly called "wives' family sociology." More recently, there has been an interest in trying to bring children's voices into our understanding of family meaning making (Kuczynski, 2003; Shehan, 1999). This has emerged out of a shift from seeing children as passive receptacles of socialization efforts by parents and other adults to seeing children as active agents in the construction of family worlds.

Family as a Private Domain

Although feminist thinkers (Ferree, 1990) have challenged the rigorous separation of the public and private spheres, for most people the deep and intricate texture of the family domain continues to be experienced as a separate and unique space that is backstage from their public presentation of self (Goffman, 1959). Families vary with respect to the permeability of their boundaries but they typically are thought of as being one of the most closed and private of all social groups. Family members coalesce in the processes of preserving and protecting their traditions, habits, and secrets. Keeping conflictual, dysfunctional, or sexual behaviors from the purview of outsiders is a key mechanism by which families construct and maintain their unique self-definitions. In this regard, families are a distinctive focus of study characterized by privacy; shared meanings that are not readily available to nonfamily members; relationships with an intended permanency that are rooted in kinship, blood ties, adoption, or marriage; shared traditions; intensity of involvement that ranges from the most loving to the most violent; and a collage of individual interests, experiences, and qualities. The field researcher who studies families faces the challenge of entering and managing an intimate space. By offering to enter participants' life worlds, rather than imposing the formality of a survey or an experiment, qualitative researchers are in a good position to understand better the private meanings of families. For example, the use of unstructured interviews, observations, or diaries and letters allows participants to discuss their experiences in their own language, in their own natural setting, and according to their own comfort in disclosing.

Although some aspects of family experience are deliberately hidden from researchers, some aspects of family reality are hidden simply because of their apparent mundaneness. Some aspects of family roles and relationships are so routine and repetitive that they are taken for granted and not considered to be important by participants. In my first fatherhood project, I heard many fathers express surprise at the end of the interview that they had so much to talk about. Prior to my visit, they were somewhat anxious about whether they would have anything to say about the topic. I attributed this to their perception that fathering was such a "natural" and routine part of their everyday world that they truly believed that there couldn't possibly be much to discuss.

In the research literature, housework serves as an interesting parallel here. It was Betty Friedan who referred to housework as "the problem with no name." Prior to housework being politicized and understood as part of a broader ideological structure, it was so mired in the mundaneness of everyday life that we could not even articulate it as a legitimate focus of study. Qualitative scholars like Anne Oakley (1974) and Helena Lopata (1971) successfully excavated this taken-for-granted domestic site and in so doing, brought about a whole new consciousness of gender practices in the home. Families have many "problems with no names" that need to be examined. For the qualitative researcher, the invitation is to question the taken for granted in order to get a more focused view of family meanings and interactions.

Family as an Emotional Domain

Emotions have been overshadowed by the rationalization of the family realm. When we focus on meaning, the tendency is to focus on this as "minding" activity, characterized primarily as a set of reasoned judgments and assessments. In contrast with our efforts to catalogue the attitudes, actions, and activities of families, we need to examine the charged language and experience of emotions as they are expressed in the experience of living in families. Much of the everyday rhetoric of living in families is about love, jealousy, anger, disappointment, hurt, tolerance, or care. Emotions are often difficult to track in families because they may involve wild swings or expressions that are inconsistent with other attitudes and behaviors. Yet in all families there are cycles of emotional contagion where individuals within families or events external to families precipitate changes in a family's emotional climate. A stressful day at work or school can create a family tone of tension or blame; the death of a parent can create an atmosphere of sadness, anger, or relief; an impending wedding brings collective anxiety and hopefulness. Qualitative methods provide a means for attending to the emotional currents of everyday family life.

For example, in the family therapy research literature, Olson, Russell, Higgins-Kessler, and Miller (2002) examined the emotional impact of extramarital affairs on the couple relationship. Using a grounded theory approach, they conducted telephone interviews with individuals within the relationship who had either been involved in the extramarital affair or whose partner had been involved. The results of this research demonstrated how the experience of the affair changed the relationship over time, how couples managed anger and mistrust in the relationship, and how they made efforts toward reestablishing trust and working toward forgiveness.

Families as Relationships

If our primary concern in using qualitative methods is to understand what family members do in their everyday lives, then our focus can fruitfully be directed at how relationships are managed in families. Fluidity and emergence are inherent in the very definition of relationship. At a practical level, family relationships can be understood at the level of daily communication with specific reference to the ways family members talk in and about their relationships (Duck, Acitelli, & Nicholson, 2000). By focusing on talk as a central component of relating, we can begin to understand how love is expressed, power is exercised, or conflict is generated in family relationships. For example, Fraenkl (1994) examined how couples talk about and experience time in their relationship in order to come to a deeper understanding of the rhythm of their everyday life.

Other research is more focused on trying to understand intergenerational relationships in families. For example, LaSala (2002) conducted 80 in-depth interviews with 20 gay and 20 lesbian couples in order to understand their perceptions of their parents' and in-laws' attitudes toward their relationship, their sexual orientation, and the impact this was perceived to have on them. Through this analysis, they examined the ways partner loyalties, parental disapproval, and management of intergenerational boundaries were handled differently when comparing gay and lesbian couples.

To make an ontological assertion that families are relationships raises a number of important questions about underlying assumptions. First, we inevitably encounter a paradox when we seek to study dynamic relationships, for as soon as we draw any observations about the course of a relationship in a family, we freeze that relationship—we remove it from its context and draw a conceptual frame around the dynamics. In the process of observing and conceptualizing relationships, we are drawn to "stasis and fixity" and, as a result, tend to overlook the "fluid and uncertain" quality of relationships (Duck et al., 2000, p. 180). Second, as researchers we must make decisions about how to conceptualize relationships in families. These can be individual-to-individual relationships (e.g., a brother and a sister), category-to-category relationships (e.g., parent–child relationships), or multiple, dynamic relationships involving various groupings (e.g., family time). The way we choose to focus our lens on these relationships will inevitably shape how we portray families in our research. Third, any relationship in a family can be uniquely understood from the perspective of each member of that relationship. While participation in that relationship is shared, the meaning of the relationship for each participant will be, in some way, different. As researchers, it is important that we pay attention to these multiple perspectives. The degree to which individuals in a relationship either have authority or exert power or control on some other basis is also critical for understanding the meanings they bring to the relationship. Fourth, the content of everyday communication in family relationships can lead to both closeness/intimacy and distance/division. Hence, it is important to be attentive to both positive aspects of relationships that contribute to feelings of love and attachment and negative aspects of relationships that contribute to anger, conflict, and abuse. Fifth, relationships within families are influenced by relationships with people outside of families. This can result in mixed allegiances or competing demands. Of interest here are the ways family members manage these multiple relationships. Finally, when we study relationships in families, it is important that we pay attention to the direction of influence in those relationships. For example, in contrast with a set of relationship assumptions that parents unidirectionally influence children, there is more emphasis now on seeking to understand the bidirectional influences in parent–child relationships (Lollis & Kuczynski, 1997).

Family Practices

Much of our traditional theorizing in family studies has endeavored to understand families as if they were suspended in time, space, and culture. Positivistic forms of theorizing look for enduring patterns of explanation that represent persistent patterns in family experience. By contrast, a focus on family practices is concerned with the emergent conditions, fluidity, and changing definitions of everyday reality. The emphasis is on how family members produce and reproduce themselves as family through the interactions, language, and organization of their everyday relations. In this regard, "family" is both a meaningful resource and a practical metaphor that is used in the production of caring relationships and mutual obligations (Holstein & Gubrium, 1994).

Morgan (1999) outlines a number of themes for understanding family practices. First, the emphasis is on the *active* ways family members carry out their routine, everyday practices. In other words, the focus is on how family members *are doing family* in their everyday taken-for-granted worlds (similar to the way men and women are *doing gender*; West & Zimmerman, 1987). What makes family practices meaningful is the degree to which family members perceive these practices as being somewhat "special," "different," or "emotionally significant." Equally important, however, is to recognize that when we focus on family practices, these are always continuous with other areas of existence. As a result, family practices must also be understood as gender practices, class practices, work practices, or age practices. For example, the conditions of work (number of hours, degree of flexibility and control) can have profound effects on the practices of parenthood. In keeping with this, it is important to keep in perspective the interplay between the *construction of individual biographies* within families and the *historical framework* within which these constructions occur. For example, the kinds of parenting practices that are forged by a mother or father are shaped in part by the cultural parenting norms at any historical moment (see for example a study by Knudson-Martin & Mahoney, 2005, that looks at the process of achieving relationship equality in two samples of couples— one from 1982 and one from 2001). Finally, according to Morgan, it is necessary to account for the interplay between the perspectives of the family member whose actions are being accounted for and the perspectives of the observer. In this regard, observed family practices must be understood as a product of perceived and experienced family activity.

Examination of family practices is concerned with understanding families as they perform in relation to perceived collective cultural codes and beliefs. Family members draw on the rituals, practices, and expectations that are available in the "cultural tool kit" (Swidler, 1986) and in the process they create themselves as a cultural form that expresses systemic beliefs and ideals. They draw meaning from the cultural matrix of which they are a part and express meanings about the kind of family they wish to appear as, all in the service of creating a definition of who they are as a family. Families do this in a variety of ways: They choose to mask or pronounce their racial or ethnic traditions and practices, they choose to follow or rebuke trends in the material world, or they create impressions about who they are as a family that either support or challenge dominant notions of family stability or normalcy.

One of the ways to access family practices is to investigate aspects of their experience that are highly visible, important, or significant. For example, Marks (2004) examined the experience of highly religious families from a diverse sample of Christians, Jews, Mormons, and Muslims. Through interviews with 12 mothers and 12 fathers ($N = 24$), he focused on the process by which families create, plan, and organize religious practices and rituals—often in the face of resistance and challenges from both inside and outside the family. The way these families assign meaning to and engage in these religious practices becomes a means for understanding marriage relationships, parenting behavior, and family beliefs and values.

The manner in which families experience love also serves as an important window on family practices. Beck and Beck-Gernsheim (1995) have tackled the complexities and contradictions of love in families as they relate to a broad array of cultural processes including industrialization, gender dynamics at home and in the work place, parenting, individuation, and loneliness. Love can serve as an important vehicle for understanding the linkages between the personal practices of family life (e.g., expressions of intimacy, working through conflict, care, or sex) and the public messages about love in the media (e.g., idealized romance). Examining family practices allows us to look at the varied and unique ways that families construct changing definitions of themselves within the broader cultural milieu.

The examination of family practices is central to understanding family processes. By articulating a logic of practice (Bourdieu, 1990), the experience of everyday family life can be examined in terms of regularities, irregularities, and even incoherences. To understand families in action is to get beyond an emphasis on only rational and logical coherence in families, in order to understand the logic of practice whereby families must make instantaneous judgments, assessments, and urgent decisions that often preclude the orderly logic that comes with the luxuries of detachment and reflection (Swidler, 2001).

Many family decisions are based on inherited traditions, practices, and beliefs. When family members live their lives in the taken-for-granted uninterrupted mode, they are typically "guided both emotionally and intellectually in their judgments and activities by unexamined prejudices" (Geertz, 1973, p. 218). These unexamined prejudices not only reflect the degree to which culture is embedded in actions and beliefs, but also highlight the relative immunity of culture from routine scrutiny. As a result, many family behaviors or beliefs that constitute proud family traditions continue unchecked until there is conflict or crisis that calls them into question. When faced with new challenges and crises, families are more likely to be reflexively aware of their taken for granted practices.

Whose Family? Issues of Voice

Families also present a challenge in terms of the "unit" of analysis. Most survey research focuses on the individual as the unit and focuses on that individual's characteristics, attitudes, and behaviors. By contrast, qualitative research can accommodate multiple perspectives and can better deal with families, couple relationships, or sibling relationships as "units." Such "units," composed of more than one member, can provide richer accounts and closer approximations of lived family experiences. Although the practical limitations of an observation or interview segment and/or the nature of some research questions may lead researchers to focus on one family member at a time, the composite family picture, with all its inherent corroborations and contradictions, is a strength of qualitative research.

As researchers, we also need to be attentive to the fact that families may have spokespersons who present the family to the outside world. Although these spokespersons can serve as key informants, they also can act as a kind of gatekeeper in the presentation of family images. Multiple member perspectives may be key in many types of family research. The question of deciding who to talk to is intricately linked to the research question and who we believe can best inform us about the phenomenon in question. For example, when the focus of investigation is parent–child relationships, data would minimally be gathered from mothers, fathers, and children. In a family therapy study of how couples deal with the sequelae of childhood sexual abuse among adult females and their partners, Wiersma (2003) conducted in-depth interviews with six couples. Here the research question was designed to elicit an understanding of each partner's perspectives on the reciprocal and dynamic effects of the abuse on each other. As a result, it was important to include both voices in the research.

There are also a number of practical challenges that are encountered when interviewing multiple members of families. For example, in a grounded theory study of families who have adopted special needs children (Clark, Thigpen, & Yates, 2006), the researchers began with interviews with one or both parents (some were single parents) and when possible sought to include the children in the research. Although their goal was to include both the adopted children and the parents, the results were primarily derived from the parents since getting information from the children was difficult for a variety of reasons. For example, some children were too young to provide meaningful information; adolescents were reluctant to participate and when they did were often "monosyllabic"; and in some cases, parents were reluctant to have their children included in the research. As a result, while multiple perspectives may be considered ideal at the outset of a project, practical considerations often get in the way of including multiple voices.

The way we articulate what it is that family members do in the course of being a family shapes how we frame our studies and where we invest our analytic energy. Whether we think of "family" as ideology, experience, process, or structure, it continues to reflect a sphere of meaning that is part of the everyday life world. Our efforts to understand this sphere of meaning through qualitative methods must be attentive to the limitations of knowledge. As Lather (1990) has suggested, all knowledge is social, partial, local, and critical. From this standpoint, the knowledge that we can expect to garner from family spheres of meaning involves an attentiveness to the way meanings are produced through interaction (social); the changing and incomplete view of those meanings (partial); how they are located in a specific space, time, and a cultural and ideological context (local); and the manner in which values are produced, maintained, or constrained in the production of that knowledge (critical).

These ontological questions present the qualitative researcher with some of the most fundamental field problems. First, because families represent particular structures, practices, forms of consciousness, traditions, ideals, discourses, and interactions, any effort to define family as a category must be based on the emergent meanings and experiences of family members. In keeping with this, research about or with families must be attentive to the conceptual boundaries associated with "the family" that have real meaning for individuals who are part of diverse families. At the same time, there must be an attentiveness to the unboundaried flow of experience that is multifaceted and that may include dimensions of family roles or practices in tandem with other outside-the-family practices and experiences. Second, researchers have an experience of family and this affects values, priorities, and interpretations in the research endeavor. Researchers need to be clear about their own family politics in relation to how, what, and why they study what they do in families. How does their positioning within their own families affect what they study and how they report the results? What is the goal of the research? Is the purpose to reflect "the way things are in families" or to bring about social change in the way that power, responsibilities, and activities are distributed in families? Does the research support current family ideologies or challenge them? What are the "ideological codes" that "infect" (Smith, 1993, p. 62) interpretations? Finally, researchers must deal with continuous change and temporal complexity within families. Individual development, family development, and historical time intersect to create unending configurations of new meaning. As a consequence, ontological questions arise with respect to the form that knowledge about families can take. Do we believe that there are nomothetic patterns of family experience that can be generated? Is idiographic, thick description the best approach for studying postmodern families (see Chapter 9 for a detailed discussion of nomothetic and idiographic forms)? If we believe that patterns are identifiable, how far do we go with this? That is, are they generalizable to larger populations? Do these reflect "generic processes"? Can we theorize about families?

These are broad, foundational field dilemmas that require qualitative researchers to adopt a reflexive and critical stance toward the study of "the family." Specifically, this means being diligent about questioning what families are and how we can know them. It means we must be explicit about our theoretical perspective on studying families, our hidden assumptions about family experience and meanings, our blind spots in understanding diverse family experiences, and the values that underlie our personal and theoretical interpretive perspectives.

Ontology Shapes Inquiry

Our ontological assumptions about the nature of human development and the nature of family experience direct the course of methodological inquiry. Each of the five methodological approaches discussed in Chapter 5 is rooted in the study of the following ontological domains.

Studying Culture as a Basis of Ethnography

Some of our earliest scholarly qualitative research occurred within the discipline of anthropology. The emphasis here was on studying collective meaning-making practices originally within what were then considered more exotic and distant cultures. There is now also an interest in examining cultures that are more immediate. We are interested in the way culture shapes individual human development and the ways ethnicity, neighborhood, and other types of affiliation affect family activity. Ethnography focuses on the study of culture.

Studying Meaning as a Basis of Grounded Theory

The Chicago school of sociology, through the articulation of a symbolic interactionist theoretical perspective, put an emphasis on understanding meaning. All human action could be understood as a process of constructing interpretive meanings that are derived from social interaction. These ideas gave rise to the articulation of a social constructionist perspective that became central in many disciplines but notably in sociology (Berger & Luckmann, 1966) and psychology (Gergen, 1985). The premises of symbolic interactionism and social constructionism have been important theoretical influences in the qualitative analysis of individual and family meaning-making processes and serve as the foundation for grounded theory methodology.

Studying Experience and Consciousness as a Basis of Phenomenological Inquiry

Although closely related to the study of meaning, Phenomenology places a focus on the study of individual consciousness. Of particular interest here are the ways individuals gear into their taken-for-granted life worlds. This includes an interest in not only the individual's subjective perceptions of that world but how that individual understands experience within the intersubjective milieu of the shared social environment.

Studying Stories as a Basis of Narrative Inquiry

Oral history, through the practice of storytelling, represents one of the most ancient forms of communicating human reality. The narrative tradition, which puts an emphasis on how individuals construct stories about their lives, has taken a central place in the study of individual and family reality. Theories based in the narrative tradition have become very important in both the clinical practice and empirical qualitative research that is conducted in family therapy. Another way we come to understand human stories is through the analysis of written texts. Hermeneutics has its origins in the 17th century as a set of guidelines for scholars who were engaged in the task of interpreting the Bible. In the same way that biblical scholars were interested in finding the "hidden meanings," hermeneutics has now broadened to look at the underlying meanings in many different types of text. For family scholars, this could mean, for example, looking at the underlying values and ideological assumptions that exist in popular parenting books.

Studying Power and Social Change as a Basis of Critical Inquiry

Power, oppression, and privilege are central to understanding the everyday realities of individual and family life. Gender, socioeconomic status, ethnic affiliation, and sexual orientation create hierarchies and maintain systems of privilege in families and communities. Critical inquiry begins with these systems of power and seeks to provide evidence for the way power structures are held in place and the way power structures can be changed through heightened awareness and knowledge.

In the next chapter, the focus shifts to the ways these ontological domains of study direct methodological inquiry.

5

Methodology

Links Among Ontological Assumptions, Theory, and Forms of Inquiry

The terms *methodology* and *method* are often used interchangeably in discussions of research practice. On some occasions, method is treated as an abbreviation of methodology. There are, however, important distinctions to be made between these terms that have implications for how we plan and carry out our research activities.

Methodology is defined in the Oxford dictionary as the science of method (*Concise Oxford Dictionary of Current English*, 1990). Tempting as it is to fall into a tautological abyss with such a definition, we can maintain a steady posture if we take seriously the relationship of the terms as they are given in the definition. To speak about methodology as the "science of method" is to make reference to a set of underlying principles, beliefs, and practices that constitute science itself. As we discussed in Chapter 2, Kuhn (1962) talked about paradigm science as being shaped by inherited concepts and theories, consisting of beliefs about scientific procedures, and guided by shared organizing principles governing perception itself. Methodology, then, refers to a set of broader scientific beliefs and practices that provide direction to inquiry. Methodology involves giving attention to the relationship between on the one hand, inherited theories, concepts, and ontological assumptions, and on the other hand, techniques and practices used in the process of empirical inquiry. Method, by contrast, is a term that is used to describe the specific tools or techniques that are used in gathering data. Methodological assumptions, values, and theoretical influences thereby give direction to the methods or techniques used in the process of empirical inquiry.

Methodology can be understood to have two roles: one political and one procedural (Seale, Gobo, Gubrium, & Silverman, 2004). The political role of methodology has to do with displaying and upholding legitimacy in the broader culture. Through the insistence on strict rules of scientific practice, rigor, and ethical codes of conduct, methodology serves as a means to elicit trust. The procedural role of methodology is a practical one: It helps to frame research topics and guide researchers in concrete terms as they make decisions in the process of inquiry.

As qualitative researchers, it is important that we be mindful of methodology in both of its forms. Politically, those who have used qualitative methodologies have had to struggle to elicit scientific respect—not only with the broader culture, but with social scientists working within more positivist-oriented paradigms. The implication is that we must be very deliberate about how we articulate our methodology. It is essential that we be clear about our ontological and theoretical assumptions and that we demonstrate the reasons why qualitative methods are warranted. Procedurally, it is necessary when making methodological decisions that we "situate" our methodology in relation to the specific demands of the research situation (Seale et al., 2004). In this regard, we treat methodology as a guide to decision making in practice that serves as a means to locate those decisions within a set of inherited collective practices.

In the qualitative tradition, the relationship between methodology and methods can be understood when we examine the following methodological approaches.

Ethnography and the Study of Culture

Theoretical Background

Qualitative inquiry has deep roots in the anthropological study of culture. Ontologically, if we wish to understand the nature of being human, we must understand humans as they are embedded in culture. As the anthropologist Geertz (1973, p. 49) has argued, "there is no such thing as human nature independent of culture." Ethnography is concerned with describing the cultural ways of human life (Vidich & Lyman, 2003).

Early anthropological efforts were interested in culture for a variety of reasons. Initially, there was an interest in understanding "primitive" cultures in order to trace the origins of the great chain of being (Vidich & Lyman, 2003). These were cultures that were viewed as less civilized than Western scientific culture and were thereby examined in order to understand the evolution of culture. These studies of culture also became part of the colonial mentality of discovery and conquest throughout the period from the 17th through the 19th centuries whereby description and understanding of the exotic became the basis for conversion to Western cultural practices. At a broader level, there was an interest in mapping these cultures through ethnography in the same way cartographers wished to map the geography of the world. Ethnographers entering into the exotic were like "cross-dressers, outsiders wearing insiders' clothes while gradually acquiring the language and behaviors that go along with them" (Tedlock, 2003, p. 166).

Culture remains at the center of anthropological studies—now with different sensitivities about interests. Although there is still an interest in the exotic, there is also a move to see culture as local, less distant, and more immediate. This reflects the drift of ethnography from its roots in anthropology to its presence in sociology. Whereas anthropology was more concerned with distant cultures, sociology took a greater interest in immediate and local subcultures. As a result, ethnography became very popular within sociological inquiry in the mid-1900s as a way to examine the exotic within home culture. Hence, there was a strong interest in using ethnography as a way to understand hidden and "deviant" subcultures (e.g., drug users, pool sharks, gangs). The study of culture has also become an important focus within psychology. Influenced by anthropology and the work of Mead (1934), Vygotsky (1962), and Bruner (1990), cultural psychology is concerned with the study of cultural meaning and the "cultural construction of the person— including thoughts, emotions, motivation, development and identity . . . within the collective meanings, identities, experiences and practices" of the culture (Kral, Burkhardt, & Kidd, 2002). At a pragmatic level, what is of interest here is the way human beings create meanings within cultural contexts of practice—what people are doing or are trying to do within a cultural context (Bruner, 1990). Qualitative research methods are particularly conducive to understanding these contexts of practice and the cultural rules that people have for making sense of their worlds (Kral et al., 2002).

The study of culture has two primary foci (Fetterman, 1998). First, there is a concern with the materialist aspects of culture, which emphasizes observable patterns of behavior, customs, and a way of life. Second, there is an emphasis on the ideational aspects of culture comprised of ideas, beliefs, and knowledge that characterize a particular group of people.

In our efforts to observe and understand culture, we have tended to focus on culture as the outcome of human values, beliefs, and practices. In this traditional view, culture is the symbolic product of all values and actions. Equally important, however, is to examine the constituting role of culture (Geertz, 1973). This is a perspective that gets us to look at culture as the source, rather than the result of human thought and behavior (Crotty, 1998). Because complex cultures contain diverse and often conflicting symbols, rituals, and guides to action, culture is not a straightforward blueprint for how to act, but is better viewed as a "tool kit" for constructing strategies of action (Swidler, 1986). It is in this regard that people can be seen to use culture or to treat culture as a pool of resources (Swidler, 2001). The relation between actions and culture is a recursive one insofar as members of a community culture are constantly playing out cultural distinctions while at the same time they are constantly engaged in the meaningful construction and redefinition of the culture in which they live. This is "culture of the moment" that changes with new ideas, words, and ways (Douglas & Isherwood, 1996, p. 37).

Culture is a dynamic and changing system of meanings and symbols that provides a means for examining the flow of family experience in context. In lived experience, culture is usually hidden from view but manifested in what we wear, how we speak, and what we believe. We make culture intelligible by breaking it down into meaningful categories such as values, rules, time, signs, status, and standards that provide guidelines and understandings for how to act. Cultural categories provide us with the "fundamental coordinates of meaning" (McCracken, 1988a, p. 73).

Theoretically, "culture" is at the root of ethnography as a methodology. In its traditional form, *ethnography* was used interchangeably with "field work." This involved full immersion in the culture, use of all the senses to take in the sights, sounds, and smells of everyday life fully, with the aim of generating a detailed portrait of the activities and practices of the culture being observed. To enter into the field is to move physically into the cultural spaces where people engage in their everyday activities. This may involve gaining access to the group by first identifying important persons in the culture who serve as gatekeepers. It also may involve seeking out key informants who have understandings of specific aspects of that culture.

In the study of families, there are a number of exemplary ethnographic accounts. Hess and Handel's (1959) *Family Worlds* provides detailed insight into the everyday lives of parents and children. DeVault's (1991) work *Feeding the Family* provides an important account of the way meanings, activities, and responsibilities associated with the provision of food are navigated within the home. In her more recent work, DeVault (2000) has conducted an ethnographic examination of families in public spaces by observing their activity and ways of relating to each other at the public zoo. The goal of this immersion was to observe what happens as family members relate to each other within the context of the organization of the public space.

Implications for Methods

The primary aim of ethnography is to understand how things work from the perspective of the participants in that cultural setting. According to Spradley (1980), it involves looking at what people do (action and behavior); what they say and how they say it (language); and how they make, acquire, and use things (cultural artifacts) in the course of everyday living. It also involves the examination of formal and informal rules, ritualistic patterns, and cultural values and ideals. Ethnography is rooted in the assumption that through prolonged interaction with participants, researchers are in the best position to understand the way individual values, beliefs, motivations, and actions are expressed in and through culture.

Observation of these components of culture provides the stories, patterns of living, and cultural themes that generate the ethnographic account. The standard of reporting for an ethnographic study is to generate "thick description" (Geertz, 1973)—that is, a cultural account that emphasizes descriptive detail. This emphasis on thick description serves the ethnographic purpose of seeking to understand, in a holistic way, the many perspectives and dimensions of culture. Ethnography can thereby be understood as both a process and a product. As a process (as in doing ethnography), it involves intensive observation of culture over time; as a product, it is a detailed, descriptive account (as in an ethnography).

Two methods have traditionally been used with an ethnographic methodology. Participant observation and interviews are the primary techniques (i.e., methods) for understanding the way a culture works. Participant observation has been called an oxymoron—because it implies the contradiction of being both involved and detached (Tedlock, 2003). Although the word *participant* implies that the researcher becomes fully involved in the practices that are being examined, there are many ways that researchers have positioned themselves in relation to the observational field. This can range from full and extended immersion in a culture—living as participants would live—to periodic observations that involve dropping in to see what is happening at different points in time. Even when the researcher is fully immersed in the culture for an extended period of time, rarely does this involve "full participation." In practice what it means is that the researcher rarely does what the participants do—but rather, lives alongside them, interacting with them as they do what they do, observing and participating enough to write feelingly about the research (Delamont, 2004). Within cultural anthropology there has always been a concern with the researcher "going native" (Wax, 1971) and the need not only to maintain distance but to "manufacture distance" (McCracken, 1988b) in the relationship with participants.

Ethnography also typically includes interviews of varying degrees of formality. Here the question arises about how "natural" the data are. When researchers observe what goes on in a culture, they can make a claim to seeing activity and behavior in a more natural form. This is known as unobtrusive observation—where researchers watch from a distance and in some ways assume their own invisibility. This is a reasonably valid assumption when their identity as researcher is unknown. When actors in that culture are aware that the researcher is a researcher, then their actions and words may have continuity with everyday activities, but are presented, at some level, as performance. If they know they are being observed, then the researcher becomes an important member of an audience to which their behavior is directed. When researchers engage members of a culture in a research interview, as a way of more directly gathering information, the information that is gleaned can be considered less "natural."

Triangulation of methods is often used in ethnographic studies. Triangulation refers to the use of multiple sources of information as a way to understand more completely the social situation at hand. This can include observation and interviews along with document analysis, media information, pictures, biographies, official records, group meetings, key informants, and other forms of statistical data. For example, in a study of families of men whose jobs require them to travel, Zvonkovik, Solomon, Humble, and Manoogian (2005) used a combination of focus groups, in-depth interviews, and in-depth telephone interviews. By including both husbands and wives in a variety of interview formats, the authors increased the range of voices and experiences brought to the data collection effort and as a result increased the trustworthiness of the data (for more on triangulation see Chapter 10).

The degree to which ethnographers participate in the cultural realities they seek to understand and questions of the degree to which data can be considered natural are ultimately questions of epistemology. In other words, these are fundamental issues having to do with the relationship between the knower and that which is to be known.

As Hammersley and Atkinson (1983) have argued, however, all research is a form of participant observation because there is no way of studying the social world without being part of it.

Variations

From its colonial beginnings and more positivist orientation, ethnography now takes many different forms or genres that reflect positioning in different paradigms.

Critical Ethnography

Consistent with the assumptions of the critical paradigm, critical ethnographers continue to follow the methodological practices of participant observation, interviewing, and immersion in cultural settings, but with a very different understanding of participation. Foremost is an explicit acknowledgment of their own political positioning in relation to participants. A critical ethnographer enters into settings with an air of transparency about political concerns. In contrast with the implicit imperialist assumption of early ethnographies where observation potentially became a means for controlling other cultures, participation for a critical ethnographer involves examining and working collaboratively to address issues of power and oppression in these cultures. The aim of ethnography shifts from pure description and representation of these cultures to confrontation of injustice, empowerment, emancipation, and political transformation. This is done through a process of examining oppressive practices, dominant and subjugated discourses, and exploitive relationships. This work is rooted in a conflict perspective that rests on the following epistemological assumptions (Kincheloe & McLaren, 2003):

- All thoughts and activities are mediated by power relations.
- Systems of class, race, and gender oppression are often mediated by the social relations of capitalist production and consumption.
- Certain groups in any society are privileged over others.
- Oppression is often invisible and inadvertently reproduced because people have come to see their positions of disadvantage as natural, necessary, or inevitable.
- Scientific practice is political and is embedded in the broader system of power relations and as a result cannot be seen as an activity separate from the power dynamics of the setting being observed.

An ethnographic study of caregiving at the end of life among African American families provides an example of how dominant cultural values and practices regarding formal care have influenced these families (Turner, Wallace, Anderson, & Bird, 2004). The paper begins with a clear articulation of the underlying critical issues where formal care is steeped in a tradition of "mistrust that many African Americans hold toward the health care system

which has resulted from years of exclusion, racism and discrimination"
(p. 427). Using ethnographic interviews and focus groups with 88 African
American caregivers, the researchers not only sought to describe and analyze
the perspectives of these families, but they were explicit about their transformative goal of suggesting ways that end-of-life services might be improved for
these African American families—especially in light of their experiences of
racism and discrimination.

Given the focus on changing oppressive social realities, the success of critical ethnography is assessed not so much by the "thickness" of description
as it is by its transformative effects on the culture being studied. Lather (1991)
has used the term *catalytic validity* as a way to assess the impact of the
research in helping the participants of a critical ethnography to enhance their
own self-understanding and process of transformative change.

Postmodern Ethnography

Traditional forms of ethnography were linked to modernist assumptions
about progress and the ideological dominance of Western authority over colonial cultures. Postmodernist ethnography abandons the interests of progress
that pointed toward the break up of "ethnos" through practices of accultura-
tion and assimilation (Vidich & Lyman, 2003). It invokes an awareness of the
perils of essentializing culture (Marcus & Fischer, 1986)—in other words, the
tendency to reify or freeze culture into a representation based on time-bound
perspectives from partial viewpoints within the culture.

With the postmodern turn, however, new epistemologies, paradigms, and
discourses have resulted in more reflexivity and concern about the products
of the ethnographic endeavor. Specifically, there has been a call for the final
public texts of ethnography to reflect various levels of interpretation and
meaning, to be socially and culturally located, and perhaps most important,
not to make any privileged claim to represent the truth or reality of the experiences being described. Postmodernity has precipitated a new awareness of
how we do ethnography:

- It calls for the abandonment of the search for monolithic and enduring truths
  and instead encourages a focus on understanding the changing complexity of
  human reality.
- It serves to demystify the orthodox tradition of objectivity in favor of a greater
  awareness of values, meanings, and interpretations.
- There is a shift from monolithic and dominant stories to the capturing of
  multiple and potentially contradictory voices. This involves a commitment
  to "polyvocality" (Gergen & Gergen, 2003), which means recognizing both

within ourselves and within those who join our research as participants the multiplicity of competing and often contradictory values and viewpoints.

- It calls into question what it means to play the role of a scientist who is interested in studying people. Under postmodern ways of thinking, the authority of the ethnographer can be questioned. Specifically, it calls into question the objectifying practices embedded in the traditional distinctions between researcher and "subjects" or "participants." In its stead, there is an acknowledgment that the researcher is a participant in the same reality and that this warrants critical self-awareness as part of the research process. In this regard, any account involves "understanding the other through self-reflection" (Kleinman & Copp, 1993, p. 55).

- It is manifested as a crisis of representation where there is a pervasive skepticism about the researcher's ability to capture lived experience directly. This crisis throws into jeopardy the assumption that there can be a direct relationship "between words and the world" (Gergen, 1994, p. 412). In the face of this, it is argued that experience is created in the social text written by the researcher (Denzin & Lincoln, 1994).

- Postmodern ethnographic accounts take many forms, from traditional written texts that would appear in an academic journal to "performance ethnographies" that might include theater, art, or poetry as ways of understanding culture (McCall, 2003).

In the face of the postmodern abandonment of positivist, objective truth, it would appear that ethnographic study has become "seriously irregular" and more pluralistic (Geertz, 1983, p. 4). This is not without its challenges and uncertainties. However, it does not automatically reject conventional methods of knowing and telling but opens them to inquiry, critique, and change (Richardson, 2003). I concur with Kvale (1995), who takes a moderate postmodern position: "While rejecting the notion of a universal truth, it accepts the possibility of specific, local, personal and community forms of truth with a focus on daily life and local narrative" (p. 21). Rather than fixing culture into "reified textual portraits," the goal of postmodern ethnography is to call into question that which appears "natural" or "obvious" (Kincheloe & McLaren, 2003, p. 465).

Autoethnography

The problem of representation associated with postmodern ethnography resulted in a greater emphasis on the researcher as both subject and as participant in culture. Yet fully including the self in ethnographic accounts was more often given lip service than serious attention. Authors would include references to "I" in their accounts, but the researcher's self would come and go in the face of a mixed allegiance between writing empirical accounts and reflexive commentary.

Autoethnography starts with an account of the researcher's personal life. It is deliberate in making linkages between the personal and the cultural. Carolyn Ellis, stating it in the first person, puts it this way:

> I start with my personal life. I pay attention to my physical feelings, thoughts and emotions. I use what I call systematic sociological introspection and emotional recall to try to understand an experience that I have lived through. Then I write my experience as a story. By exploring a particular life, I hope to understand a way of life. (Ellis & Bochner, 2003, p. 206)

Increased vulnerability is one of the repercussions of doing autoethnography. As Allen and Piercy (2005) describe, "telling a story on ourselves, we risk exposure to our peers, subject ourselves to scrutiny and ridicule, and relinquish some of our sense of control over our own narratives" (p. 156). At the same time, this vulnerability is a basis for a deeper understanding of our own biases and projections such that the "vulnerability is returned for strength" (p. 156).

Autoethnography seeks to maintain an emphasis on three components: the research process (i.e., *graphy*), culture (i.e., *ethno*), and self (i.e., *auto;* Ellis & Bochner, 2003). Accounts arising from an autoethnography are usually written in a first person voice, thereby reflecting the inward-outward dynamic associated with doing this research. In keeping with this, autoethnographies offer little allegiance to the traditions and practices of scientific reporting and as a result are more likely to appear in a variety of formats. These can include biographical accounts, personal journals and stories, photo essays, and even poems and fictional constructions.

Autoethnography rests on the assumption that the researcher's self and the participant other are not separate entities. Rather, there is an understanding that both are vulnerable experiencing subjects connected by embodied, lived experience (Tedlock, 2003). In the process of writing these cultural narratives, autoethnographers seek to bridge their own knowledge and experience of the culture from outside the fieldwork with their experience of culture in the process of doing fieldwork. Hoppes (2005), for example, provides an autoethnographic account of his experience of care during his father's illness and death. In this narrative account, the author draws on cultural values that shape caregiving practices and that had an effect on how he saw himself as a son and managed the boundaries for care in relation to other family members, and the meanings that he gave to caregiving and his awareness of death.

In a type of joint or coconstructed autoethnography, Davis and Salkin (2005) present a reflexive account of their experience of being sisters in a relationship where one has experienced a physical disability. Through inter-active interviewing with each other and the coconstruction of a narrative, they report on their family dynamics and perceptions of their relationship in a way that is "multivocal" and accepting of their differences.

Feminist autoethnography involves a deliberate effort to be reflexive about one's own experience as a woman in order to confront or explore what are often hidden or sensitive topics such as anxiety or sexuality (Allen & Piercy, 2005). As Allen goes on to describe the process, it begins with a confronta-tion of one's own vulnerabilities: attentiveness to difficult emotional touch-stones such as anxiety, embarrassment, or loss in order to come to a deeper appreciation of the voices of those in marginalized positions. The goal in fem-inist autoethnography, as it is for all forms of autoethnography, is to tell the story of one's own struggle or experience as a basis for connecting with the reader so that readers might in turn reflect on their own experience (Allen & Piercy, 2005).

Applied Ethnography

Applied research in general is typically concerned with gathering data as part of a process of making assessments and decisions in relation to a partic-ular issue, problem, or client. Chambers (2003) suggests that applied ethnog-raphy is based on the assumption that ethnography has practical value when it prepares cultural profiles of human groups as a way of informing decision makers who are responsible for policies and programs that affect the lives of the people in those groups. Diversity raises questions about how cultures with different values and interests can live side by side. Applied ethnography has a role to play in understanding the way various cultural social groups express and reconcile their cultural interests in a multicultural society.

Applied ethnography can also be used as a tool for bringing about organi-zational change or improvements to clinical practice. Understanding the cul-ture of an organization from a variety of perspectives can play an important role in evaluating the effectiveness of programs and introducing organizational change (Patton, 1997). For example, an ethnographic analysis of the culture of the workplace can be a means for devising strategies to change work-life prac-tices and policies. In the field of family therapy, ethnography can also be used to inform clinical practice (Tubbs & Burton, 2005). Here ethnography is used to understand the meanings and dynamics of a cultural subgroup, which in turn is used as a basis for developing appropriate intervention strategies. Clinical intervention and ethnography are parallel processes that involve, on the one hand, clinicians' engaging clients in a process of understanding their difficulties in order to help solve their "problems," whereas ethnography involves engaging participants in their cultural space in order to understand their culture. Tubbs and Burton provide an example from their own ethnographic research where they examined parenting issues in low-income, urban families with a particular emphasis on families of color. Using a large sample of 256 families, the researchers were particularly interested in the way decision making in these families related to parenting, and the way child development was influenced by welfare practices and policies. Using the principles of evidence-based practice and "translation research," the researchers first sought to understand the cultural rules that shaped parenting in various neighborhoods and then used this as a basis for modifying existing intervention strategies so that they might be more sensitive to these cultural conditions. The goal here was to shape interventions that are attentive to an in-depth understanding of the cultural milieu so as to maximize their effectiveness—in terms of cost and problem resolution—in a way that ultimately improves the lives of clients (Tubbs & Burton, 2005).

Phenomenology: The Study of Conscious Experience

Theoretical Background

Phenomenology has its roots in philosophy. The late 19th-century philosopher Edmund Husserl (1859–1938) began with the problem of how objects, actions, and events appear in the consciousness of the actor. Experience is a central focus for phenomenology and can be understood as consciousness of physical things, values, moods, activities, and feelings. Phenomenology is rooted in an epistemology that inextricably links subjective and objective insofar as the primary focus is on the way individuals subjectively assign meaning to the objects of their consciousness. Of particular interest in phenomenology is the way people are geared into their everyday lifeworlds (*lebenswelt*). Known as the natural attitude, phenomenology is concerned with taken-for-granted aspects of everyday reality. As a philosophical perspective, this lifeworld was a reality that was prescientific and self-evident.

Alfred Schutz (1971) played a key role in taking the philosophical ideas of phenomenology and bringing them to social scientific inquiry. Influenced by Weber's methodological principle of *verstehen,* Schutz was interested in opening pathways for conducting scientific research that would allow for the "sympathetic understanding" of the conscious experience of everyday life. For Schutz, the construction of reality occurs on two levels. First, individual actors interpret their everyday world within a specific context according to their own biography and spheres of relevancy. Second, scientists observe and record how these individual actors do this, and in the process, they interpret and attribute their own meaning to the observed meanings.

Within psychology, phenomenology has also been adapted for scientific inquiry. Given the shared interests in understanding the mind, awareness, and consciousness as a basis for action, there was a natural affinity between these two perspectives. Early efforts focused on how to adapt the principles of phenomenology for use in both psychology and psychiatry (Spiegleberg, 1972). More recent efforts have outlined the ways phenomenology can be used for qualitative psychological research (Giorgi & Giorgi, 2003). The primary aim of this research is to examine the psychological meanings that constitute an experienced phenomenon through the process of examining lived examples of the phenomenon within the context of the participants' lives (Giorgi & Giorgi). Direct description of experience, rather than analysis or explanation, is key to gaining access to the lived, everyday lifeworld (Kvale, 1996). The primary goal of this research is description. Phenomenological approaches are also now prominent in the fields of nursing (Benner, 1994) and education.

Phenomenology is also well suited for use in family therapy research. The starting point for the clinical researcher who uses a phenomenological approach is that "a priori assumptions about how families work or do not work become the core of our inquiry" (Dahl & Boss, 2005, p. 65). Specifically, there is an intense curiosity about the taken-for-granted aspects of family life and the language used to describe it, an awareness that knowledge generated from studying families is tentative and subject to a variety of meanings within the family, and that phenomenological researchers/clinicians are not separate from the phenomena being studied.

Phenomenological research is shaped by a number of key theoretical concepts that provide a language and a focus for this analysis:

The Natural Attitude. The natural attitude is the everyday mode of consciousness that is characterized by the belief in an existent system of meaning in the world. In this everyday form of consciousness, there is a suspension of doubt about the nature of reality.

Intentionality. Subject and object are inseparable in phenomenology. To be conscious is always to be conscious of something. *Intentionality* is the term used in phenomenology to describe the ways we direct attention toward objects in our experience. Hence, intentionality is not concerned with purpose or deliberation in action, but rather is concerned with the active relationship between conscious subject and the object of the subject's consciousness (Crotty, 1998). Intentionality puts an emphasis in research on the ways that individuals subjectively make meaningful the objective world they interact with and participate in. In practical terms, the object cannot be adequately described apart from the subject and the subject cannot be adequately described apart from the object (Crotty, 1998).

Taken-for-Granted Reality. When we operate within the natural attitude, we take for granted that the lifeworld exists in a way that is, for practical purposes, uniform and somewhat predictable. This is our everyday consciousness that is guided by shared meanings and common sense.

Intersubjectivity. In order for everyday life to be taken for granted and somewhat predictable, it must be embedded in a system of shared meanings. For phenomenologists, intersubjectivity is rooted in the idea that consciousness of the everyday lifeworld is never fully private, but is part of a common, shared, social reality. When we act in that world, we assume that the other shares a consciousness of the same basic reality. Although the other brings a subjective perception of that reality, there are common elements and shared meanings that provide the platform for social interaction. Furthermore, in the process of interacting with others, individuals contribute to the intersubjectivity of their everyday worlds. In this regard, intersubjectivity is an ongoing accomplishment (Gubrium & Holstein, 2003a).

Gearing Into the World. We not only act within an intersubjective framework, we actively act upon it. In other words, we actively gear into the world and shape and transform the situations we experience. Hence the preexisting lifeworld shapes our actions while at the same time we modify that lifeworld through our actions.

Stock of Knowledge. Our ability to operate in this world of common sense is shaped by sedimented layers of knowledge that we have of the world. Our understanding of the world at any point in time encompasses our accumulated personal experiences that arise through our participation in the social world. Our stock of knowledge is our subjective point of reference for understanding the everyday lifeworld.

Typifications. One of the functions of our current stock of knowledge is to give the lifeworld a sense of predictability. Based on our past experiences, we come to expect that future events will fit into our scheme of a familiar reality. Familiarity with the past allows us to anticipate the future: that which was "typical" in the past can be expected to be "typical" in the future.

Typifications, then, are based on the premises of uniformity and continuity of everyday reality. The familiarity of past events also serves as a means to contend with new experience. Specifically, our ability to explain and integrate new experiences is based on our ability to typify from past experiences as a means of knowing what to expect with new ones.

Problematics. When new experiences fit into one's typifications, this simply validates one's stock of knowledge without interruption. When an action is incongruent with previous typifications and past experience, however, taken-for-granted reality is brought into question. Dramatically unexpected events, accidents, or shocking revelations often call for an explication of the everyday lifeworld. These are problematics, defined by Schutz as moments when "hitherto sufficient typification appears insufficient." In the study of families, examples of problematics would include being told at a later age that you're adopted or learning of an affair within marriage. These types of events involve a radical reorientation of everyday reality.

The Nature of Objective Reality. Although the emphasis in phenomenology is on subjective and intersubjective experiences (and the interpretation and meaning of experiences), these experiences must be viewed within the context of an objective world. There is a system of order in the world that represents a set of constant relations, including our organization of time or temporality (e.g., hours, days, life cycles), space or spatiality (houses, cities, countries, offices, etc.), and social structure (families, churches, agencies, etc.). In addition, all experience can be understood because it is rooted in a lived body (i.e., corporeality) and in relation to other human beings (i.e., relationality; see van Maanen, 1990).

Superimposed on intersubjectivity is an objective frame of reference that is historically and culturally derived. The natural and social world is the "arena" of our consciousness, and this is part of the taken-for-granted world. As the preceding discussion of intentionality would suggest, objective reality exists but it can never be understood fully apart from the subjective perceptions of it. Each person stands in a different relationship to this objective reality and interprets it through his or her own position or standpoint in that order. Objective reality has a different meaning for the actors who experience it because of their different position and relation to it.

Implications for Methods

The purpose of a phenomenological study is to investigate the lived experience of one or more individuals in relation to a phenomenon of interest.

In keeping with the concept of intentionality, the focus of inquiry is on the way individuals subjectively make meaningful the objective world they interact with. The goal of phenomenological research is to understand and describe the participants' experience of their everyday world as they see it. As is the case with many other qualitative approaches, this may involve the formation of characteristic themes that emerge from the collective experience of the phenomenon.

In order to examine how a particular aspect of lived reality is constructed, the researcher must always begin by "bracketing" that reality. This involves suspending any judgments about that reality in order to see it as the participant would see it. Gaining an understanding of the participant's reality involves invoking the "phenomenological epoché." This is, in itself, an interruption of the taken-for-granted flow of experience and a call to reflect on the lived experience of their reality. This shift to a description of experience from the experience of experience of course changes the experience at hand, but becomes a necessary aspect of conducting research. Senter and Caldwell (2002) conducted phenomenological interviews with nine women who had successfully ended an abusive relationship. In these interviews, their goal was to capture the women's "naïve descriptions" of their experience and to then identify the common elements of those experiences among the participants. They report on the ways these women redirected their energy and intention by drawing on spirituality as a strength and resource in the change process. In an in-depth study of six Latino fathers, Parra-Cardona, Wampler, and Sharp (2006) draw on the phenomenological concepts of bracketing, lived experience, intentionality, and lifeworld as a way to understand the way these young fathers experienced their participation in a therapeutic/educational parenting program.

Phenomenological studies often use in-depth interviews as a way to elicit detailed descriptions of this reality. This may involve repeated interviews with the same participant or interviews with a range of people experiencing the same phenomenon. The emphasis of these studies is often an effort to understand how people experience the mundane, taken-for-granted aspects of their everyday experience. In this regard, "ordinary language is the modus operandi" (Gubrium & Holstein, 2003a, p. 218). Specifically, the goal is to understand how participants use everyday language to give shape and meaning to their typified, familiar world. This can include descriptions of what was experienced and how it was experienced. Montgomery (2002), for example, focused on the life experiences of young adolescent women (14–17) who planned a pregnancy. Based on phenomenological interviews with eight pregnant adolescents, she identified 11 themes that provided insight into their motivations and expectations for the pregnancy. Included in these were their desire to have something they could call their own and care for, and the desire to be perceived as grown up with increased responsibility and independence. Similarly, in a study of 12 African American grandmothers who were primary caregivers to one of their grandchildren, Gibson (2002) sought to understand the lived experience of these women. She began with the "grand tour" phenomenological question—"What is your experience as the primary caregiver to your grandchild?"—which she then followed with questions having to do with the circumstances that led to caregiving, their perceived role, and the impact of absent parents on the child.

In some of my own work, I have used the concept of problematics as a way to gain a better understanding of the disruptions in the taken-for-granted aspects of reality. In this research, I looked at the experience of infertility as a problematic in the desire and effort to become biological parents. When the taken-for-granted flow of experience (expectation to become biological parents) is interrupted in this way (infertility), participants have heightened awareness of the taken-for-granted aspects of their experience. Focusing on problematics not only gives insight into the unusual and unexpected, but it brings sharply into focus the typical reality that is no longer experienced in the same way (in this case the "normal" experience of becoming parents). Phenomenologists might also use observation and life histories as ways of understanding lived experience.

The task for the phenomenological analyst who wishes to study families is to examine the meanings that are a part of family experience by examining their taken-for-granted, intersubjective consciousness. Specifically, the effort is to describe and classify family experiences as they appear in the minds of the family members. Families can be understood as representing a unique "province of meaning." Schutz talks about the fact that there are multiple realities that exist in the world and that we move in and out of these realities: religious experience, science, art worlds, and family are all different provinces of meaning. The goal is to understand individual and collective experiences of this unique province of meaning called family. An important concept for understanding family is that relationships within a family are a special type of "we-ness" that involves touch, intimacy, dependency, ancestry, intensity, and a unique mutual knowing.

By virtue of living together in close proximity, families share a unique "we-relationship" that arises from shared face-to-face interactions in time and space. This sense of we-ness and intimacy is the basis for sexual intimacy as well as violence in the home. High levels of intimacy and familiarity and the corresponding routinization of behaviors within the family make for a high level of typification in the family. These typifications become the basis for examining predictable patterns of behavior in families.

Variations

Phenomenological approaches appear in many different disciplines and as a result have come to have a variety of specialized labels. As Cresswell (1998) has outlined, there is reflective phenomenology, transcendental phenomenology, dialogic phenomenology, empirical phenomenology, existential phenomenology, hermeneutics, and social phenomenology. In addition, ethnomethodology, influenced by both symbolic interactionism and phenomenology, is sometimes treated as a form of phenomenological analysis. While each of these variations puts emphasis on different aspects of lived experience, they share the fundamental assumptions of bracketing prejudgments; examining the intentionality of consciousness; and seeking to understand the essential, invariant structure of experience (Cresswell, 1998).

Grounded Theory Methodology

Theoretical Influences

When Barney Glaser and Anselm Strauss introduced grounded theory methodology in 1967, a complex set of theoretical influences shaped the articulation of their approach. These authors were both sociologists but they came from very different backgrounds. Glaser trained under Paul Lazarsfeld, who was a leading quantitative sociologist at Columbia University. The late 1950s and early 1960s was a period when positivist approaches clearly dominated the social scientific research agenda. The dominant approach was to use ever more sophisticated quantitative techniques in order to support grand theories that would serve as a basis for explaining contemporary social problems. The theories of Talcott Parsons and Robert Merton were broad and far reaching and were treated as the social gospel of the day. Strauss trained at the University of Chicago and was influenced by the work of John Dewey, George Herbert Mead, Charles H. Cooley, and the emerging ideas of symbolic interactionists like Herbert Blumer and Everett C. Hughes. Within this tradition, there was a focus on understanding the complexity and changing nature of human experience that involved a growing interest in developing theoretical explanations that reflected the emerging, process-oriented components of social action.

Both Glaser and Strauss came to the partnership with a primary interest in the way theory is created. Most grand theories of the day were put forward from the minds of "great man" thinkers. These thinkers were revered and immortalized. They organized, coordinated, and created systems of ideas and meanings that were seen to define the frontiers of knowledge and thinking for social scientific communities of which they were a part. They were seen as the mechanism that gave social science a privileged voice in the culture. As Glaser and Strauss point out in the preface to their original book, however, there was a gap between grand theory and research. Great man theories were taught with a "charismatic finality that students could seldom resist" (Glaser & Strauss, 1967, p. 10). There were two underlying concerns here—one was the tendency toward deference to great theoretical ideas without any supporting empirical research; the other was the methodological preoccupation with verification strategies that concentrated on the improvement of methods for testing theory. It was out of these concerns that Glaser and Strauss put forward a set of "guides, along with associated rules of procedure" (p. viii) directed toward "improving social scientists' capacities for generating theory that will be relevant to their research" (p. vii). Grounded theory methodology was introduced as a systematic way to gather and analyze data for the purposes of generating theory.

Given the importance for Glaser and Strauss of making linkages between empirical research and theory-generating practices, the original version of grounded theory methodology reflected the language of positivism. Theory was to be built up from the "facts," shaped by the "accuracy" of the evidence, moved forward by hypotheses, and constructed with empirical generalizations with the aim of creating formal theory about the forms of social action. Although a social constructionist or interpretive paradigm is usually associated with the use of a grounded theory approach, many of the positivist assumptions prevail when researchers use this method as a means to represent an objective reality.

The primary theoretical influences that shaped the direction of grounded theory as a methodology were those that were being formulated under the name of symbolic interactionism (SI). Although the Chicago school had a rich tradition of doing qualitative work, it wasn't until Blumer published his book *Symbolic Interactionism* in 1969, after the publication of *Discovery of Grounded Theory* in 1967, that SI theory became more formalized, with a set of key assumptions and concepts. Nevertheless, the developing ideas of the Chicago school profoundly shaped the assumptions of a grounded theory approach. These theoretical ideas included the following:

- The self is a social product that can be understood by taking the perspectives of others (role taking).
- Language is a product and a medium of human association and is central to understanding the way humans make life meaningful.
- We are born into a world of shared symbols that provide a means for interaction and communication.
- All social action is based on the definition of the situation, the interpretation of meanings that arise in interaction, and the emergence of shared meanings in a situation.

- Social reality is complex, changing, and subject to unfolding contingencies.
- Social life is a process that is emergent.

These theoretical ideas that emphasized process and the changeable nature of human experience served as the basis for constructing grounded theory methodology as an approach built on the principles of an emergent, open-ended, and flexible design. If meaning-making activity involved an ongoing project of constructing identities and interactions, then the methodology had to be designed in a way that attended to this changing reality. In keeping with this, the kinds of explanations offered by a grounded theory approach involved theory that is generative rather than definitive. Consistent with the emphasis on process, there is a recognition that the theoretical products of a grounded theory study are subject to change in the same way the experience and conditions of participants' lives are subject to change. Hence a discovered theory is ever developing and momentary. In the language of our consumer culture, it is likely to have a short shelf life due to the changing conditions of people's lives.

Given the highly changeable nature of family reality, grounded theory approaches are well suited to understanding shifting roles and emerging meanings in families. In family therapy research, the "discovery orientation" of grounded theory methodology provides a good fit for examining the diversity of families seen in clinical practice (Echevarria-Doan & Tubbs, 2005). There is a "kinship" between the process of conducting a grounded theory study and the process of doing clinical work with families (p. 55): Both forms of inquiry are essentially inductive in nature; seek to understand meanings and perceptions; are well suited to asking questions about sensitive topics that are complex, ambivalent, or changeable; and include questions that invite alternative perspectives, diversity, and uniqueness. In the same way there is a correspondence between the theoretical assumptions of family therapy and the grounded theory methodology, there is also a good fit between the outcomes of grounded theory research and clinical practice. In this regard, a grounded theory approach can "expedite" the research-to-practice link because the emergent theory can highlight family strengths and possible intervention strategies that are rooted in the lived experience of the participants (Echevarria-Doan & Tubbs, 2005, p. 59).

Implications for Methods

In an emergent or open-ended design, the researcher begins by being attentive to the phenomenon of interest and allows participants' experiences of this phenomenon to shape the direction of the research. Instead of using fixed questionnaires or surveys that involve a set of assumptions about key issues and the most important questions to ask, a grounded theorist tries to suspend preconceived ideas and be attentive to what participants are describing about their own experience. In an emergent design, the researcher typically begins with broad observations of activity or starts an interview with nondirective questions. As discussed in the first chapter, this requires the researcher to start the project with a "beginner's mind" in order to be fully attentive to the reality that is being presented. Underlying this approach is the belief that participants will highlight what is important in their experience, offer clues about the salience of key issues, and give direction to the researcher about the right questions to ask.

All of the procedures outlined in the grounded theory approach are designed to generate theoretical explanation of a particular social phenomenon. As a result, the methodological language is concerned with theory, not only as the product of the analysis, but as a central guide to the collection of data. The goal of the research is to create a substantive theory that offers explanation of the empirical area of inquiry. In order to generate that theory, the methods used are attentive to theory as the desired outcome. The key process in generating theory is to construct categories that reflect the main thematic patterns in the data. Categories are constructed through the process of comparative analysis that involves comparing one instance or aspect of a phenomenon with other recurring aspects of that same phenomenon. Categories are named and refined and become the basis for the emerging theory.

There are two types of theory in a grounded theory study: substantive and formal. Substantive theory is the creation of a theoretical explanation within a specific empirical area of inquiry. This is the primary aim of a grounded theory study to generate an explanation of a particular phenomenon that is grounded in and supported by the data. In some of my own research on the experience of infertility (Daly, 1988, 1989, 1999), I developed a substantive theory that included a category on the unique experience of loss in infertility. Properties of this category included loss of body function in reproduction, loss of the social role of parenting, and loss of a fantasized child. Formal theory, by contrast, is concerned with the creation of more abstract theoretical ideas that provide explanation about patterns of social action. Prus (1994) has referred to these as generic concepts. These are explanations that go beyond the specifics of an area of empirical inquiry and offer explanations at a broader level. Hence in my own work on infertility and adoption, I explored the meaning of resocialization of adult identity as a formal theory of social action (Daly, 1992b). By comparing across a number of substantive domains, I was interested in trying to understand some of the common elements in such a process. Most grounded theory work does not include formal theorizing activity, but rather tends to focus on offering full and comprehensive explanation of the specific processes within the chosen area of empirical study.

Grounded theory has become one of the most followed qualitative methodologies because it provides a methodological language that serves as a guideline for conducting emergent qualitative studies. Three key features of this emergent methodology are inherently theoretical:

Theoretical Sensitivity

In the original formulation of grounded theory (Glaser & Strauss, 1967), theoretical sensitivity focused on the way concepts emerged in the process of collecting data that gave shape to the developing theory. It was by being attentive to emergent ideas and concepts in the data that the researcher was grounding the developing theory of the experience of participants. In subsequent work by Strauss and Corbin (1990, 1998), theoretical sensitivity is described as a process that begins before data collection and goes on throughout the collection and analysis of data. There are several sources of theoretical sensitivity at the outset of a project: existing concepts and theories, the empirical literature, and the personal and professional experience of the researcher. For example, in a study of how mothers grieve the loss of a child, Farnsworth (1996) drew on her own experience of being a bereaved mother as well as theoretical ideas from family stress theory and feminist perspectives on motherhood. Theoretical sensitivity is a process of taking stock of how these perspectives on the research problem can shape the direction of the subsequent inquiry. While the goal is to understand what some of these influences are, the practice involves holding these understandings provisionally. In other words, they serve to shape the beginning line of inquiry but must be held lightly and reconsidered when information emerges in the data to suggest alternative explanations.

In traditional, positivistic theory, concepts are often put forward as being definitive in their explanation. The aim is to offer certainty of explanation. In an inductive approach where the goal is to discover theory from data, *sensitizing concepts* (Blumer, 1969) serve as a means to guide inquiry. Like theoretical sensitivity, sensitizing concepts are theoretical ideas that come from existing theory. Rather than using these concepts as "prescriptions for what to see," they can be used more fruitfully in inductive inquiry as ideas that "merely suggest directions along which to look" (p. 148). Gilgun (1995) for example, used justice and care as sensitizing concepts in her analysis of the moral discourse of incest perpetrators in order to better understand how they invoked discourses of caring as the reason for their abusive behaviors. Once again, the data matter most and it is from the data that the developing theory can be forged.

Theoretical Sampling

Theoretical sampling is based on the idea that the researcher makes decisions throughout the research process about where to look for information in order to best develop the emerging theory. In an emergent design, one of the most important parts of discovery is to learn to ask the right kinds of questions. Questions are formed on the basis of emerging puzzles: As we seek to understand experience, we are left asking how and why participants make the choices they do; we encounter puzzles about the meaning of critical events and we begin to see the beginning shape of patterns—but typically with incomplete explanations for what is going on. Theoretical sampling involves actively pursuing these explanations. The focus is on sampling for ideas rather than sampling people. Although there are times when we must sample a certain kind of person in order to get at the ideas, the underlying motivation is to help fill in a piece of our emerging puzzle. As a result, theoretical sampling is directed by the incompleteness of our theoretical explanation and involves sampling for certain kinds of events, situations, unique perspectives, or experiences that people have had that would shed light on these missing elements. In practical terms, these decisions may involve making observations at a particular site or interviewing a person in authority who might help us to understand certain kinds of organizational practices.

Theoretical sampling is often confused with traditional methodological sampling practices. Indeed, even in a grounded theory study proposal, it is usually necessary for the purposes of research ethics approval or to satisfy a graduate committee to outline a set of procedures for how the sample will be obtained and the criteria used for sampling. Whereas the emphasis in survey research or large quantitative designs is on getting a random sample that is representative of a population group, in qualitative research the sample size is usually restricted by the time-consuming nature of interviews and observations. As a result, qualitative research is more likely to use a purposive sampling strategy that defines a narrow set of parameters for who will be included in the study. Participants are chosen purposively because of their relevant characteristics and experiences with the phenomenon to be explored. A grounded theory approach typically involves both of these sampling strategies: purposive sampling to decide who to speak to and theoretical sampling that involves decisions about where to go for missing pieces of information.

Theoretical Saturation

Through the process of constant comparative analysis, the researcher begins to build a theory based on emerging categories and their properties. Properties are characteristics of a category that give it range and organize its meaning. Categories that are developed in the data collection process must be saturated through the process of theoretical sampling. As researchers seek additional information in order to solve the puzzle of what is going on, they gain a greater sense of confidence in the explanation they are able to bring to the phenomenon at hand. This growing sense of confidence that comes as the explanation deepens is referred to as theoretical saturation. Our emerging explanations become saturated with supporting data.

Theoretical saturation can be understood in a number of ways. First, it is an ideal that is never fully achievable. In fact, it stands in contrast to the underlying assumptions of grounded theory that any theoretical explanation is tentative and subject to change with new information. Hence to talk about saturation is to suggest that researchers need to go as far as they are able in saturating their categories—knowing that these can never be complete or definitive. Second, theoretical saturation is a standard that is used to make decisions about when to stop data collection. Hence in a grounded theory study, the key issue is not how many people you talked to (or the size of the N) but rather whether the number of interviews or the range of the observations is justified by having reached theoretical saturation of the key categories in the theory. The third way of thinking about theoretical saturation is to treat it as a guide for the construction of the emerging theory. The practice of saturating a category involves theoretical sampling for information and monitoring the level of confidence we can have in our emerging explanations. Theoretical saturation as a standard refers to the point at which we put forward our theory as a product (tentative as that may be), whereas theoretical saturation as a guide refers to the ongoing process of constructing the theory.

Variations

Postmodern critiques of grounded theory have drawn attention to the objectivist assumptions of traditional grounded theory approaches. As Charmaz (2003b) has argued, grounded theory aligns quite well with the objectivist assumptions of both traditional positivism and postpositivism: positivism with the emphasis on an objective, external reality that can be discovered and represented, an emphasis on unbiased data collection, use of standard, technical methodological procedures, and the use of verification strategies; postpositivism with acknowledgment of participants' voices, the potential conflicts between participant's reality and the researcher's reality, and recognizing art as well as science in the analytic process. Charmaz argues for another paradigm position, which is constructivist (again, this might also be referred to as constructionist) grounded theory. Objectivist and constructivist grounded theory approaches can be seen as lying on a continuum.

Objectivist Grounded Theory. The objectivist form of grounded theory has the following characteristics and procedures:

- Assumption of a reality that can be researched, understood, and represented through theoretical explanation
- Treatment of data as if they had an objective status: "let the data speak" or "the reality of the data"
- Use of systematic procedures for the collection and analysis of data
- Concern with researcher bias and strategies to control this bias
- A direct and mechanical link between observation and theory, rendering the researcher somewhat invisible: For Glaser (1992), theory emerges directly from data through the process of comparison, and it is essential to keep out the theorist's preconceptions
- Accordingly, there is a tendency to report data and research findings as distanced experts

Constructivist Grounded Theory. In constructivist grounded theory the researcher plays an active and deliberate role in organizing and assigning meaning to the data as a way of constructing higher order categories and theory. Rather than assuming the pretense of a blank slate in approaching phenomena as in objectivist approaches, the researcher approaches a problem with a greater emphasis on theoretical sensitivity to prior experiences, concepts, ideas, and theory. In contrast with the objectivist approach that emphasizes the importance of accurately representing external reality while minimizing researcher influence, the constructivist approach is concerned with the interpretive process by which theory is meaningfully constructed. The key elements of this approach are the following:

- Data are coconstructed between the researcher and the researched
- There is now one reality to be understood and represented, but many perspectives on the same reality that emerge in the interactive research process
- Emphasis is on "strategies" rather than rule-oriented methods
- Researcher gains "intimate familiarity" (Blumer, 1969) through involvement, understanding, participation
- Recognition that theoretical products reflect complex changeable meanings

- Deliberate inclusion of the researcher's self in research reports and theoretical constructions
- Reflexivity is apparent in the written texts in order to illustrate the researcher's meaning-making process

These variations of grounded theory are on the same continuum and, as such, they share many of the same methodological principles and practices. The key difference between these approaches is an epistemological one that involves a different way of thinking about the relationship between the researcher and the subject matter. The key in thinking about how you position yourself on this continuum is to consider your own paradigm beliefs about the construction of knowledge. These are by no means exclusive categories, only points on the continuum with many possible positions in between. The onus is on you as the researcher to justify your own position and make it transparent to your audience.

Narrative Inquiry: The Study of Story

Theoretical Background

Narrative approaches introduce a number of important bridges into qualitative inquiry. With its close affiliation to literature and fiction, narrative serves to connect the broad domains of art and science. With its popularity in family therapy, narrative serves to blur the boundary between research and practice, theory and therapeutic change. With its inclusion of the everyday and the extraordinary, narrative bridges the mundane and the exceptional. With its emphasis on lived, embodied experience and the nuances of private life, narrative bridges the emotional and the rational. The narrative approach, with its roots in many domains, thereby offers many opportunities for exploring lived experience in many forms and at many levels of analysis.

Narrative analysis has become an effective methodology for understanding family realities. For example, the MacArthur Family Narrative Consortium (FNC) defines family stories as "verbal accounts of personal experiences that are important to family, and typically involve the creation and maintenance of relationships, depict rules of interaction, and reflect beliefs about family relationships" (Fiese & Sameroff, 1999, p. 440). Furthermore, individual family members may present different narratives to the researcher or provide a recounting of how their own experiences affect the collective workings of the family (Fiese & Wamboldt, 2003).

What Is Narrative Inquiry?

The texts produced under the rubric of what I call narrative inquiry would be stories that create the effect of reality, showing characters embedded in the lived moments of struggle, resisting the intrusions of chaos, disconnection, fragmentation, marginalization, and incoherence, trying to preserve or restore the continuity and coherence of life's unity in the face of unexpected blows of fate that call one's meanings and values into question. (Statement by Arthur Bochner in Ellis & Bochner, 2003, p. 217)

Stories are a primary means by which we organize human experience and make it meaningful. Our collective account of experience, history, has emerged out of our oral tradition of giving meaning to our lives through the told record of a combination of everyday life, celebration, tragedy, catastrophe, and unusual events. The word *story* is at the root of *history* and reflects the centrality of narrative for the construction of past events. Like any story, history is at some level an "artifice" and a product of individual imagination (Carr, 1986, p. 10).

Individuals use story to make sense of their own lives. Narrative offers a way to plot the course of individual human development (Daiute & Lightfoot, 2004). Families, through photo albums, rituals, and traditions, form the story of their lives together. Stories at all levels serve to construct and interpret not only events and actions, but to construct and reconstruct identities and culturally embedded selves. Life stories, however, are never complete—although episodes in the life course have beginnings and endings, plots and characters, "the life course itself is an incomplete collection of narratives" (Clausen, 1998, p. 193).

In the *Poetics*, Aristotle talks about *mimesis* as the basis for understanding the dramatic story. Stories imitate life in action. In this regard, Paul Ricoeur talks about *mimesis* as a "metaphor of reality." Metaphor and mimesis lie at the root of narrative insofar as the story "refers to reality not in order to copy it, but in order to give it a new reading" (Ricoeur, 1981). Narrative approaches are strongly influenced by hermeneutics because the story can be constructed in many ways and read with many interpretations. What is key here is that narrative does not seek to copy reality; rather its goal is to help make sense of that reality. As a result, telling a story of one's experience necessarily involves selection, imagination, and embellishment. Stories also involve choices about what to leave out of the description. Motivation for telling the story takes into account who the audience is and how the teller will appear in their eyes. How the story is told becomes part of "presentation of self" and "impression management" (Goffman, 1959).

Narratives come in many different forms. These are referred to as *genres,* which are culturally developed ways of organizing narrative experience (Daiute & Lightfoot, 2004). At one level we can think about broad genres like tragedy, comedy, adventure, or romance. At another level we can think about fairy tales, movies, autobiographies, novels, poems, online stories— each with their own format and structure. In addition, there are many different styles of presenting stories, including realistic, confessional, impressionistic, literary, and critical (Van Maanen, 1988).

Narrative inquiry has several key characteristics. The first of these is concerned with the ontological basis of narratives: They are provisional constructions that constitute reality. One of the first criticisms of narrative approaches as a mode of conducting social scientific inquiry was to question the validity of the story and the degree to which it corresponded with reality. This, of course, is an objectivist or positivist question concerned primarily with the truth or falsity of the story in relation to the "real" events. The hallmark of the narrative approach, however, is its fundamental "indifference to extralinguistic reality" (Bruner, 1990, p. 44). The power of narrative is not measured by the degree of correspondence between the plot and events, but rather by the unique way the story has been constructed and told. As Riessman (1993) has argued, narratives "do not mirror a world out there"; rather they are "constructed, creatively authored, rhetorically replete with assumptions, and interpretive" (p. 5). In this regard, it is critically important to examine what the storyteller has accomplished by telling the story in the way he or she chose to tell it. As part of this, stories are always at some level incomplete. Although we use the expression, "I want the whole story," this too is a fallacy insofar as a story might always include more detail if constructed in a different manner. As Stake (2003) has argued, "the whole story exceeds anyone's knowing, anyone's telling" (p. 144).

The second characteristic of narrative is the inherent sequentiality of the story (Bruner, 1990). The sequence of events, experiences, and characters comes together to form the plot of the story. The organization of the plot is in marked contrast to the "ill-structured" nature of experience itself, which is neither pedagogically nor epistemologically neat (Stake, 2003). Stories have beginnings and endings, events are organized in coherent and meaningful ways, characters are introduced at strategic and dramatic moments. Narrative inquiry is therefore interested in the way the story is put together. The sequence of a story does not necessarily follow the chronology of events. Rather, the story is constructed in ways to highlight events at different points of time and to move between the past, present, and future in order to capture memories, current experiences, and anticipated events. Sequence gives the narrative a sense of structure, and events become meaningful when we understand their placement in the narrative. Narrative accounts allow the individual to see life events as systematically related and that there is a coherent connection among life events (Gergen & Gergen, 1984).

Related to the sequence of the story is the inherent temporality of any narrative. Narrative typically serves as a means of making meaning of the past. Stories are always told from the conditions of what G. H. Mead referred to as the specious present and, as a result, the events of the past are always subject to different forms of retelling where certain events take on greater importance while others drift into temporary insignificance. Stories told within the contingencies of the present always rearrange, redescribe, invent, omit, and revise (Ellis & Bochner, 2003). Although we tend to think of narratives as the construction of past actions, they are always shaped through the filters of present conditions and are likely to include hopes, dreams, and expectations of the future. Narrative is a "reconstitutive process" that involves an interweaving of the events of the past, the past's effects on the present, and the symbolic reconstruction of the past in the present (Ezzy, 1998). Stories move freely in the temporal dimension and can offer insight into both lives as they have been lived and lives that are yet to be lived. It is in this regard that narrative plays a critical role in understanding identity: A person is defined as a "self-narrating organism" who creates a biography in the process of telling a life story (Maines, 1993). Telling the story of your life provides a means to select key experiences to include, and to describe these in a manner that provides continuity and the creation of the kind of person you want to be seen as. For example, in a narrative study of adoptive adolescents, the adolescent is viewed as creating and recreating a life story that makes meaning of, and gives purpose to, his or her experience of adoption (Dunbar & Grotevant, 2004).

The fourth characteristic of narrative is concerned with the cast of characters. Of particular interest in any story is how the central protagonist of the story (usually the teller) is presented to listeners or readers and how the protagonist sees the story. Protagonists play a critical role in interpreting the events of the story and offering meaning to the overall narrative (Bruner, 1990). These interpretations are passed on to the audience, who in turn interpret these interpretations in their own way. Every story has significant players who are brought to the foreground of the story: Some bring surprise and suspense to the story while others are noticeably left out of the story when one would otherwise expect them to be present.

The fifth characteristic of narrative is that a story has many functions in social life. When the emphasis is taken off whether a story is true or not,

attention shifts to what the story *does*. Stories are part of the existential struggle to move life forward (Ellis & Bochner, 2003). As Bochner argues, stories
come with many questions: "What are the consequences my story produces?"
"What kind of person does it shape me into?" "What new possibilities does
it introduce for living my life?"

To think of narratives as agentic and producing consequences for how we
live is the basis upon which White and Epston (1990) outlined the narrative
approach to family therapy. In family therapy, families re-visit, re-experience,
and quite often re-story the past events of their lives in order to sort out their
present conflicts and to construct invitations to a different future. The structuring of a narrative is also a selective process whereby people "prune" from
experience those events that do not fit with the dominant evolving stories—
as a result, a good part of experience goes unstoried. In living our lives, then,
our stories are full of gaps. In telling the story, however, some of these gaps
must be filled in by "performing the story." People are "re-authoring their
lives" insofar as they enter into them, take them over, and make them their
own (White & Epston, 1990, p. 13). It is in this regard that Kvale (1977)
refers to remembering as a search for meaning that involves an imaginative
reconstruction of past events. Therapy, then, is a "context for the re-authoring
of lives and relationships" (White & Epston, 1990, p. 17). Persons can tell
their stories, "perform" their stories, arrive at new outcomes to their stories,
ascribe new meaning to their stories, perform alternative stories, elaborate
stories, and perhaps most importantly, separate themselves from their stories
so that they can experience a sense of personal agency. By "breaking from the
performance of their stories, they experience a capacity to intervene in their
own lives and relationships" (White & Epston, 1990, p. 17). Research questions, like therapeutic questions, are "interventive" insofar as the interview
does not just elicit a story already known but contributes to the creation of a
new story with its own effects (Burck, 2005).

Part of this process involves opening spaces for "subjugated knowledges"
(White & Epston, 1990, p. 32). Whereas the dominant stories are "problem-
saturated" stories of family life, the subjugated stories are previously neglected
but vital aspects of lived experience. "Re-authoring" of stories through
therapeutic means is a way of arriving at new meanings of past events. By
plotting alternative stories of one's past and bringing forward previously subjugated stories, people arrive at "unique redescriptions" of themselves and
their relationships, which in turn can serve as an opportunity to "re-vision"
their relationships with themselves and others. Though White and Epston
(1990) emphasize the importance of narrative for therapeutic change, these
principles of looking at alternative and subjugated stories also can be a useful device in the research endeavor.

Implications for Methods

In the qualitative tradition, narrative is highly valued because it is rooted in time, place, and personal experience and serves as a vehicle for understanding identity, human agency, and the embeddedness of individual lives in the broader culture. One of the appeals of narrative analysis is that it allows us to understand people's lives in a more holistic way. The primary emphasis in narrative analysis is to understand the story in order to understand how the individual lives life. In contrast to constant comparative analysis in grounded theory, where the aim is to identify patterns across cases, the primary goal of narrative is to understand how individuals construct their storied experience within the context of their life. If we are collecting a number of stories, as is often the case, we may wish to identify common elements from various stories that help us to understand the nature of shared, cultural experience. For example, Sevón (2005) presents the stories of four pregnant women who spoke about their expectations and ambivalences of becoming a mother in relation to the dominant cultural narratives of "good" mothering. Similarly, Savvidou, Bozikas, Hatzigeleki, and Karavatos (2003) conducted a narrative study of mothers who were hospitalized by a mental illness. They wanted to understand how these women coped with the dominant social discourses that reinforced their sense of incapability as mothers. Using semistructured interviews, they asked these 20 hospitalized women to describe their children and their relationship with them. Through the analysis of these narratives, the authors report that these women discovered it was extremely difficult to use alternative discourses that portrayed their competence, since they often felt trapped in the extremely powerful, scientifically based dominant discourses about mental illness.

Like ethnography, narratives offer a window on culture, for it is through the process of storytelling that we can understand how culture is constituted. As Vygotsky (1978) has argued, stories are implicitly collaborative endeavors that involve the storyteller's drawing from those who are familiar with the way things work in the culture. Stories therefore straddle personal experience and public tales. Since stories help us to understand both cultural conventions and deviations from these conventions, they can be seen as having both moral and epistemic status (Bruner, 1990). In other words, stories help us to comprehend our individual and cultural values (moral status), and they are a means by which we come to know our cultural practices (epistemic status). In this regard, narrative analysis goes beyond the lessons of the individual story: It is also a means to generate knowledge that disrupts traditional explanations and allows us to see the complexities of human lives as they are shaped by changing cultural practices.

A number of methods have been used to elicit and examine the stories of people's lives.

Narrative Inquiry

In its simplest form, narrative research involves sitting with participants and asking them to tell the story of their experience as it relates to an area of joint interest. Using an interview format with minimal direction, researchers sit down with participants and ask them to tell the story of their experience. The interviewer would typically begin by framing the area of interest. For example, in a study of adoption reunion, the researcher might start with a statement like: "I am interested in how adoptees have experienced reunion with their birth parents. Can you start by telling me when you first started thinking about this as a possibility?" The primary line of questioning is to encourage the telling of the story and may include simple prompts such as, "And then what happened?" or, "Can you say more about what that was like?" The approach is to ask open-ended questions with a minimum of interruptions, using occasional prompts to encourage the provision of detail in a particular area. The challenge for the interviewer is not to let a preordained set of questions get in the way of the story to be told. Ultimately, however, it is important for the researcher to acknowledge that the story told in the context of an interview setting is essentially a jointly constructed narrative. While the story essentially belongs to the participant, the researcher plays an important role through gestures, prompts, and questions in shaping the form and structure of the narrative.

Narrative inquiry can also take a more focused approach to the examination of individual lives. In human development research, McAdams (2004) has used narrative inquiry as a means to understand the experience of generativity in adulthood. Using intensive life story interviews with 74 middle-aged adults, McAdams and his colleagues identified themes that were characteristic of highly generative adults, including an early experience of being advantaged relative to others, sensitivity to the suffering of others, and the transformation of bad scenes into good outcomes.

In a study of domestic violence, Enosh and Buchbinder (2005) identify a number of different narrative styles that emerge in the coconstructed interview between the researcher and battered women and batterers. These narrative styles are identified as struggle, deflection, negotiation, and a self-observation process, with each of these styles having implications for thinking about relational patterns and power dynamics between researchers and participants. This research provides an illustration of the importance of examining not only the content of the story, but how the story can be constructed in different ways depending on the participants, the researcher, and their interaction.

Life Histories

Life history is a term used to describe the way participants provide retrospective accounts of their lives in response to questions from an interviewer. It is focused on how the participants see their own lives—often within the broader social, political, and economic contexts of history. It is concerned with how participants select events to highlight from their lived experiences in order to create a coherent sense of who they are. Life history research has played a central role in both human development studies and family sociology. In human development studies, Bernice Neugarten (1968) used the term "interiority" to describe the increasing desire in middle and later years to look within in order to assess the way that one has lived one's life. In developmental studies of aging, Robert Butler (1963) put forward the life review method, which was designed to have participants reflect on their life as a whole in order to come to a greater understanding and acceptance of how their lives had been lived. The principal means of conducting these reviews was to encourage participants to reminisce about their lives (Bornat, 2004). Life history is also known as the biographical method or the life story method. Although Neugarten and Butler emphasized the importance of life review in middle and later years, the term has also been used more broadly to elicit life stories that occur at any time throughout the life course (Clausen, 1998).

In family sociology, life histories were a central part of early Chicago school sociology. The classic study by Thomas and Znaniecki (1918/1958) titled the *Polish Peasant in Europe and America* employed a life course perspective and was based on a collection of written autobiographies and memoirs. Like many life history studies that followed in the Chicago school, these analyses took into account "both the influences of social structure in providing opportunities or constraints for the actor along with the actor's own ability to perceive these opportunities/constraints subjectively and to react to them creatively" (Miller, 2000, p. 6).

The biographical method is often concerned with key turning points in a person's life—how these are retrospectively constructed and presented as part of a biographical story. Although there are times when researchers are interested in how entire lives are reconstructed, biographical methods are also used to discover how participants describe a particular phase, situation, or transition in their lives (Rosenthal, 2004). John Clausen's Berkeley longitudinal study provides a classic example of life history research in human development studies. He collected information on individuals' personalities and social backgrounds over a 50-year period. In the life history interviews, he was interested in identifying major life turning or decision points, dominant influences on development, perceptions of careers and relationships, and major sources of satisfaction and dissatisfaction (Clausen, 1998). "Turning points" were a central focus in these interviews, and they involved looking at the major roles that were affected, the perceived cause of the turning point, the timing of the turning point, and the ultimate consequences as viewed by the participant (Clausen, 1998).

Case Study Analysis

A case can be defined in a variety of ways ranging from the story of one individual to the collective stories of participants in an organization who, together, constitute the case. Hence we can do case study analysis of a father in a family, or we can treat the family itself as the case. Similarly, a case can be an individual, a family, a town, a school, or any other institution (Gilgun, 2005b). Storytelling is central to understanding the "particulars" of the case. As Stake (2003) has argued, case study researchers are primarily interested in what makes the case unique and what sets the story apart from other stories. This involves paying attention to the emic meanings held by the person or persons within the case. This includes understanding its atypical features, happenings, relationships, and situations. Yet how we learn from the singular case is inherently comparative insofar as we can know its particulars only by showing how the case is like or unlike other cases. Accordingly, most researchers concentrate on describing the present case in sufficient detail so that the reader can make good comparisons.

Case studies often use a variety of techniques for understanding the case. In addition to asking individuals to tell the story of their experience, researchers might also engage in observations; interviews with close associates; and the analysis of relevant documents including diaries, letters, or reports. Case studies provide a means to understand the idiographic experience of individuals, families, and groups. For example, Fravel and Boss (1992) did a family case study that involved talking to the parents of three children who went missing almost 40 years earlier. Their purpose in conducting this single-case study was to gather information that might broaden our understanding of families' experience of ambiguous loss and how they talked about behaviors, attitudes, or other resources that had been helpful to them.

Narrative Analysis

- Why was the story told in the way it was?
- What is the order and sequence of story?
- What is in the story—what is left out of the story?
- How is the self presented in the story?
- What is the relationship between biography and history in the story? That is, how is the story located in relation to other events?
- What purpose is being served by the narrative? What is accomplished?
- Who was the audience the storyteller had in mind? How is the story positioned in relation to the audience?
- What were the dramatic turns in the story?
- How does the story help us to understand cultural practice?

Variations

Narrative analysis can take many forms depending on how one sees the structure and purpose of the narrative. These reflect different ontological assumptions and correspond with different paradigm positions.

Positivism/Postpositivism

Stories are used by some to try to establish a set of actual events or experience. The story is examined to find clues to *what really happened*. The story *represents* that reality. This approach to narrative, often used in the examination of historical documents, is used as a means of reconstructing *real* events. In this approach, the language and structure of the story are viewed as representing reality with an expectation of correspondence between the narrative and experience. Establishing the "truth" of past events is paramount in this approach, and like a journalist's story, may involve fact checking.

Social Construction/Interpretive

In this paradigm, language and reality are no longer separate realms. Reality is as it is constructed through our language and stories. There is no reality out there, only an unfolding reality that is created through our verbal constructions of it. It is in this regard that narrative *constitutes* reality: "it is in the telling that we make real phenomena in the stream of consciousness" (Riessman, 1993, p. 22). From a social constructionist perspective, narrative is not a "window into something else" but rather it is "of the world, not about it" (Daiute & Lightfoot, 2004, pp. x–xi). Hence, when we do narrative analysis from a social constructionist framework, the story is not about a life that is lived; instead it is constitutive of that life because "life and narrative are inextricably connected" (Ellis & Bochner, 2003, p. 220)

Critical

Narrative is *persuasive* and often brings about change in the way people see their own experience. Included here is an examination of power relations in the production of narratives. What is the purpose of the story, and is there an underlying effort to bring about some kind of change by telling the story? As Sarbin (2004) argues, one of the goals of a critical narrative is to lead readers or listeners to action. In keeping with the assumptions of this paradigm, ideologies and interests are infused into the story. We examine who is telling the story and seek to decipher how that person's position may give rise to a particular agenda. Analyzing narratives within this stream involves an examination of themes of morality, justice, and equity. These themes are reflected in stories of gender or racial discrimination, mental health, experience in oppressive institutions, or experiences of marginalization or exclusion.

Postmodern

A postmodern approach to narrative celebrates the presence of many different stories. There is an underlying skepticism about "metanarratives" (Lyotard, 1984, p. xxiv). Whereas modernist metanarratives emphasize grand unilinear depictions of the world, postmodern views are more likely to involve discontinuities and contradictions (Giddens, 1990). Instead of seeking truth by finding the most accurate story, there is an effort to bring forward the many possible stories that highlight different vantage points and experiences. As a result, these stories may be contradictory and inconsistent, but there is an understanding that this is consistent (ironically) with the way that lives are lived. There is a deliberate intention to move beyond any one dominant story to examine the subjugated stories that offer alternative ways of understanding experience. The goal of narrative analysis here is not truth or coherence but understanding complexity, diversity, and contradiction. Postmodern researchers have used the term *testimonio* as another way to examine the ways reconstructions of the past offer insight into the present condition (Tierney, 2003). There is an emphasis on understanding multiple voices and an effort to understand the ways the narrative is situated.

Critical Approaches: The Tradition of Feminist Inquiry and the Example of Participatory Action Research

Theoretical Background

Feminist inquiry has played a strong role in the development of qualitative family research. Classic qualitative studies of housework by Anne Oakley, of poverty and abuse by Lillian Rubin, and of widowhood by Helena Lopata have served to foreground women's experience of family life. In keeping with the assumptions of the critical paradigm, feminist inquiry developed a methodology that was reflexive and based on nonhierarchical principles of collaboration between researcher and participant. It is a form of inquiry that is conscious and inclusive and built on the inextricable relationship between personal life and scholarly inquiry (Allen, 2000). While feminist research has taken many forms, approaches share a concern with reciprocity, exchange of thoughts and feelings, and efforts to avoid objectifying the participant. At the root, feminist inquiry is built on the common cause of highlighting women's voices in the name of challenging patriarchy and eradicating women's oppression in the home and beyond. In this respect, feminist research is built on the principle of *praxis,* which is an active and reflexive process that provides a means for demystifying power relationships and fosters the desire for social change with the goal of unsettling the normativity that gives privilege to an elite few (Allen, 2001; Thompson & Walker, 1995).

Building on some of the foundational principles of feminist inquiry, participatory action research (PAR) is emerging as an important qualitative methodology in the critical paradigm. It is driven by the need of researchers to engage in research that is responsive to contemporary social issues but also results from external pressures by funders and taxpayers to conduct research that involves real social change (Small & Uttal, 2005). It is concerned with the examination of injustice, inequality, marginalization, and the distribution of power. The primary aim of research in the critical paradigm is not simply to explain, but to serve the call for justice through a process of social *action.* Specifically, through a process of data gathering and analysis, participatory action research works to develop research-informed strategies that can serve as catalysts for social change. It is also by definition *participatory.* Although researchers bring their research skills to the organization of the research process, there is an understanding that participants bring different kinds of expertise to the research endeavor. This is research that involves all relevant parties in actively examining, together, current action that they experience as problematic in order to better understand it, change it, and improve conditions. As such, participatory action research is concerned with the generation of practical knowledge that can serve people in the process of transformation as they struggle with the conditions of their everyday life. Accordingly, participatory action research is consistent with the paradigm assumptions of postmodernism, feminism, and critical theory.

PAR and Traditional Science

The traditional model of science has the following characteristics:

- Researchers take an expert position and define what is important to study
- Clear distinction between researchers and researched—with the "researched" called on to provide information
- Purpose of the research has to do primarily with the researcher's agenda: gathering data, testing hypotheses, and developing theory

By contrast, Participatory Action Research has the following characteristics:

- *It deliberately shapes the research questions* or research problems by involving those people who are experiencing the issues (participatory)
- *It is concerned with action and change*—it involves a process of collaborative definition of concerns, raising of questions, reflections on current and past activities, planning of a data gathering phase in response to created questions, analysis, collaborative drawing of conclusions, plan for collective action
- *Research serves the process of social transformation*—rather than the emphasis on prediction in traditional science, PAR is concerned with moving toward and realizing possibilities—hence it involves constructing a preferred future based on principles of equality and collaborative effort
- *It is driven by the yoked energy* of the need to know and the desire to bring about social change

---

Participatory action research has emerged out of a number of theoretical traditions, including Marxism, liberation theology, and the contributions of the Vienna Circle to critical theory. Some of the most noteworthy PAR projects have originated in third world countries where the conditions of oppression have been most evident. Paulo Freire's (1972) work, described in his book entitled the *Pedagogy of the Oppressed* is concerned with a process of social transformation with the poor through a process of education. Freire worked in the rural areas of northeastern Brazil in the early 1960's on a program of literacy that was designed not only to teach language but to awaken critical consciousness of their oppressive social conditions (e.g., not being allowed to vote). Freire's work was built on the ontological assumption that the reality in which people are embedded is not static but rather is fluid and *transformable.* As a result, his method of social action was built on the premise that people can rise above what they might perceive as their unalterable fate, and through the process of critical reflection they can find ways to intervene in their own lives.

Like Marx, Freire was concerned with *praxis*. Praxis is like the spine of the critical paradigm because it involves the unification of knowledge and social action (the spine connects the thinking head and the doing legs!). In Freire's own words, praxis is "reflection and action upon the world in order to transform it" (p. 28). He pointed out clearly that these must occur together, for reflection without action was "armchair revolution" whereas action without reflection was "pure activism" (p. 41). At the center of his idea of praxis was the importance of education for raising consciousness and thereby mobilizing women and men to reflect on the conditions of their lives and become agents in the process of changing themselves and the conditions of their lives.

One of the key characteristics of the PAR approach is the leveling of the traditional scientific distinction between the researcher as powerful expert and the participant as the unknowledgeable contributor. Freire cast this relationship in very different terms. He argued that this hierarchical distinction was very much a part of traditional education. He called this the "banking" model of education where the teacher/expert deposits information or knowledge into the account of the unknowing student. This is a unidirectional, empty-vessel model of education that serves to inhibit social change because of its emphasis on acceptance of the status quo knowledge. In response, Freire advocated for a participatory model of education that was dialogical. In this model, students and participants tell teachers what is important in their lives and provide insight into the conditions of their experience. Teachers share their understandings and serve as a catalyst for deepening the dialogue, but students are treated as the experts on their own experience. This collaborative process of learning, reflection, critical consciousness, and intervention was the basis of his beliefs that lie at the root of his approach called the pedagogy of the oppressed. It also served as the basis for the development of participatory action research that is collaborative, critically reflective, and concerned with the process of social transformation.

PAR and Values

Given the central importance of values within the critical paradigm, PAR can be seen to uphold the following values (Stringer, 1999):

It is *democratic*, enabling participation

It is *equitable*, acknowledging people's equality of worth

It is *liberating*, offering freedom from oppressive, debilitating conditions

It is *life enhancing*, enabling expression of life potential

Implications for Methods

The blurring of the distinction between researcher and participant serves as an important starting point for understanding how participatory action research is carried out. In traditional research, investigators would typically exert a monopolizing authority over all aspects of the research project. Using prior research and theory, they would articulate the research problem, design a set of procedures for gathering data, gather the data from participants who consent to give the information, and analyze and interpret those data and draw conclusions about them. In this model, researchers extract information from participants and explain what they have found. In PAR, participants and researchers must be viewed as members of a shared lifeworld where participants are treated as "knowing subjects who are not only 'others' but autonomous and responsible others" (Kemmis & McTaggart, 2003, p. 365). This represents a fundamental shift from doing research *on* people to doing research *with* people (Ladkin, 2004).

Given this shared participation and responsibility, one of the aims of PAR is the transference of research skills to participants so they become owners of the tools for their own inquiry. Even without specialized research training, participants can become researchers who generate their own evidence for decision making. This has implications at all stages of the research. Rather than formulating the research problem on the basis of prior research or theory, participants are engaged in a process of defining what the needs or concerns are in their own situation. The goal, as Habermas (1996) has argued, is to open "communicative space." The research begins with the people who would traditionally be seen as the "end users" of the knowledge produced. This process may be developed as a program of activities rather than a traditional research design. It provides a means for opening dialogue among various stakeholders and allows the opportunity to identify important issues and develop strategies for collecting additional information. A key component of PAR research is the process of gathering data in order to inform decision making. This can take many forms, including roundtable discussions, document analysis, focus groups, individual interviews, and observation of meetings, events, or social activities. In the spirit of PAR, this may involve peer interviewing or the training of community members to conduct interviews or focus groups among themselves.

For family researchers working with community partners in research, participatory action research has become an important approach for solving puzzles that emerge in practice. PAR introduces a new vision for practice and research that involves a shift from seeing the social service practitioner as "mechanic/technician" to "creative investigator and problem solver" (Stringer, 1999, p. 3). This involves collaboration between researchers and service professionals that emphasizes sharing systematic approaches to inquiry, developing investigative skills, and generating sustainable solutions based on analysis of data. Specifically, they work together to design the project, collect data, reflect on and analyze the data, and then continue to work together to construct plans for the resolution of the problem. In their action research with mothers living in poverty, Dodson and Schmalzbauer (2005) included community informants in the early stages of research design, hired members of the community to carry out interviews, and used interpretive focus groups, drawn from the community, as a way to gain a better understanding of what they had heard in earlier interviews so that they could assess "what it is really like" or come to know "what people face" every day.

Working in collaborative relationships involves challenges. As Ladkin (2004) points out, there are many issues to bear in mind:

- Leadership is still important; a balance must be found between providing direction and providing space for the inquiry to unfold. For university researchers, the primary role may be to serve as a *catalyst and support* to the project.
- There must be ongoing attentiveness to group dynamics in order to ensure distribution of responsibility and collaboration.
- Flexibility is important when working within organizational settings in order to contend with some institutional constraints.
- Collaboration involves a set of changing dynamics that results in shifting ownership and the emergence of new choices and directions.
- Relationships are central in PAR and must be attentive to power dynamics, equality issues, and the open negotiation and renegotiation of shared goals and outcomes.

Throughout the process of doing PAR, attention is given to the articulation of an agenda for social change. From the outset of the research, PAR is intentional about its commitment to social change. This occurs early on as awareness of key problems begins to emerge. It is reformulated throughout the project as new evidence brings to light different aspects of the problem and gives rise to new solutions. Actions are taken and the outcomes and implications are examined. Changes are then monitored, reflected on, and evaluated, with new actions and plans emerging as a result. Key throughout the process is that these actions and strategies are collaborative, reflective, and responsive.

In keeping with Freire's original ideas, PAR proceeds through a cycle of action and reflection. In this process, an individual or a group of people take action, together or alone reflect on that action, consider a new action to try, and then again reflect on that action (Ladkin, 2004). In contrast with highly controlled traditional research, these cycles can be messy and take unpredictable routes (Ladkin, 2004). These processes of social change can be potentially liberating for some groups and threatening for others. For example, not only can the research give rise to controversy among the participating partners because of differing interests, but recommendations generated may actually be experienced as intimidating by some because of the possibility that they could lead to organizational or personnel changes that participants may not view as being favorable (Small & Uttal, 2005).

One of the key differences between researchers and participants that must be kept in mind is that participants may be more likely to live directly with the consequences of the transformations they make. Harmonizing insider (participants) and outsider (researchers, practitioners) perspectives becomes a central challenge in PAR research. Authenticity can serve as an important standard for evaluating the degree to which there is success in "seeing things intersubjectively, from one's own point of view and the view of others" (Kemmis & McTaggart, 2003, p. 347). Striving for authenticity involves reconciling an ongoing tension between what participants regard as important or of consequence and the insights that might be brought to the situation by the eyes of the outsider.

In the effort to meet some of the practical challenges of understanding participants' worlds, there is often a tradeoff between the rigors of scientific methods and the practical expediency of community-based problem-solving strategies. This tradeoff is rooted in a different set of epistemological assumptions that recognize the importance of practical and experiential knowledge alongside theoretical and empirical knowledge. Although collaboration is an important concept in this kind of research, there is often conflict between the agenda of university trained researchers and community participants. Whereas university researchers are more likely to enter into a project with research training and expectations for publication of results, community participants may be intimidated by the researchers' experience, may lack confidence in their own knowledge, and may come with suspicions about the merits of the research processes (holding memories of data being extracted from them in the past).

The key to contending with this tension is to return to the underlying paradigm issues associated with critical perspectives. Research with the primary goal of bringing about social transformation is less concerned with accurately representing reality through rigorous methods and more concerned with addressing issues of inequality and marginalization from an informed perspective. The process of doing the research is every bit as important as the outcome of the research. That is not to say that there is no place for rigor in PAR; rather, it can serve as an important means for enhancing the process of social transformation on the basis of convincing and influential data.

Variations

A variety of labels are used to describe participatory action research. Kemmis and McTaggart (2003) suggest that the variation in the nomenclature itself reflects the contestation of the field that is consistent with its home in a critical paradigm. They offer an overview of many different varieties, each with "action" at its core: critical action research, action learning, action science, and industrial action research. It is also referred to as emancipation research, community mobilization or action research, and dialogic research. At the root of all of these approaches are seven underlying characteristics:

1. It is a social process that links individual and social concerns.

2. It is participatory: It engages people in examining their own knowledge.

3. It is practical and collaborative: It involves working toward improving the conditions of participants' own lives.

4. It is emancipatory: It helps people to release themselves from constraints of unjust social structures that limit their self-determination.

5. It is critical: It contests and seeks to reconstitute language that contributes to oppression and to relationships that are exploitive.

6. It is recursive in that it encourages self-reflective knowledge of practices and action that brings about desired change.

7. It is transformative for both theory and practice.

In the family field, there are a number of excellent examples of participatory action research. William Doherty and colleagues have used models of catalytic community partnership and action research as a guide for researchers and parents within a community to participate in a process of social change (Doherty & Beaton, 2000; Doherty & Carlson, 2002). Under the banner of "Family First," Doherty and colleagues spearheaded a collaborative project that involved mobilizing families to take back control over the scheduling of their family time. In the face of pressures to have children involved in all kinds of extracurricular activities, parents were ending up feeling like "recreation directors on the family cruise ship" (Doherty & Carlson, 2002). This is a model based on the principles of citizen engagement and involves bringing families together into communities to reflect on their own experience and to map out strategies for change. In another project, Mendenhall and Doherty (2005) worked with parents and adolescents in a health care setting to build a democratic relationship with health care providers in an effort to create a different model of care. Researchers serve as a guide and a catalyst to the project but also hold an awareness of transferring leadership to community members who wish to play a leadership role in the process of their own transformation. Like PAR, what is of utmost importance for the success of the catalytic community partnership is to break down the distinction between the producers and consumers of knowledge: consumers become the producers of their own knowledge, which is used in the service of change.

Community action research also has been effectively used with economically disadvantaged families. For example, Peter Fraenkel (2006) has created the collaborative family program development model (CFPD) in his clinical work with families in New York City who are homeless and attempting to move from welfare to work. Rather than viewing families as difficult and problematic clients to be changed, the therapist becomes an appreciative ally who interviews families using a collaborative, research-based approach that involves creating a community-based program. Families are research collaborators in investigating the nature of their situation, generating interpretations of their experience, and creating program formats that are useful and relevant for making change. In a similar vein, McBride, Murray, and Brody (2004) created partnerships with representatives of African American family communities in rural Georgia as a means to work collaboratively toward a research design that was meaningful for participants and had ecological validity. They conducted focus groups with members of the community to gather information about their experience and to get reactions to proposed intervention models. One of the research results from these focus groups was that the team should consider how to include the African American church in the resultant model of competence-promoting influences in the lives of these rural African American children.

In my own research, I am a director of a participatory action research project on father involvement. This project, which is national in scale, is part of a federally funded research program in Canada that encourages PAR. This is called CURA—Community-University Research Alliance—and its aim is to promote collaborative research, education, and knowledge transfer activities. Below is an outline of the steps that we undertook to set up this project:

- The formation of a small working group of three people who were interested in developing a research agenda on father involvement in Canada (myself as a researcher, a Health Canada representative, and a person representing a community based parenting consortium)
- Seed funding to host a roundtable session of various stakeholders in father involvement: fathers themselves, practitioners who work with fathers, policy makers, and researchers

- A one-day roundtable session for 110 stakeholders (including fathers themselves); at the end of the day 10 strategic issues were identified through a "dotmocracy" process (i.e., a process of voting with colored dots on the issues and ideas that had been generated over the course of the day)
- The formation of a Steering Committee with representation from each stakeholder group through a process of nomination
- The development of a vision and set of strategic goals based on the 10 themes identified in the roundtable session
- The creation of a research strategy with input from all stakeholders that was built on the 10 strategic issues
- The use of PAR as the primary means of building collaborative partnerships in each of these areas and outlining a strategy where each partnership would define its own research goals and ways to reach those goals
- The project was funded, with the result being a network of seven cluster groups in different parts of Canada, each examining the conditions and practices of fathering in one of the following subgroups:
  - Immigrant fathers
  - Gay fathers
  - New fathers
  - Young fathers
  - Indigenous fathers
  - Separated and divorced fathers
  - Fathers of children with special needs

For each of these groups, researchers worked with fathers and practitioners in the following activities:

- Engaging a group of fathers in a set of roundtable discussions about the experiences and challenges associated with being a father
- Setting a plan for broader data collection using interviews, questionnaires, and focus groups: How are these conditions of fathering experienced by other fathers in this same category? What are other issues they face?
- Opening conversations about what they would like to change in their life—or what would help to improve being a father?
- Engaging participants in a process of using creative imagination: How might it be better?
- Who is important in bringing about change? How might they be engaged (if not already engaged in bringing about change)?

Summary

Methodologies play a key role in bringing together our underlying values and beliefs, our epistemological and paradigm assumptions, and the strategies we devise to gain knowledge about individual and family life. The five methodologies outlined in this chapter are among the main methodologies used to study individuals and families. However, one of the challenges we face in immersing ourselves in these methodologies is that each has many variants and boundaries between them are blurred. Positioning oneself in relation to these different methodological approaches can be a challenge for the novice qualitative researcher. The key to finding our methodological home is to engage actively in a process of reflexivity where we consider the values we hold to be important, the assumptions we make about human nature, the focus and purpose of our inquiry, and the kind of outcome we wish to move toward.

In the next chapter, we examine the specific methods and techniques we can use in the service of these methodologies.

6

Methods of Data
Collection and Creation

In this chapter, we will explore some of the main methods used in qualitative inquiry. In contrast with methodology, which is concerned with a broader set of beliefs and theoretical assumptions, *method* refers to the specific tools or techniques used in gathering and generating data. Specifically, we will examine observation methods, interviewing approaches, and focus group techniques.

Before we look closely at some of these methods, it is important to examine how the language of method highlights certain kinds of epistemological assumptions. Our usual language of referring to "collecting" or "gathering" data highlights the separation between the researcher who is the gatherer and the researched who provide the data. Researchers are thereby presented in a relatively passive mode—they are the recipients of data rather than the creators of data. This language reinforces an objectivist approach to data collection. Social constructionist and postmodern approaches, which place a greater emphasis on the subjectivity of the researcher as well as the researched, would be more inclined to use language that talks of data being created or coconstructed in the process of interaction.

The opportunity to provide full descriptions of events and activities through a direct, holistic view of those events led Becker and Geer (1970) in their classic paper on the relative merits of participant observation and interviewing to refer to participant observation as the "yardstick" against which to measure the "completeness" of data collected in other ways. This was based on the underlying assumption that observation allowed the researcher to see directly what people do rather than attempting to understand their actions on the basis of what *they say they do* in an interview. As a result, interview accounts were seen to be more subject to "distortion" and observation "of what really happened" served as a guard against such interpretive reconstructions. The use of observation to see reality fully and the effort to represent this reality accurately, in an undistorted way, is of course indicative of an objectivist stance. Direct observation of reality, it was argued, was a way to access the "truth" of what happened as opposed to the constructed descriptions in an interview of what had happened.

More recent debates on the relative merits of observation and interviewing problematize both methods and seek to move beyond the dualistic argument that observation is "natural" and interviews are "contrived" (Atkinson & Coffey, 2002, p. 809). Instead, both observation and interviews are treated as different forms of social action that involve both the work of observing and the activities of the observed and the work of interviewing and the content of the interviews (Atkinson & Coffey, 2002). In both observation and interpretation, doing and talking are activities that don't just happen, but are forms of social action that are indicative of morals, activities, accounts of action, and reflections of experience. Consistent with interpretivist and postmodern assumptions, the researcher is participant in the creation of data and, in both forms of social action, plays a role in the way the reality is shaped, constructed and communicated. In order to describe an event that is either observed or recounted in an interview, the researcher must always play a role in the way the event is narrated.

In the discussion of methods in this chapter, it is important that we be mindful of the way epistemological assumptions can influence the way we think about and use these methods.

Observation

Observation approaches have long been central to the ethnographic tradition. There is a tendency when describing observation to use the terms *fieldwork, participant observation,* and *ethnography* interchangeably. Although fieldwork is rooted in the anthropological tradition of entering into exotic cultures, it is now used to describe observation work in any kind of site whether that be a community, an institution, or the family home. Ethnography is commonly used to represent both the process of conducting an observational study of culture and the product of that study, written up as an organized, conceptual account. Finally, the term participant always involves a matter of degree: the researcher can be fully engaged—doing as participants are doing, interacting with them as they are engaged in their own activities, or somewhat more disengaged and watching participants carry out their activities. In all cases, however, researchers are participants by virtue of their presence in the social setting.

Perhaps more than any other method, observation requires the use of all of our senses in order to comprehend the fullness of experience we are seeking to understand. Smells, tastes, sights, and sounds present us with so much information that it is difficult to record all that is going on at any given time. As we discussed in Chapter 1, observation demands that we cultivate a "beginner's mind" and be attentive to the shapes and patterns of our participants' worlds. As observers of social settings we are also participants in those settings, and as a result, we can never simply cognitively record events from a dispassionate standpoint, we must also contend with our emotions, judgments, preferences, and need to create impressions.

One of the chief advantages of doing observations is that they provide opportunities to see social life in a *natural* form where people are observed in situ. As we engage in these natural settings, we can watch how people move in time and space, interact with one another, and navigate a variety of social settings. This approach to observation reflects the relative invisibility of the researcher and is rooted in the assumption that portrayals of that reality can be accurate and essentially unmediated by the researcher's perspectives. While this approach is still prominent in observational studies, it must also be balanced with the understanding that the observer is part of the social processes that are observed and that the observer helps to narrate (Atkinson & Coffey, 2002).

In the study of families, one of the challenges in using observation is the traditional norms of privacy we associate with family life. As a result, we have relatively few research accounts that provide a window on the private activities that go on within families. Work by Annette Lareau (2002) and classic studies of "whole families" (Hess & Handel, 1959) are notable exceptions. Work by DeVault (2000) on how families interact and behave in public places such as the zoo provides another way of understanding family activity through the observation method. Videotaping newlywed couples in an "apartment lab" for 12-hour sessions is also a means of minimizing the effects of the observer on the couples' interactions (Driver & Gottman, 2004). While work such as this is effective in watching, for example, behavioral patterns of conflict in relationship, it is important to bear in mind that the camera and the eyes behind it are never fully eliminated from the awareness of the participants.

Doing successful observation work with individuals and families involves a number of challenges.

Access and Permission

Gaining access to settings is one of the first challenges of doing observational research. One of the key steps in this process is to obtain the necessary permissions. In small, intimate settings where your role as a researcher is going to be obvious, it is necessary for those who are being observed not only to give their permission, but to provide their informed consent. For example, conducting an observational study of family mealtime would require consent and an open discussion of when and how the observation might occur. One of the implications of an observation such as this that is fully open and negotiated is that the presence of the researcher does change the natural flow of activity and relationship dynamics. Sustained use of video cameras would be one way of reducing the impact of the researcher on the observational setting. At another level, researchers interested in studying wedding rituals might negotiate a different kind of access. Although it would still be necessary to get permission to observe and to have consent from the wedding couple, the researcher could be more inconspicuous during the activities, thereby preserving some of the natural activity in the setting. By dressing appropriately for the occasion and joining in as a participant, researchers can observe how the formal marriage ceremony is conducted, they can listen to and observe how speeches are given, and observe how relatives and friends interact over the course of the evening. In more public settings, like a mall, a museum, or a playground, discretion is required as to whether it is appropriate to obtain permission. In public settings such as a park when the researcher is able to be a natural participant in the activities, it is not necessary to obtain permissions. In fact, to do so would likely end the observational episode. For example, if I am interested in observing fathers interacting with their children at the playground, my own presence at the playground with my children would provide me with the opportunity to observe other fathers without being noticed. By contrast, if I wanted to observe patterns of relationship formation in a nursing home, I would need to seek the permission of the directors of the home in order to be on site on a sustained basis. Finally, certain kinds of sites may have very restricted access that makes observational research difficult. For example, centers that provide services to families in crisis (e.g., medical, abuse, welfare) may restrict access by researchers in the interests of protecting vulnerable family members. This kind of research is not impossible, but access may be more limited. For example, when I was doing my doctoral research on adoption readiness, I began with some participant observation work in an infertility support group. I was a participant in this group and so I began by informing them of my interest in this broad area of research and requested their permission to draw on some of my understandings from the group as a way of developing my research ideas.

While we typically think of gathering ethnographic data once we have access to a setting, it is also important to record and monitor the process of both entering and leaving field sites that are of interest to us. The process of negotiating access to a field site provides important insights into the presence of both physical and social-psychological boundaries. Specifically, the field researcher who studies families faces the challenge of entering and managing an intimate space. Although families vary with respect to the permeability of their boundaries, they typically are thought of as being one of the most closed and private of all social groups. Family members coalesce in the processes of preserving and protecting their traditions, habits, and secrets. Hence the way we as researchers are able to access families through these boundaries becomes an important part of the data we collect. When I have done interviews with family members in their homes, I am there as an observer as well as an interviewer and my senses are very awake as I enter into the family's space. Some of my memories of entering family space are indicative of their informal rules, practices, and habits. For example, where we sit in the house (living room with the TV on, kitchen table, or closed off in a separate room) provides insight into how visitors are managed in the home; the way children are controlled during an interview at home (parents spell each other or a babysitter in the other room) provides insight into parenting boundaries and practices; or the way the house has been tidied (or not) provides insight into aspects of the family's impression management. These provide important observational insights into family behavior when we are accessing family space. Similarly, when we leave family space we can gain insight into some of the ways families return to their normal routines and practices as we are leaving. In a sense, entry and exit from the family's space offer opportunities to see some aspects of family culture.

Focus for Observation

In any social setting, one is quickly confronted by the complex dynamics that are occurring at any given time. Indeed, one of the anxieties that naturally arise in a field study stems from being unable to absorb or comprehend all that is going on at any point in time. Hence, one of the first challenges in conducting an observation study is to determine an appropriate focus. The focus for an observation is shaped by the underlying research question and may be modified as determined by what the researcher discovers along the way. At the outset, it may be helpful to "foreshadow" problems or ideas that will help to shape the inquiry, guide access, and bring focus to the observational activities

(Delamont, 2004). At a very practical level, this involves planning contacts, getting direction from people who have experience with the field you will be entering, and using the literature as a way of thinking about the subject matter you will be pursuing. As part of this process, it is important to identify key informants and gatekeepers in the subcultures you will be approaching. In the tradition of ethnography, these are typically important and powerful people in the subculture (e.g., elders, community leaders, bosses) whose approval and support may be necessary for successful research. Preparation to enter the field may also involve anticipating practical issues such as timing, recording strategies, and strategies for self care while in the field.

Finding the appropriate focus for observation also becomes a unit of analysis question. There are many possibilities here:

- *Individuals in context:* If we are interested in questions of identity or role, we may focus on the way individuals manifest certain kinds of behaviors while operating within relevant contexts. For example, if we were interested in understanding how live-in nannies provide care for children, we might observe and examine how they interact with children, the things that they do and say, and the kind of vocabulary used in the description of what they do. We might be interested in observing any activities that relate to this role: this could include observations of household routines and activities or how they interact with children at the playground.

- *Single relationship dynamics:* If we are interested in relationships, our focus would be on what people do and say as they live out and manage their relationships within a variety of settings. For example, we might be interested in understanding how fathers relate to their preschool children. Observations could take place in a number of different places, including a Saturday morning play program for dads, or observing fathers playing with their children at the local playground. One might also observe fathers picking up their children at the child care center in order to understand how they reengage with their children at the end of a busy day.

- *Complex family dynamics:* The number of dynamics and interactions within families can very quickly become complex, thereby creating challenges of focus for observers of family activity and interaction (see Kreppner, 2005, for a discussion of this). One can imagine the possibilities for doing a study of family mealtime in order to understand the meaning and importance of mealtime, the way it is organized and structured, conversation dynamics, and how various individuals within families carry out roles and activities. One can imagine a focused observation of all family members sitting at the table engaged in an orderly conversation; one can also imagine a set of dynamics that would be more difficult to focus on, when several conversations are occurring simultaneously, when people are coming and going from the table, or when family members are in different places while eating the meal.

- *Families in public spaces:* One of the places where I often feel like an informal ethnographer is when I am doing the grocery shopping. This is an interesting field for observing how parents use various strategies to control children's behavior. The observer in these settings sees how families manage activities within the context of a set of expectations for orderly and well-mannered behavior. The focus of our observation is how families attend to implicit cultural pressures to demonstrate controlled, and controlling, parental behavior. Here we might observe bribes, tantrums, threats, cajoling, promises, and physical restraint. In addition to seeing families in grocery stores, there are opportunities to observe families in shopping malls, airports, parks, playgrounds, buses, funeral homes, and movie theaters. Public spaces also allow us to observe how family members say goodbye to one another (e.g., airports), how families grieve with one another and manage expressions of sympathy (funerals), or how family members relate to each other during a family reunion in a public park.
- *Interaction of family members and social institutions:* The interface between families and various public and private institutions (e.g., schools, childcare centers, courts, churches, and workplaces) also offers an opportunity to observe the way families relate to these cultural institutions. When family members go to church, attend parent–teacher interviews, or attend company picnics, they typically must present themselves in these settings in a way that is consistent with the culturally appropriate norms associated with the institution. The focus of observation here is on how families modify their actions in an effort to align themselves with the expectations of the setting.
- *Families in neighborhoods and communities:* Observation can be a useful tool for understanding how families live within their spatial contexts and for observing families as they relate to one another within local communities. For example, when a new subdivision opens in a community, one might conduct an observational study of how families within that subdivision develop a sense of neighborhood. One might also observe gendered patterns within a neighborhood in order to understand who in the family accesses services and the implications of this for family dynamics.

Although it is important for the researcher to have a focus and a clear sense of direction, it is also important to maintain some flexibility in the field about where the focus should go next. Thinking about the levels of analysis described above allows us to focus observation and inquiry. As in most qualitative research, one of the strengths of choosing relatively unstructured approaches is that we open ourselves to discover what is important in the social setting. Maintaining and finding the right focus in an observation study is part of the emergent philosophy in qualitative work. We construct for ourselves a line of inquiry, but we allow participants in the field to shape and redirect that inquiry in the process of discovering what is important and significant from their perspective. In this regard, focus always involves an interplay between staying within the parameters of the objectives of our research and having the flexibility to pursue and examine unanticipated and surprising contingencies within those guiding objectives.

In practical terms, we can think of observational work as being developmental in nature. We begin with a research question and set of specific interests and we observe broadly in relation to the question. In these early stages, we can begin with broad orienting descriptions of time, place, and features of the setting. We can describe how people appear (in terms of dress, comfort, proximity to others), the kinds of activities and interactions they are involved in, and the kinds of things they say to one another. At this early stage, we deliberately try to keep a wide lens to gain an appreciation of the setting and the context. As we become more familiar with the setting, we can increasingly sharpen our focus by examining particular individuals, relationships, or episodes of activity. If our goal is to deepen our understanding of the phenomenon, then we can become increasingly selective in the way we focus our observation in order to understand sequence of activities, timing, unique language use, and the conditions under which certain activities occur.

Guiding Questions for an Observational Episode

When we enter into any field setting, it is important that we assess and record our observations so we have field notes to help in the analysis and interpretation of the data. The following questions can serve as a guide:

- Where is the activity taking place? Provide a description of the physical setting.
- When is the observation taking place?
- What were the preceding activities?
- Who is present in the situation?
- How are these people related?
- Have they come together with a particular purpose in mind?
- What is the nature of their participation?
- What are they doing and saying?
- What kinds of organizational practices are evident? (i.e., are they relating to each other in certain roles? Is authority being exercised? Are there rules being followed?)
- What are the unique aspects of this setting?
- How am I being perceived in the situation? What are my role and the nature of my activity in the setting?

Positioning Ourselves

In a traditional observation study, researchers were expected to make a decision about the degree to which they would participate in the social setting, ranging from a position of being the detached, passive, outsider with no active involvement in the setting to the other extreme of being a full participant in the activity (Spradley, 1980). In addition, there were a number of positions in between that allowed for a balance between engagement and distance. In this approach, a number of arguments have been made to support the merits of both distance and proximity. On the one hand, being a full participant allows for complete immersion in the setting and a fuller understanding of the nuances of the experience. It allows the researcher to gain access to events, experiences, and talk that might not otherwise be achieved. On the other hand, it has been argued that being immersed in the social setting is likely to contaminate the natural dynamics occurring in the setting and blind the observer to the tacit cultural rules at work. In order to see clearly what is occurring, the researcher should try to manufacture some distance so as to see the setting more fully and objectively. Implicit in these arguments is the degree to which researcher positioning is going to create or minimize bias in the observational setting. The concern with bias, coupled with the assumption that one can stay on the outside of an observed setting is indicative of a set of objectivist assumptions that are concerned with the accuracy of the representational effort.

For researchers who approach observation from constructionist or postmodern assumptions, there is no option but to be engaged in some way in the observational setting. From this perspective, the researcher is an actor in the setting and plays a role in the way the setting is organized and in the way other actors make decisions and perform their own roles. Even when observers make a decision to minimize impact on the setting, their mere presence shapes other activities, their attention is drawn to particular aspects of the setting, and their efforts to construct an account of the setting are influenced by and have an influence on other participants. With an acceptance that we as observers play a role in any social setting, the observation shifts from an emphasis on *what* others are doing to a focus on *how* all participants, including the researcher, play a role in the construction, narration, and evaluation of events and activities in the setting.

When researchers enter into the family domain, they temporarily become part of the family system. They are typically welcomed into the home, and although they may be treated with caution, they nevertheless become part of the network of interacting personalities. When we enter into family spaces, it is important to be reflexive about our role as we attempt to manage the flow of information within the family system. Although the traditional norms of question and answer typically guide the course of our focused research conversations, there are occasions when the unpredictable happens and researchers are called upon to manage their role in the family delicately. This can include unanticipated disclosures and the dangers of being co-opted or triangulated into the family (Daly & Dienhart, 1998). These are occasions when we hear more than we may have wanted to hear or find ourselves in power alliances within the family. As participants in these experiences, it is important that we reflect on our role, monitor comfort levels with participants, and reposition ourselves as necessary.

Observing and Interpreting

When we emphasize not only what was said or done, but how the researcher and participants play a role in the construction of events, we engage in a process of observation *and* interpretation. While it is necessary to have a running record of what occurred, it is also important that we make sense of how these activities were constructed and performed given the conditions, the players, and the audience. Even the thought of creating a "running record" of events reflects a set of selective choices that the researcher imposes on the complex setting. Hence, the running record is a form of narrative—infused with the observer's meanings, selections, and interpretations where the distinction between observation and interpretation is blurred.

Making Field Notes

Part of positioning ourselves in the field is to make decisions about how to record our field notes. Field notes are a record of our observations and interpretations of what has occurred in a field setting. Depending on how we position ourselves, there are a number of possibilities for how we might go about this.

Being unobtrusive: Those who wish to remain as inconspicuous as possible and to blend into the setting as participants might make their field notes at the end of a participatory episode. In the tradition of ethnography, there are tales of researchers running to bathrooms to record notes or retreating to quiet corners in order to outline sequences of events. In some settings, such as a meeting room or even a park, note writing can pass as a natural activity for the setting. A small handheld recording device can also serve as a valuable tool when driving home from an observation setting—allowing the researcher an opportunity to record both observations and insights about the setting.

Being discreet: In some settings, there is an opportunity to make brief notes without interfering with the activities being observed. Often this is a matter of striking a balance between paying attention to what is going on in the setting and jotting down key phrases or terms that capture the essence of the episode. These can then be revisited at the end of the episode and expanded in greater detail. Sometimes it is important to take down exact quotations that are especially pertinent. When this is not possible, it is best to try to capture the approximate wording as best you can.

Using audio- or video recorders: In situations where it is possible to record the events in a setting, the researcher still needs to make decisions about where to put microphones and, in the case of videotaping, how to position the camera(s) in order to optimize the gathering of information. Like any composition, these decisions will determine what aspects of the setting can be used for analysis. More than any other recording methods, however, these kinds of instruments are most likely to elicit performances from actors in the setting. When the red light is on, actors are "speaking into the mike" and as researchers, we need to be mindful of this effect.

Recording activities, making interpretations: In field notes, it is a good idea to include both what might be considered "factual information" (i.e., what you have seen and heard) as well as a record of your insights and interpretations. In a field note book, it is a good idea to devise a system that allows you to make a record of both. Some prefer to integrate observations and interpretations (especially if you are working from a paradigm [e.g., interpretive] that blurs this distinction to begin with); others prefer to have two columns on the page—one for a running record of what is observed, the other a record of how you are making sense of this and how you are perceiving your own role in the setting. This gives an opportunity to record your reflexive insights as well as emerging interpretations and theoretical insights. As Richardson (2003) has argued, the process of recording and writing is a process of analysis.

Being diligent: The goal of ethnographic work is to create a "thick description" (Geertz, 1973) of the phenomenon, and this requires attention to detail. One of the most important things about taking field notes is to make sure that you get in the practice of making time to develop your field notes. This should be done immediately after a session and should involve expanding cursory notes taken during the session. It is also critical at this time to record your early impressions and interpretations of what was happening in the setting, including a reflexive commentary on your own role and impact in the setting.

Organizing as you go: An extensive and prolonged field study can involve masses of notes. Make sure your materials are dated, and organize them into a meaningful file system as you go along. For hard copies of notes use numbered notebooks, a binder, or file system; for computer files, you can create meaningful directories that correspond with certain sites, time periods, or activities.

Interviews

Interviews are conversations with an agenda. Although the word itself has a built-in symmetry that suggests an interplay between two viewpoints, it is typically the case that the interviewer initiates the conversation, shapes the direction of the conversation by asking the questions, and takes the information obtained through the conversation for the purpose of constructing knowledge about some aspect of the participant's reality. In the qualitative research tradition, this is consistent with the postpositivist idea of "gathering" data from participants in a unidirectional kind of way. In its most traditional form, we can think about this type of interview as the "Dragnet model" where, in the words of the well-known detective, we are interested in "just the facts, ma'am." In the analysis of interviews, emphasis is placed on what participants said, and this is treated as a representation of their reality outside of the interview. The interviewer's goal is to draw this out without getting in the way of the interviewee's account of the experience. Objectivity, neutrality, and distance are guiding principles for the interviewer.

Feminist qualitative researchers were some of the first to call attention to the power imbalances inherent in the interview relationship. Anne Oakley (1981) drew attention to some of the inherent power dynamics and hierarchies associated with traditional interviewing techniques and called for greater attention to understanding the interview as a relationship where the standpoints, interests, and perspectives of interviewers and interviewees must be taken into account. Feminist researchers also played a pivotal role in emphasizing the importance of reflexivity in order to monitor the ways our own experiences shape the form and outcome of the interview process (see Allen, 2000, for an overview).

Approaching an interview as a relationship plays an important role in making more visible the ways in which the researcher participates in the joint construction of research data. Research interviewing is a social form that may resemble other forms of talking in a relationship, but that has a unique style of social and personal interaction (Johnson, 2002). Whereas a postpositivist approach to an interview would place a greater emphasis on what participants say and how they answer the question, a postmodern interview would more likely emphasize the contributions of both interviewer and interviewee in the construction of the account. Rather than researchers trying to remain separate, distant, and objective, they are more likely to engage fully with their own experiences, reactions, and disclosures. In contrast with a unidirectional Dragnet model, this is more akin to the Parisian café model where both participants in the interview share experiences, answer questions, and offer information. This type of interview is more "dialogic" in its approach and involves the researchers and participants in a process of give and take aimed at a complex understanding of the topic (Rossman & Rallis, 2003).

So what happens to the research agenda when we shift power dynamics in the interview from unilateral to bilateral forms? Between the two extremes of exploitation and mutual sharing is a position that strikes a balance between the open recognition of the research purpose as creating the interview relationship in the first place, and the acknowledgment that the interviewer is an active subject in shaping the way that social reality is being constructed. In my own experience, I have struggled with this as a tension. On the one hand, as I became increasingly aware of these power dynamics and recognized how my own preferences and ideas were shaping the construction of the data, I felt it was important to be mindful of the relationship aspects of the interview. On the other hand, I was trained to conduct interviews under a postpositivist model of gathering data. Hence, I recruited participants and used the principles of establishing rapport, building trust, sharing information when necessary, but generally guarded against giving too much away in the interview setting. These activities were shaped by the principles of objectivity—insofar as my primary aim was to understand interviewees' experience and to minimize the impact I would have on the way they communicated their experience to me. Paradoxically, I was building trust for the purposes of my own exploitive aims! This is a tension that continues in my interviewing practice. I do not believe that when I interview I can ever get beyond the perception that it is a conversation with an agenda—an agenda shaped by *my need* to inquire about an aspect of another person's *reality*. While I still believe that issues of trust and rapport are important, I am aware of the fundamental ways I coconstruct the data with interviewees. Furthermore, as I have more fully embraced constructionist and postmodern values, I am aware that it is not possible for me to be neutral in an interview setting as my preferences, gestures, and ideas are always shaping the course of the interview interaction. In the words of Gubrium and Holstein (2003b), the interview has been "reconceptualized as an occasion for purposefully animated participants to construct versions of reality interactionally rather than merely purvey data" (p. 32).

In the end, I think it is useful to think about the tension between "gathering data" and coproducing data as a continuum upon which we position ourselves at different points. These are epistemological positions that come with beliefs about the nature of knowledge itself. Our position may shift on this continuum depending on how we ask the questions and what our purpose is at any given time. Hence, there may be times when we ask our questions in a structured way without any discussion of our own experience, putting us closer to an objectivist stance on that continuum; alternatively, there may be times when the interview is an unfolding conversation on a topic, which would position us on the subjectivist end of that continuum. Regardless of where we position ourselves, at some level the interview is interpretively active, interactive, and unavoidably collaborative for both interviewers and respondents (Holstein & Gubrium, 1995).

One of the practical models for carrying out interviews is proposed by Rubin and Rubin (2005), who talk about "responsive interviewing." Based on interpretivist assumptions, responsive interviewing accepts that both the interviewer and interviewee are human beings who form a relationship with the goal of generating deeper understanding. While acknowledging mutual influence, there is also recognition of the ethical obligations of the interviewer; the responsibility to give direction to the interview; and the need for the interviewer to be self-aware of influence, biases, and expectations. This moderate approach accepts both the unique roles and responsibilities of the interviewer while at the same time recognizing the mutual influences of both researcher and participant in the relationship.

Neutrality in an Interview

Rapley (2004) has summarized the literature on neutrality in interviewing and argues that there are three positions:

1. An essential practice: Researchers must remain neutral; otherwise they will unduly bias the story and contaminate the data

2. A bad practice: Neutrality is established to uphold a pretense that treats the participant as an object and maintains a hierarchical, patriarchal, and asymmetrical relationship with the participant

3. A misleading practice: Neutrality is simply not possible in an interview context because interviewers are always active and influencing the course of the interview; as a result, it is misleading to make a claim to that effect

What is your position? How is your position related to your paradigm beliefs?

Finding People to Interview

In most projects, whether a thesis or a formal grant-based study, we outline for ourselves a recruitment strategy that we hope will be effective in bringing us into contact with the people we wish to speak with. Whereas survey research is concerned primarily with representativeness in sample selection, qualitative interviewing is more concerned with contacting participants who have "narrative competence" (Gubrium & Holstein, 1995, p. 21) or the ability to tell a story that overall enables and encourages representations of diverse and complex experience. Typically we begin with an ideal plan that we describe in our research design. It may include the following:

- Recruiting through an organization that has agreed to contact prospective interviewees on our behalf
- Setting a goal for the approximate number of interviewees that we think will be necessary to achieve our goals
- Making a deliberate attempt to get a range of viewpoints or experiences in order to achieve a broad understanding of the phenomenon
- Building in enough flexibility to choose participants that will allow us to inquire in more depth about emerging themes in the research is in keeping with the principles of theoretical sampling and saturation.

In almost all projects I have been involved with, these well-laid plans must typically be modified because of the difficulties in recruiting participants into studies that require a significant investment of their time. For example, in most of my research on dual-earner couples, who are almost by definition living within time-stretched schedules, it is extremely difficult to find couples who are willing to give up an evening for an interview. Increasingly, this seems to be the case with many aspects of family-related qualitative research where it is challenging to find participants willing to volunteer some of their time to your research effort. I would argue that it is normative practice to have to brain-storm beyond our initial recruitment strategies and to use contacts, acquaintances, snowballing techniques, media, and alternative recruitment sources in order to engage people in the process of interview-based research.

Structuring the Interview

In preparation for conducting interviews, we need to decide how formal we want the interviews to be. How we make these decisions is determined by our epistemological beliefs, our assumptions about neutrality, and the way we position ourselves in the interview setting. There are a number of possibilities for structuring interviews.

Unstructured and Emergent

One of the strengths of qualitative research is that it provides an opportunity to understand the process by which meanings are constructed. An open-ended interview structure is one that begins either with general conversation in the area of interest or with general orienting questions that provide an opportunity for participants to talk about their experience. In this approach, the researcher begins with relatively little structure and is more concerned with opening conversation in order to understand how a participant is thinking about a particular set of experiences. Although we use the term *unstructured*, research interviews always have some level of structure as they are concerned with some focused aspect of reality.

These are often referred to as *in-depth interviews* because the goal is to understand meanings, perspectives, and life experiences. Given the active engagement of the researcher in this in-depth exploration, this approach would typically involve a positioning at the subjectivist end of the continuum. These interviews invoke a greater expression of the interviewer's self and seek to build a kind of intimacy in the relationship that occurs over several different interview sessions (Johnson, 2002).

In grounded theory work, this approach is consistent with the principles of emergent design: Rather than trying to anticipate the right questions to ask, the researcher enters into exchanges with participants and seeks to understand their meanings and ways of experiencing reality. Whereas predetermined questions require anticipating what areas are important, one of the advantages of an open-ended design is that you allow participants to lead you into areas that they perceive to be important. In the course of these conversations, we come to understand which questions to ask.

In a narrative approach, an open-ended interview might begin by simply asking participants to tell their stories in relation to the research focus, followed by a series of probes and follow-up questions. Here the aim is to let participants tell the story in a way that communicates what they see as the key components of their lived experience.

When conducting unstructured interviews, the researcher must find a balance between asking a question that is too general and therefore unanswerable and one that is general but is answerable in relation to specific experiences. For example, Rubin and Rubin (2005) suggest that asking, "What makes your marriage work?" may be too general and complicated a way to start the interview. While the researcher is ultimately interested in this, it may be better to start with broad questions about the marriage that will ultimately provide some insight into what makes the marriage work. This might involve asking questions about expectations when they got married and whether those expectations have been fulfilled, or questions about how they reliably get what they ask for from each other. These initial orienting questions can become increasingly focused as participants begin to talk about their experience. Furthermore, it is important to allow these initial orienting questions to change and evolve as you discover which questions are most effective in opening the conversation about their experience.

Semistructured

The term *semistructured* has come to mean many things in the qualitative research tradition. In its broadest sense, it means following an outline or set of interview guidelines that give the interview some organization and structure. This can include a list of general questions to which other questions are added; a list of preliminary questions that are modified, discarded, or replaced as the inquiry proceeds; or a set of key domains within which a set of flexible questions are asked. The main advantages of semistructured interviews is that they can help to maintain a focus on the key research questions, they can serve as a resource or a reference point for interviewers so that they can concentrate on what is being said and then come back to the guide, and they can facilitate data analysis by generating data within some general domains.

In many qualitative interviews, the researcher begins with a set of questions that have arisen from a reading of the literature or an understanding of preexisting theory. For example, in my own research on fatherhood identity, I was influenced by symbolic interaction theory, which directed me to ask questions about the influence of significant others, socialization, and role-taking activities. Although I did not use this theoretical language in my interviews, I did ask questions about who they perceived as being important influences in the way they saw themselves as fathers (i.e., significant others), how they were prepared to become fathers (i.e., socialization), and how they assessed their own performance as fathers in the eyes of others (i.e., role taking). These questions were part of approximately 15 questions that I used as a foundation for my inquiry. As the study progressed, I changed how I asked these questions, changed the order of the questions, dropped some and added others, and in each interview followed different tangents that were of interest. One of the chief advantages of a semistructured approach was that the questions served as a touchstone that helped to maintain some level of focus while at the same time allowing for the flexibility to follow the conversation as it unfolded uniquely in each interview.

Another approach to semistructured interviews is to begin with a set of broad domains that you have identified as being important to your research. These domains might come from your understanding of the literature or they might be aspects of your own experience that you see as being important. For example, if you were conducting a study of work–life issues for single parents, you might wish to ask questions about the degree of flexibility in the work place, parenting and custody arrangements, leisure preferences, scheduling strategies, and perceived control over time. How questions are asked in those areas is flexible, but the interviewer tries to include each of these areas. Semistructured formats also allow interviewers to add new domains to the list as they emerge in the course of the interviews. In a study of welfare families in three American cities (Roy, Tubbs, & Burton, 2004; Tubbs & Burton, 2005), researchers used a system they called "structured discovery" that involved a number of researchers conducting in-depth interviews and observations. The goal of this approach was to ensure that the same areas were covered in each interview (family economics, child development, parenting, intimate relationships, etc.), but at the same time, the intention was to allow enough flexibility to capture unexpected findings.

Highly Structured

Interviews with a preset, rigid format are especially useful in instances where comparability is paramount. These tend to be used when the researcher is looking for very specific information on topics or is involved in large-scale projects where answers are to be coded, categorized, and counted for quantitative analysis. In cases where there are multiple interviewers, it is important to have a set of questions to follow so there is coherence in the data collection effort. In this approach, which is also known as survey interviewing, these data are collected either face-to-face or via the telephone (Singleton & Straits, 2002). Interviewers are trained, questionnaires are pretested, and participants are identified through random or probability sampling techniques.

In highly structured interviews, questions are either open ended or have a series of fixed responses with an opportunity for elaboration. This typically involves an objectivist positioning and is concerned primarily with bringing the participants' answers forward and keeping the interviewer's perspectives in the background. Accordingly, neutrality is valued in a structured interview. Highly structured interviews are most likely to result in a combination of quantitative and qualitative analyses. The advantage is that we can gain a good understanding of the distribution of responses within a population with some understanding of how and why participants responded as they did; the disadvantage is that the a priori structure of the questions may not tap fully into some of the significant meanings and experiences of the participants.

Stages of an Interview

Interviews must be "stage managed" in order to meet the purposes of the research (Legard, Keegan, & Ward, 2003). Specifically, Legard et al. identify 6 stages in the organization of an interview:

1. Arrival: involves "small talk," trying to put the participant at ease, getting comfortable in the surroundings, accepting the hospitality of the host, getting settled with equipment

2. Introducing the research: reiterating the purpose of the study, reviewing confidentiality and consent issues, and seeking permission to record the interview and then waiting until the environment is suitably comfortable for the interview to proceed

3. Beginning the interview: asking background and contextual information about relevant domains (e.g., age, family characteristics, work information) and then easing into general questions about the research focus

4. During the interview: introducing key questions that either follow the interview guide or that explore domains of interest; using probes to get deeper information on an issue of importance; taking the opportunity to explore in greater detail emergent ideas deemed to be important

5. Ending the interview: provide the participant with a signal that you are nearing the end of your questions, using phrases like "the final area I want to explore with you is . . ."; provide participants an opportunity to express any ideas they would like to bring forward or finish off with any additions to previous comments. I like to end with the question: "Were there any things that you were expecting to talk about today that I didn't raise in my questions?"

6. After the interview: take time to thank participants and indicate how their contribution will help the research; change the conversation so that it returns to everyday small talk; it is important to stay with participants if they have more to say; they should be left feeling "well"

Methodology Shapes the Type of Interview

The way we conduct our interviews will be shaped by our methodological orientation. As discussed in Chapter 5, our methodology gives direction to the course of inquiry. For example, if we are doing a phenomenological study, the interview would be structured to encourage participants to talk about the details of their lived experience, how they understand it and make sense of it, and what it means for the way they live their lives. A narrative approach to interviewing would begin by asking participants to tell the story of their experience. The kinds of questions we would ask in these interviews would seek to understand the story more fully by asking about how events unfolded, who the characters were in the story, and what the key turning points were in the story. In a grounded theory approach, interviews would be constructed based on emerging themes and ideas. Given that the purpose of grounded theory analysis is to create a substantive theory based on comparative analysis, the task is one of asking questions to saturate our understanding of key themes as they unfold in the course of a number of interviews. In keeping with these ideas, Morse (1994) argued that different methodologies result in different kinds of interview questions: in ethnographies, there is a tendency to have questions that orient toward a *description* of culture; in grounded theory studies, questions have an orientation toward *process*; in phenomenological studies, *meaning* questions are directed toward understanding lived experience. Although these kinds of questions reflect an area of emphasis in each of these methodologies, they are just that and should not be taken as mutually exclusive.

These methodological considerations also have implications for whether we do a single interview with a participant or conducted multiple, repeated interviews. In life history research, it is often the case that interviews stretch over many sessions and may sometimes involve years of follow up (Miller,

2000). For example, in an ethnographic study of dying patients who had received hospice care, Wright (2003) was both a participant observer in the hospice setting and chose to do repeated interviews (up to 10) with participants when they were willing and had the stamina to talk. This removed some of the pressure to "get it all at once." It allowed the conversations to unfold at a more leisurely pace, and provided participants with the opportunity between interviews to reflect on the conversations and to bring forward additional thoughts or experiences.

Face-to-Face Versus Telephone Interviews

Conducting interviews by phone is often perceived as an efficient strategy for both researchers and participants. This can save travel time as well as preparation time associated with getting the space ready (i.e., housecleaning to receive the researcher). It is also an effective means of sampling participants across a larger geographical area. Although it is often more difficult to establish rapport over the telephone, this might be offset by the fact that participants may be more open in the telling when there is not the intimacy of the face-to-face telling. Telephone interviews can be used to conduct either structured or unstructured interviews, and they can be audio recorded. For example, Zvonkovic, Manoogian, and McGraw (2001) examined the experience of separation among fishing families by carrying out open-ended telephone interviews about families' experience of being apart and reuniting. They also used telephone interviews as a way of following up with participants who participated in face-to-face focus group sessions.

Recording Interviews

Most in-depth interviews involve audio recording the conversation as it unfolds. Although less common, some researchers use video recording devices that allow the researcher to see gestures and events occurring in the research setting. Recorded interviews are usually transcribed verbatim and analyzed on a line-by-line basis. The advantage of recording interviews is that the researcher can be fully attentive to the conversation and not have to worry about what is said. Furthermore, the data can subsequently be analyzed in a way that allows the researcher to reexamine what was said with greater care and attentiveness.

Although researchers are often preoccupied with making sure the tape recorder is set up properly, participants may be more concerned with the meaning of the recording device for the ensuing conversation. I know when I talk to a journalist, I am always a little more anxious when the red light of the recorder goes on. Suddenly, everything I say is on the record and I feel like I must talk carefully and, I hope, intelligently! When the red light goes on for our participants, we need to be mindful of the impact it may have on them. Initially, the recorder may introduce some awkwardness or hesitancy in the conversation. There are many reactions that participants might have including concerns about confidentiality and who will hear the tapes; a tendency to overdramatize one's experience in order to make it appear interesting or worthwhile to the researcher; or inhibitions about telling the truth for fear of being judged by the researcher (Rapley, 2004). As the conversation becomes more engaging for participants, they may start to relax with the tape recorder. Usually they are just starting to relax when the tape runs out and clicks the machine off—reorienting the participant to the machine! Digital recorders are a good alternative and are typically smaller and therefore inconspicuous. They also minimize interruptions because there is no tape to turn.

One of the experiences interviewers may have when using a tape recorder is that participants will provide important information when the tape recorder is off. These may be requests made in the middle of the interview to turn the tape recorder off so they can tell you something "off the record." They may also wait until you are packing up your equipment at the end of the interview. I call these "door handle" disclosures. They present the researcher with a difficult dilemma. On the one hand, these disclosures often provide insight into some of the most private and otherwise difficult-to-see aspects of participants' experience. On the other hand, there is an implicit ethical quandary because these are intended to be off the record and therefore excluded from the formal data analysis. Several responses are possible here: one is to respect the desire to keep this off the record and therefore to keep it confidential; second, if there is some uncertainty about whether the comments are intended to be on or off the record, the researcher can ask the participant; finally, the researcher keeps the specific comments off the record but uses the new understanding as a form of sensitizing to the experience and as a way of exploring subsequent interviews in greater depth in.

When we use interview guides in either structured or semistructured formats, we go into the interview with the guide on a clipboard, which allows us not only to ask our questions in an orderly way, but to record responses as they are given to us. In a study of infertile couples that I conducted (Daly, 1988), I used an interview guide that had a combination of fixed response categories and open-ended questions. I didn't record these conversations, but rather, checked off the categories and then wrote down what participants described to me in the open-ended part of the question. Although it was impossible to write everything verbatim, it was an effective and efficient method for recording key phrases or statements and capturing some of key aspects of their experience.

Regardless of the degree of structure in the interview, I usually carry a clipboard and pen with me into the interview situation. This serves several purposes. I carry the consent forms here and perhaps a cover sheet with a list of "sample characteristics" questions. I also carry blank paper that I will use to jot down a variety of information including: the setting; observations about mood, gestures, or actions that wouldn't be captured on audiotape; events occurring in the background that might be influencing the participant; questions that were effective; and analytic insights or memos that help me to understand a particular experience. Carrying paper and pen into the interview setting is not neutral, either. Although participants can assign many meanings, two are possible: one is that the act of writing something down means that what they are saying is important; alternatively, they could also see this as intimidating and therefore inhibiting.

Cultivating Good Interviewing Skills

When we begin a research project that involves interviewing participants, we can usually expect a number of typical experiences as we prepare ourselves to interview. One of the most common experiences is that *"I'm imposing."* Because participants are usually difficult to recruit, we often feel like we are intruding on their lives. Although this is always somewhat true, participants often welcome the opportunity to be heard on a topic that is important to them. In many of my interviews I have had the experience of participants thanking me for listening to their story. They found it cathartic, and for some therapeutic, to have someone listen and understand their experience. Nevertheless, it is important that we thank our participants for their contribution to our research. Another experience is to *overprepare* for an interview as a way of dealing with our initial anxiety about "doing it right." This might result in a "stilted" or mechanical interview where we ask questions without listening to responses, rather than being attentive to the conversation as it unfolds.

The way we become good interviewers will of course depend on how we position ourselves epistemologically in the research process. When conducting highly structured interviews we would therefore strive for a standard of neutrality, resulting in the need to maintain distance and not become overly engaged with participants. If, on the other hand, we strive for a Parisian café model of interview as conversation, it is important to cultivate our relationship skills. In all interviews, however, there are some fundamental skills that can be learned and developed.

Beginning the Relationship

There is an extensive literature in qualitative research that deals with the establishment of the research relationship when doing interviews. It places an emphasis on sharing information not only about the research but about oneself as a way of establishing trust and rapport. Reciprocity is important for building trust and can be achieved by sharing personal experiences, feelings, and viewpoints. It can also be enhanced by sharing with participants some of what we have already discovered that can validate their own experiences and feelings and open opportunities for them to talk about their own circumstances and perspectives.

Being Attentive

In the opening chapter, I said one of the hallmarks of good artists is their ability to *see*. In order to be a good interviewer, it is important to be fully awake and attentive to the interview as it unfolds. We can do this by making sure we are prepared, so that during the interview we can focus fully on what is being said. Especially in an unstructured interview, we want to be listening attentively so we can build the conversation on what has already been said.

Stay in the Present

When we enter into research relationships with relative strangers, sometimes our anxiety keeps us stuck in the future. We worry about whether the interview will go well, or while participants are talking we try to plan the next question to ask. When we are preoccupied with what is going to happen, we lose our attention on what is happening.

Maintaining Naiveté

When we open inquiry into experience to understand how it works, we have to contend with our inclination to jump prematurely to explanation. This may be particularly challenging when we have a high level of familiarity with the subject matter and might tend to impose our own taken-for-granted understanding of the situation. When we are interviewing, our goal is to understand as many viewpoints and meanings as possible. We maintain naiveté by keeping ourselves open to the new and possibly contradictory ways participants might describe the same phenomenon.

Holding to the Course

When we do research interviews, we are operating within a particular focus shaped by our purpose and research questions. The research interview is not a free-form conversation that can go off in any direction, but rather is grounded in a specific track of inquiry. Learning to be a good interviewer means finding the balance between exploring new pathways in the interview and staying within the parameters of our research goals and objectives. This involves striking a balance between providing guidance and practicing constraint (Holstein & Gubrium, 1995).

Monitoring Personal Engagement

Our epistemological positioning shapes the extent to which we see ourselves as either trying to maintain a neutral stance or investing ourselves in the conversation. Through reflexive practice, we can find the right positioning given our underlying assumptions. Are we seeking to minimize hierarchy in the relationship? Are we contributing to the interview conversation or seeking to elicit information from the participant?

Maximizing the Coconstructive Potential of the Interview

If we believe that the researcher and the participant are collaborators in the production of knowledge through the interview, then one of the ways we can optimize the joint production of our understanding is to engage participants in the interpretive process. In this regard, the participants not only tell their stories but they too become researchers who "consult repertoires of experience and orientations, linking fragments into patterns and offering theoretically coherent descriptions, accounts and explanations" (Holstein & Gubrium, 1995, p. 29).

Asking Questions in the Interview: Tips and Pitfalls

- Allow time for the relationship to build; asking questions that are too personal at the beginning may simply encourage avoidance or lies
- Recognize that discussions about sensitive topics may need to build over several interviews
- During the early stages of the interview, provide lots of opportunity for participants to give the story a direction that reflects their experience; for example, "Tell me what it was like for you to have gone through that transition." "How would you describe your experience of that relationship at that time?"

- Ask first about what the people involved actually do (i.e., recount their behavior) and then ask about how they felt about their experience (Matthews, 2005)
- Specific, targeted questions can be useful later in the interview to reach a deeper understanding of emerging themes
- Avoid leading questions or responses that encourage affirmation of your own viewpoint; for example, instead of responding to a participant by saying "that must have made you very angry," you might ask, "How did that make you feel?"

Focus Groups

Focus group research was first used in the 1940s by Robert Merton, who looked at perceptions of wartime propaganda (Morgan, 1988). It wasn't until the 1980s that it became more popular as a form of marketing research where potential customers were asked about lifestyle, product preferences, or habits of everyday living. This research had a very pragmatic focus, which was to find successful ways to sell products to consumers. Focus group research is now used widely in a variety of disciplines as a way of understanding group perspectives on a particular issue. Accordingly, *group interviewing* is often a preferred term because it helps to differentiate it from its marketing roots.

One of the unique characteristics of focus group research is that it emphasizes the importance of group interaction in the discussion of a particular issue determined by the researcher (Morgan, 2002). In this regard, the interviewer or facilitator is there to encourage group discussion of an issue that is of concern to group members. In contrast to participant observation where the researcher seeks to observe naturally occurring phenomena, the facilitator in a focus group usually exerts a fair amount of control in order to keep the discussion on track. Typically, group members are brought together because they share experience of a particular topic or issue. For example, you might be interested in exploring how caregivers of stroke victims manage their own personal support networks. Bringing people together who have a shared experience such as this creates a forum for them to provide not only their personal narrative but their shared stocks of knowledge, common meanings, and collective symbols (Holstein & Gubrium, 1995). Although focus groups have been criticized for being contrived situations, Holstein and Gubrium argue that the proceedings may in fact more closely resemble the complex multivocality of everyday life compared to the standard single interview. Focus groups can be particularly useful as a means of understanding complex arguments or situations, controversial issues that involve many positions, or in situations where participants have ambivalent feelings (Macnaghten & Myers,

2004). Jarrett (1993), for example, reports that focus groups are effective in enhancing discussion among low-income mothers who may see the group as an opportunity to discuss difficult experiences that might otherwise be difficult to reveal.

Advantages of Focus Groups

- Efficiency: Opportunity to collect data from a number of participants at the same time
- Opportunity to see group process, dynamics, and interaction
- Power dynamics are more lateral compared to an individual interview (because participants prompt each other)
- Opportunity to observe "indigenous" language as it is used with peers
- Focus groups are "synergistic"—participants elaborate and build on contributions of others in the group
- Group context of people with similar experience can provide a supportive environment for disclosure of experience

---

Focus groups usually range from 6 to 10 participants (Morgan, 1988). The optimal number that combines manageability and sufficient breadth is around 7 or 8. Although there are no rigid conventions about the number of focus group sessions to be conducted, usually between three and five are required in order to identify recurring themes and issues. Focus groups can consist of a preexisting group (e.g., a support group, a family) or as is more often the case, bring together individuals who have a shared stock of knowledge about an experience. For example, I did a small focus group with three mothers of twins because I wanted to understand some of the unique challenges they faced in managing a home schedule. This was part of a broader interview study of dual-earner parents. Although this was a smaller number than is usual, these mothers quickly began to share experiences and identify common challenges that effectively oriented me to some of their unique experiences. I have also held a focus group with 12 representatives of provincial ministries responsible for adoption in order to understand philosophical differences in their approach to adoption openness. This focus group was held as a way to develop a data collection strategy for a national study of adoption in Canada.

Focus groups serve many purposes in research. In the adoption example above, the focus group experience helped to orient and sensitize me as a researcher to key issues that I needed to explore. It was a useful way for me and fellow researchers to be immersed in the perspectives and politics of adoption issues, which helped us to design a study that was attentive to these nuances. As a result, it helped us to make decisions about who we needed to talk to next, formulate our questions and help us to understand the provincial differences that we would need to be attentive to. Overall, its purpose was to help in the development of the broader research strategy.

Focus groups are also used as a stand-alone method to provide data on a particular topic for later analysis. Focus groups have the advantage of giving the researcher an opportunity to observe people interacting and offering perspectives on a shared experience. This is valuable in that these groups provide intense and focused discussions on the topic. For example, the focus group for caregivers of stroke victims would offer an opportunity to observe how members talk to each other about support, who they identify as being important, ways that have reached out for support from others and common experiences they may have had in terms of frustration, challenges or satisfaction.

In family therapy research, focus groups can be used in a variety of ways (Piercy & Hertlein, 2005). At one level, they can be used as a means to understand family dynamics, including patterns of communication, emotion management and relationship issues. They can also be an effective means to evaluate and improve clinical practice. This can include using focus groups to identify client needs, understand the experience of family problems, and evaluate services in order to improve them (Piercy & Hertlein, 2005).

Setting Up a Focus Group

There are several unique features associated with setting up focus groups that involve a number of decisions.

Moderator

The moderator is either the researcher or someone who has been hired to run the focus group. The advantage of the researcher being the moderator is that you can control the flow of the questions and move the group into areas of discussion that emerge as being important. Hiring a moderator with experience requires more discussion and structure prior to the focus group in order to ensure that it stays focused on the research aims. Given their pivotal role in the production of data, moderators who are brought into the project may also need to be engaged in the process of recruitment, question writing, and analysis (Morgan, 2002). One of the advantages of having a moderator is that the researcher can observe what is being said in the focus group without having to worry about controlling the direction of the session.

Recruitment

People are usually brought into a focus group because of some specialized knowledge or shared experience. As a result, recruitment typically follows the principles of purposive sampling, where individuals are identified based on specific experiences or characteristics. Seven or eight participants is optimal, and it is generally a good idea to over-recruit by one or two (Morgan, 1988) and in some circumstances by 50% (Wilkinson, 2004) in order to account for no-shows.

Interview Guide

The degree to which the interview guide is structured depends on the purpose of the research. At early and exploratory stages of a project, the moderator may wish to ask more general questions in order to encourage participants to speak about their experience, and in so doing to identify salient aspects of that experience. Only two or three questions may be necessary. If the research is at a stage where it is focused on more specific issues, then specific, targeted questions are appropriate. Even at this stage, however, the number of prepared questions is relatively small (e.g., from five to seven) in order to allow for interaction and discussion with the group.

Scheduling and Duration

Focus groups are more challenging to schedule because of the number of people involved. It is therefore important to plan a session well in advance so people have an opportunity to put it on their calendars. Covering a range of topics and giving participants the opportunity to discuss the issues in depth usually requires 90 minutes.

Space

The right space for a focus group is often determined by a number of practical considerations. The space must be convenient to get to and preferably in an area familiar to participants, the room setup should allow for optimal interaction among participants (i.e., they need to see each other), and the room must be arranged in a way that allows for recording.

Achieving Balance in the Group

Given the emphasis on observing interaction within the group in response to a question, the moderator needs to strike a balance between allowing this to happen naturally and encouraging shy or timid group participants to contribute to the discussion. Generally, the larger the group, the harder the moderator needs to work to ensure that everyone is heard.

Recording the Session

Focus groups are usually audio- or video recorded in order to transcribe the data verbatim. One of the advantages of video recording the session is that it simplifies the identification of the speaker in the transcription. When doing audio recording, it is necessary for someone to take notes during the session to identify the speakers.

Asking Different Kinds of Questions in a Focus Group

As a form of interview, focus groups can take different questioning approaches depending on the kind of information being sought. In traditional marketing focus groups, there was a tendency to ask specific questions that sought to identify consumer habits, interests, or preferences. In the same vein, some research focus groups are designed to elicit information responses and as a result tend to be highly structured, with questions focused on who, what, when, and why. In our example of support networks for stroke victims, the focus would be on asking about who is in the network, when they provide support, and why those individuals were chosen as part of the caregiver's support network. In this approach, the emphasis is on ensuring that all participants respond in order to elicit a range of information. By contrast, focus groups that are interested in understanding meanings, experiences, and perspectives would tend to use a less structured approach that provides more opportunity for interactive discussion. These questions are more likely to be prefaced by how things work or are perceived. In the caregiver example, we would ask how group members came to recognize the need for support, how they drew on that support, and how that support affected their perception of their own role as a caregiver. In this approach, the moderator would encourage participants to share their experiences with one another in order to gain a fuller understanding of how it was experienced. For Morgan (2002), the ideal focus group is an unstructured one that begins with an engaging and interesting question that participants themselves explore in a way that deals with all of the issues that the moderator might have probed. Rather than the moderator having to control and redirect the discussion, a smile and a nod is all that is necessary (Morgan 2002).

Assessing the Validity of Focus Group Data

One of the main criticisms of focus group data is that compared with observation studies, they are from highly contrived social settings. Furthermore, when compared to individual interviews, there are questions about the extent to which the expression of viewpoints in the focus group is shaped by group pressures for conformity. Questions of validity of this sort can always be traced back to questions of epistemology. From an objectivist perspective, questions of validity would focus on whether the moderator is being neutral, whether participants were biasing each other, and whether they were responding in ways that reflected their "real" experience. When operating within this framework, moderators can take steps to minimize their impact on the group and to encourage participants to discuss their own experience.

If we shift to the subjectivist position of interpretivism or postmodernism, how we think about validity changes. A focus group, like an interview, is a socially produced conversation (albeit more complex), and as a result it is entirely likely that participants will talk differently in individual interviews compared with a group interview. The moderator does play an important role in orchestrating the conversation and producing the results. Within these parameters, the question is not whether one is more valid than the other; it shifts to an analysis of the conditions and context within which the data are produced. Whereas interviewing individuals might provide insight into individual experiences and perceptions, a group interview provides an opportunity to observe how participants relate to and influence each other, the kinds of norms that may be operating in the group, and how relationships among peers are managed. Morgan (2002) gives the example of Daniel Wight's (1994) work where individual interviews with adolescent males revealed a sensitive understanding of girls' expectations, whereas the group interviews brought out a set of macho dynamics among the boys that were not evident in the individual interviews. The conditions under which the data are produced were radically different but both forms of data provided different insights into the boys' ways of perceiving girls.

Focus Groups Within the Critical Paradigm

Given that focus groups are rooted in market research, they have more traditionally been used as a means of extracting information rather than as a vehicle for the discussion and analysis of social justice issues. Madriz (2003) argues that focus groups are consistent with the feminist principle of collectivism (rather than individualism) and the postmodern principle of multivocality. As a result, they are an ideal method for bringing together groups of women to talk about "their everyday experiences of subjugation and their individual and collective survival and resistance strategies" (Madriz, 2003, p. 364). A feminist focus group format builds on the tradition of African American, Latina, and Asian American women coming together to talk about issues that are important to them and to become involved in political activism (Madriz, 2003).

Feminist research using a focus group method also is concerned with breaking down some of the traditional dichotomies between thoughts and feelings or passionate and dispassionate research (Madriz, 2003). Rather, the understanding of life experience must include both. Similarly, the traditional distinction between researcher and participant also breaks down insofar as the researcher's voice becomes one of the many voices expressed in and through the research.

Of importance in the running of focus groups within the critical paradigm is the role of the researcher and/or moderator in the formation and delivery of the research questions. In critical paradigm research, more emphasis is placed on empowering the voices of participants who have been marginalized. As a result, it is important to engage participants in setting the course of the group interview. For example, in participatory action research (PAR), the researcher does not presume to know the right questions to ask, but rather, engages participants in a discussion of key issues or unanswered questions that they have. Participants ask questions of each other as they try to understand their own collective experience. The direction of the research is shaped by participant need rather than by predetermined research objectives. The role the researcher plays in these group interviews is to empower participants by supporting their objectives and directions for the research. In this regard, the research becomes a means to change awareness and consciousness as well as a means to generate data that can enhance understanding and promote social change. Focus groups produce a "collective testimony" (Madriz, 2003) that demonstrates that problems of oppression are not just individual troubles, but structurally rooted problems.

Participant observation, interviews, and focus groups serve as the primary tools for generating data. Researchers often use these in combination as a way to triangulate results. In the next chapter we look at the ways in which researchers can put it all together: methodologies, methods, and specific strategies for designing the research.

7

Research Design

Constructing a Research Proposal

W hen I was learning about qualitative methods in the early 1980s as a doctoral student, I remember speaking at the time with a faculty member who suggested I stop worrying so much about "how to do it right" and "get out there and rap with them." While this was not exactly an epiphany, or a formula for succeeding in my methods comprehensive exams, it was one of those pivotal but paradoxical moments. Of course it was absolutely true—at the heart of qualitative research, we interact with others, we listen, and we seek to understand, at close range, how others experience life. Sometimes the biggest challenge is getting our heads out of the how-to books and investing our time in "rappin'" with those we want to understand. You might take this literally, and close this book and go out and find someone to interview!

The paradox is that this advice nearly paralyzed me because of my desire to "do it right." I needed structure for the experience, and while I realized I needed to get "out there," I also knew that there was a long tradition of methodological guidelines that I needed to be attentive to. I actually did get "out there" quite early in my learning about qualitative methods, and it served as a valuable experiential base for making sense of what I was reading about.

In the qualitative tradition there is an important balance to be achieved between the rigidity of prescriptive methodology and the adaptive use of methods in the process of shaping an inquiry that is malleable and sensitive to arising conditions. One of the negative reputations that qualitative research has picked up over the years as a result of this need for adaptability is the suggestion that doing qualitative research is easy and requires minimal training (compared to stats!); that qualitative research is "soft" or a form of journalism that is not systematic or "rigorous"; or that there is no "right way" and as a result, just about anything goes as long as you can justify what you did. Anyone who seeks to publish qualitative work, write a qualitative dissertation, or apply for a qualitative research grant knows that the "anything goes" motto is not likely the key to success. Developing a sound research plan is one way to rationalize methodological approaches adopted for a study while at the same time maintaining flexibility.

Historically, a number of practices have resulted in some ambivalence about the role and nature of qualitative research proposals. First, given the inductive, discovery orientation of qualitative work, researchers have been advised to minimize an a priori structure in the research in order to approach social reality with an open mind and fresh eyes. The directive was to begin as a tabula rasa in order to see the world as our participants see it, rather than trying to fit them into our preconceived ideas about their experience. Researchers were warned not to read the literature beforehand as it would predispose them to see complex reality according to the categories already established by previous research. By way of illustration, one of the pitfalls researchers were warned against in the original grounded theory book (Glaser & Strauss, 1967) was that of "exampling," where researchers search the data for examples of preexisting concepts (this is still an important thing to be careful about when doing inductive analysis). Given this tradition, there is a lingering ambivalence about the degree to which highly structured proposals and research designs are even necessary.

Second, one of the hallmarks of qualitative research is the notion of an emergent design. From this perspective, one of the dangers of articulating a rigid research proposal is that it locks us into a set of strategies that may not be practical or even relevant once the research is under way. The strength of an emergent design is that we articulate a direction for the research but make decisions along the way in order to saturate our understanding of the phenomenon we wish to understand. Research proposals that use an emergent design are set as guidelines, and they require flexibility on the part of both the researcher and external reviewers (like graduate committees or grant reviewers)—not to mention an element of trust and good faith.

Finally, in contrast to the position that little should be done at the outset of a project is the tendency to do too much. In response to challenges about the rigor or legitimacy of qualitative research, some have responded by developing tome-like methods sections of the research that justify every micro-decision with extensive references given for even the most mundane aspects of the design. This reactive and defensive approach adds to some of the confusion about what constitutes an appropriate design or proposal for a qualitative research study.

The literature on qualitative methods across most social science disciplines is now well established. One of the implications of having an extensive literature is that there are many choices to be made. Some might argue that this is like the broad choice we have in our Western consumer culture; a choice so broad that seriously entertaining all the possible choices is undermined by the excess of choice. Nevertheless, given a broad menu of possibilities, the onus is on the researcher to make choices and to demonstrate to the reader how and why the choices were made.

What Kind of Chef Are You?

When we make choices about how we are going to carry out a qualitative research project, a good place to start is to assess our own personality and style. Cooking in the kitchen may serve as a useful metaphor here. Some people who put on a chef's hat are keen to search out the right recipes for the occasion and to follow the ingredients and instructions exactly as they are outlined. Follow the rules; no substitutions allowed! Others may rely on recipes but are quite happy to substitute and/or add ingredients they think they will taste good. Still others might have a dish at a restaurant and go home to create something like it—using similar ingredients to capture the essence of the dish but freely adding spices and ingredients to make it come out as imagined. These chefs cook with flair and are quite happy to contend with unexpected challenges in a recipe.

When doing qualitative research, some feel more secure in following the recipe exactly, whereas others are quite happy to treat the methodological literature as a set of guidelines that can be used to shape a successful project. Most qualitative methodologies have a strong tradition of emphasizing the guiding rather than the prescriptive role of these methods. Nevertheless—there is room for a wide spectrum of approaches—from those who do wish to outline in detail the "rules" they are following, to those who are willing to adapt and modify the methodological guidelines to suit their specific purposes.

Functions of a Good Research Proposal

- Locates the research within a set of epistemological beliefs
- Links the research to established methodological practice
- Provides focus and boundaries for the inquiry
- Outlines specific methodological procedures to be followed
- Demonstrates that the proposed research is practical and doable within the constraints of time and resources
- Provides thesis or funding committees with a basis for evaluating the merits and feasibility of the project
- Justifies key decisions in sampling, data collection, and analysis
- Serves as a touchstone for direction when the researcher gets lost in data collection or analysis
- Provides a basis for external assessment of the ethics, feasibility, and merits of the project

In constructing a research proposal, there are many merits to describing your goals and objectives, underlying values, proposed methodological procedures, and strategies in sufficient detail. However, given the historical emphasis on emergence, induction, and discovery in qualitative research, proposals are perhaps best viewed as guides that provide direction but have a flexibility that allows for adjusting and reconsidering choices made early in the project but that no longer seem feasible in the midst of emerging practical challenges. Most traditional, positivistic research proposals are set out as a series of hypotheses that are then tested in a linear fashion—insofar as you make a proposal about the nature of reality and you see if you are right. By contrast, qualitative research is more likely to involve a series of general orienting questions, with the questions themselves being reframed and reconsidered along the way. As a result, it may be more appropriate to think of a qualitative proposal as involving a series of "loop backs" that reorient the project based on emerging information. It is in this regard that Hammersley and Atkinson (1995) emphasized the importance of thinking about research design as part of an ongoing reflexive process that involves refocusing, redirecting, and introducing new strategies throughout the research process. Maxwell (2005) argues that research design must be both interactive and sensitive to environmental influences: "you will need to continually assess how this design is actually working during the research, how it influences and is influenced by its environment, and make adjustments and changes so that your study can accomplish what you want" (p. 3).

In this chapter, I outline a number of components that are part of developing a flexible, interactive research plan. There are two levels at which to think about research design: one is a more general, philosophical level that positions the researcher in relation to the philosophical and methodological literature; the other is more pragmatic and outlines specific strategies for moving forward with the project. Both are necessary. In this chapter we will explore how to develop a research design at both levels.

Level I: Philosophical and Methodological Positioning

In Chapter 2, I used the metaphor of a cascading stream to describe the process of decision making when formulating a research project. In Figure 2.1, epistemology is the source that bubbles up and gives momentum to the flow of inquiry. This is followed by paradigms, concepts, and theories that give direction to the movement of ideas. Methodology outlines the procedural assumptions as they are determined by epistemology, paradigms, and theory. Methods are the techniques we use in data collection. The stream ultimately spills into a pool that we can think of as the collected data that eventually emerge from this process. The cascading process consists of making a series of successive decisions that start with the articulation of broad philosophical assumptions, values, and beliefs and ends with a set of specific decisions about data gathering techniques and procedures. A well-crafted research design should provide the reader with a transparent view of how the researcher is positioned in each of these key areas.

Table 7.1 outlines some of the possibilities within each of these five categories. Designing the study involves positioning the research question within the context of values, presuppositions, theoretical ideas, methodological strategies, and specific methods techniques. How we position ourselves in each of the columns is shaped by a combination of individual preferences, beliefs, and values; the nature of the research question itself; and a set of pragmatic considerations regarding the most appropriate tools and techniques to help us reach our research goals.

Although it is quite possible and indeed even desirable (for the sake of internal coherence) to position ourselves in relation to one element in each of the columns, the lines between elements are often blurred, and we might appropriately choose more than one for the research purpose at hand (please note that there is no intentional ordering across rows in this table).

Table 7.1   Options Within Epistemology, Paradigms, Theories,
Methodologies, and Methods

Epistemology	Paradigms	Theories	Methodologies	Methods
Objectivism	Positivist/ Postpositivist	Symbolic interactionism	Ethnography	Individual interviews
Subjectivism	Interpretive/Social constructionist	Phenomenology	Grounded theory	Focus groups
	Critical theory	Ethnomethodology	Narrative analysis	Life history
	Postmodernist	Narrative	Participatory action research	Case studies
		Life course	Phenomenological analysis	Observation
		Developmental theory		Multiple methods
		Conflict theory		Document analysis
		Feminism		
		Systems theory		
		Ecological theory		

Source: From Crotty, Michael, *The Foundations of Social Research: Meaning and Perspective in the Research*, copyright © 1998. Adapted with permission of Sage Publications, Inc.

Here are examples from some of my own studies:

Example 1. Study of transition to adoptive parenthood (see Daly, 1988, 1989)

My research focus for this study was to examine the way that infertile couples make the social psychological transition from seeing themselves as biological parents to seeing themselves as adoptive parents.

Epistemology. Toward the objectivist end of the continuum, as my focus was how they constructed and experienced this transitional reality in a patterned way. At the same time, I have acknowledged in my writings on this work my "insider" status as part of a couple who experienced infertility and adopted a child (Daly, 1992c).

Paradigm. Postpositivism, as my aim was to represent their reality by minimizing my influence on the data.

Theories. Symbolic interactionism (SI) and phenomenology—was particularly interested in exploring this as a disruption or problematic in their taken-for-granted reality (phenomenology) and the process of role making in the formation of a new identity (SI).

Methodologies. Ethnography and grounded theory methodology (GTM)—infertility brings into focus many cultural values and practices associated with parenthood (ethnographic inquiry); I was also interested in understanding the process of change and identity formation (GTM).

Methods. Carried out observations at infertility support groups in order to understand shared meanings and challenges among couples; also conducted semistructured interviews with couples in order to understand their constructions of their changing identity.

> *(Note: This research was one of my first qualitative projects. I have tried to capture what my beliefs and positioning were at that time. If I were to do it again, I would more likely position myself with a different set of beliefs: I would be closer to the subjectivist end of the continuum—recognizing the effect that my own experience had on the shaping of the results, with an interpretivist paradigm reflecting my understanding of the way data are coconstructed.)*

Example 2. Meanings and negotiations of time in dual-earner couples (see Daly, 2002)

I was interested in how couples with small children subjectively perceive and negotiate time in a relationship where both partners are working in the paid labor force.

Epistemology. The subjectivist end of the continuum—interested in the meaning-making processes associated with time. My own thinking about time and my experience as a member of a dual-earner family shaped and influenced the interview discussion.

Paradigm. Interpretivist/social constructionist and critical theory—how do individual partners construct the meaning of time? How did they interactively talk about and negotiate time in the relationship? How did time emerge in our interview conversations? (social constructionist) How did individual partners talk about entitlements to time and control over time? In what ways was time gendered? How did they want to change how they experienced time? (critical)

Theories. Symbolic interactionism (meanings of time, negotiated order) and feminism—gendered territories, division of labor

Methodologies. Grounded theory methodology—open-ended questions, emergent design, use of theoretical sampling and saturation

Methods. Open-ended interviews with dual-earner couples—interviewed couples together and apart

Example 3. Community mobilization project on father involvement

The objective of this research was to engage seven different groups of fathers (immigrant, teen, new, separated and divorced, indigenous, gay, fathers of special needs children) in a process of articulating a research agenda, generating data on the nature of their experience, and developing strategies for change.

Epistemology. Toward the subjectivist end of the continuum in order to understand the diverse ways fathers live their experience. Again, my own involvement in the project was rooted in my experience as a father interested in advocating for change in father involvement.

Paradigm. Primarily critical theory—driven by a political agenda—we were interested in understanding why fathers are often marginalized in services, ridiculed in cultural portrayals, and cast as deficient in their role. We were deliberate about engaging fathers in a process of change.

Theories. Feminism, theories of praxis and transformation in an effort to understand gender dynamics and pathways for social change

Methodologies. Participatory action research as a way to engage fathers in a process of reflecting on and constructing their experience as a basis for developing shared information, tools, and resources that would support greater involvement

Methods. Multiple methods, but primarily focus groups and individual interviews

As I reflected on each of these projects and how I would characterize my position, I experienced some hesitation in saying that the approach was exactly as outlined. This is attributable to the fact that these are highly complex belief systems and procedures that come with blurred boundaries and regular exceptions. Hence, I think it is normal that we experience some ambivalence in the process of trying to position ourselves in each of these domains. The value of the effort is that by scrutinizing our values and procedures we can proceed with a stronger sense of reflexive awareness and research integrity.

At a general level, then, research design involves a preliminary process of thinking through how we are going to approach the process of inquiry. It involves reflecting on what we can know, how we can come to understand it, and what some of the methodological strategies are for achieving our objectives. At this level, these design considerations help to clarify our underlying scientific values, help us think through a coherent plan of inquiry, and communicate to outside observers of our research the way we think about the logic of our approach. Given the philosophical nature of these considerations, it is best to articulate them as clearly as possible at the outset, but to hold them lightly so that you can come back to them throughout the process of research to reflect on how underlying values may be changing and to consider the introduction of alternative pathways for achieving research objectives.

Level II: Developing a Research Proposal

Familiar to most researchers is a more standard set of research protocols that serves as a practical guide to the conduct of the research. These protocols take many forms, but given their rootedness in the positivist tradition of social science, they are often given in an objectivist form. When we position ourselves in paradigms that involve different assumptions about the nature of knowledge, we need to consider a number of options for constructing a research proposal.

Statement of the Research Question

- Where do I find a researchable issue?
- How do I know whether this is a worthwhile subject to study?
- How do I get started on the project?

One of the first challenges in any research project is to find a researchable topic. This is a familiar anxiety that we all have encountered throughout our educational careers as we have searched for paper topics or research questions. Especially when we embark on our first qualitative research study, this can be a particularly daunting challenge as the stakes seem suddenly higher when we are investing so much time with the added pressures of generating a thesis and possibly publications from the research.

This early stage of the research design is referred to as the "armchair walkthrough" by Morse (2004, p. 494). The goal of this pre-proposal stage is to venture into the literature on topics of interest, reflect on personal and professional experience, and consider social problems of interest to us that might lend themselves to analysis. A number of activities are important in the process of identifying a researchable question:

- Read in areas that are of interest to you
- Read different kinds of literature—theoretical, practical (e.g., clinical, community development), popular press (e.g., magazines, self-help), and empirical; what is missing in our understanding?
- Talk to people who work, study, or do research in this area. What do they identify as important missing information?
- Be reflexive—write down your rudimentary ideas, develop them, scratch them off, talk to someone about them

Once you latch onto something that is of interest, go back to the literature. Consider how this emerging question might make a contribution to our understanding of the broader issue. In draft form, articulate an early version of your research question. Then ask yourself the following:

- What do we know about this already?
- What could answers to this question tell us?
- How might this study move our thinking into new territory?

Once you have your preliminary question, it is useful to begin imagining who you might talk to and what you would want to ask them. Doing a preliminary brainstorm on questions you would like to ask in the field may also serve in the process of articulating the broad research question.

Once you have gone through this process, it is important to draft your primary research question. Though this may be modified as the project design develops, it serves as an important guidepost in moving the research forward.

Significance of the Research (Justification)

- For whom is this research significant?
- How will this research be important?
- How does this research question fit with existing research, theory, and practice?

When you begin to narrow the research question, it is important to pay attention to the motivation and significance of the research. All research, at some level, reflects an underlying set of values, interests, and concerns. As a result, it is important to reflect on your own personal stake in the research as well as the potential benefits that might come from the research for those directly involved or for the general public.

Most researchers study topics that hold some personal interest to them. As I have written elsewhere, we are often insiders to some degree in areas that are of interest to us (Daly, 1992c). Having a personal interest in the topic may also serve to motivate and sustain us in the research effort. Unless we believe that the question is important enough to ask, dissertations may go unfinished or publishable results might never be brought together. Passion for the topic is an important ingredient for success. Hence, it is critical to be reflexive at an early stage about why you personally think this is an important topic to explore. When issues are very personal, be careful not to use the research to sort out personal problems. To this end, you might ask yourself the following:

- What is my personal agenda in this research? What do I see as being important?
- Am I motivated by personal unmet needs? In other words, do I want people to hear my story—through the voices of others? (Maybe I should explore this at a personal level first, with people I trust)
- Am I attached to a particular set of answers or experiences because they support my own beliefs? Am I willing to listen to a range of experiences?

When the research proposal is being developed as part of a funding proposal or for a thesis, it is also important to outline how the research question will contribute to the public good in terms of new knowledge, social change, and/or practical recommendations. Specifically,

- How will this contribute to our understanding of the phenomenon?
- What are the potential contributions to the theoretical and empirical literature?
- How will it serve participants?
- Does it have practical implications for clinical work or policy?

Most importantly, this section of the research proposal needs to convince the reader (or reviewer) that this research is important and worth doing. Accordingly, it must have a clear purpose, be attentive to specific interests and values, and demonstrate the scholarly and practical values of the research.

Contextualizing the Study: The Literature Review

- Should I do a literature review?
- Is a qualitative literature review different from one in other kinds of research proposal?
- What kinds of literature should I be looking at?

In the process of finding and articulating the research question, you will have initiated your literature review for the project. Although arguments are made that one should avoid consulting the literature in order to enter into the experiential field unencumbered by prior ways of thinking, it is now more typically the case that researchers do review the literature in order to situate the research question in relation to our prior understandings. There are a number of advantages to doing a literature review: It allows us to determine the extent to which the topic of interest has been explored, it provides a preliminary set of insights into how the phenomenon has been construed in the literature, and it provides a basis for justifying the importance of the proposed research in relation to the work that already exists.

Conducting a literature review as part of a qualitative research project is different in some respects from other kinds of research projects. In a traditional quantitative project, the researcher would conduct a review of both theoretical and empirical literature in order to formulate hypotheses about the nature of reality that are then subjected to empirical tests of verification or falsification. In the development of a qualitative research proposal, however, the literature is more likely to serve a sensitizing function. At a broad level, a review of the existing literature can highlight those aspects of reality we need to know more about, and in so doing facilitate the development of our primary research question. At a more specific level, the literature can help us to see dominant values and discourses by the way issues have been construed in the literature thus far, it can sensitize us to think more deeply about the issue by reading about aspects of the phenomenon that take us beyond our personal experience, and it can also offer different experiential perspectives on the issue.

A literature review for a qualitative proposal can include many different kinds of literature. Although the emphasis is still typically placed on the empirical and theoretical literature, it is becoming increasingly common— especially in postmodern approaches—to bring in literature from a variety of sources to develop a deeper sensitivity to the issues involved. These might include works of fiction with detailed descriptions of a related experience, poetry, media accounts, or other kinds of cultural portrayal (drama, advertising, the Internet).

Statement of Specific Objectives

- What is the reality or human experience that I am going to focus on?
- What is achievable within the scope of this project?
- What are the specific outcomes that I wish to have at the end of this project?

Research objectives are essential for articulating what is achievable in the research. They break down the broad research question into a set of outcome-oriented activities that must be manageable within the constraints of time, effort, and money.

One way we can narrow our research focus is to think through conceptually what we wish to understand. These foci are shaped by a number of paradigmatic, theoretical, and methodological considerations. At the broadest level, we must first consider which strengths of qualitative inquiry we want to emphasize.

- Is our focus on meaning-making activity, interaction, storytelling, negotiations, lived experience, cultural activities, context, or process (or some combination of these)?
- What is our unit of analysis? Is our intention to focus on the individual, the family, a relationship, or a system of relationships?

In a study of adults' preferences for future care if they became frail, researchers used a number of lenses that arose from the use of a life course perspective (Roberto, Allen, & Bleizner, 2001) that combined several levels of analysis. In order to understand how adults anticipate their future care plans, these authors examined individual, family, and historical perspectives. Specifically, they looked at how individual future plans were related to previous experience, how family relationship histories influenced contemporary family relationships, and how broader structural influences such as economic conditions, cultural ideologies, and geographical location affected their plans for care. In this type of design, several levels of analysis are effectively brought together in the qualitative inquiry.

In order to formulate objectives, it is necessary to have considered possible methodological approaches that determine how we can go about asking our questions. This presupposes consideration of both epistemology and paradigms that outline our assumptions about what is knowable and our role in the generation of that knowledge. In this regard, one of the important considerations in the articulation of objectives is choosing between the use of naturally occurring data and the construction of data. Examples of gathering naturally occurring data include examining existing diaries or documents, unobtrusively observing natural settings, or conducting conversation analysis of dialogues that occurred outside of a research context. Constructed data are those that result from the active participation of the researcher and would include participant observation, interviews, and focus groups. Key questions in the formulation of the research objectives would be:

- How does my involvement in the research shape the anticipated outcome?
- Am I seeking to represent their reality in a patterned way (i.e., nomothetic outcome)?
- Or am I interested in the unique and idiographic stories that might emerge in the research? (see Chapter 9, "Analytical Strategies," for further discussion of nomothetic/idiographic)

Description of Methodology and Methods

- What is the methodology (e.g., ethnography, grounded theory, narrative)?
- What is the fit between the research question, methodology, and the method(s) chosen?
- How will I go about generating data? Interviews? Observations? Focus groups?
- To what degree is this a highly structured versus emergent design?

This section anchors the entire research proposal, for it is in this section that the research question, justification, objectives, and literature review come together with the chosen methodology and data generating methods.

As discussed in Chapter 5, methodology is not concerned simply with how we conduct the research, but also with how we seek to conceptualize and understand reality. In this section of the proposal, it is important to review the related methodological literature and to use the language of that literature as it relates to your research question. For example, if you are planning to do a grounded theory study, it is important to use the language of grounded theory—emergent design, theoretical sensitivity, constant comparative analysis, or negative case—and to demonstrate how you will use these design features in the service of analyzing your own research question. By so doing, you achieve a number of important objectives. First, you communicate to readers how you have positioned yourself within a tradition of research that comes with recognizable guidelines and procedures. Working within these established procedures means that you are operating within a set of shared meanings about the methodology that does not require extensive explanation. Second, by clearly articulating the reasons why you have chosen a methodology, you enhance the focus of your research by demonstrating the theory–methods linkages. For example, if you are using a phenomenological analysis as your chosen methodology and are concerned with lived experience, taken-for-granted reality, and intersubjectivity, your discussion of methodology provides the opportunity to demonstrate how those theoretical concepts provide a methodological basis for examining the phenomenon of interest in your own research. In this section of the proposal you demonstrate how you are constructing your questions and exploring the issues on the basis of these concepts. Finally, articulating the methodology serves as a basis for reflecting on role, data collection or generation strategies, and further refining of the research question.

Decisions about data collection and methods are contingent on thinking through a variety of issues related to the research question. As a result, methods should be justified in relation to the following:

- The level of analysis (individuals, relationships, family dynamics, cultural values, a social setting)
- The perspective you wish to examine (individual perspectives, multiple perspectives, coconstructions)
- Naturally occurring or constructed data (see above)
- Individual or group perspectives
- The focus of our inquiry: Behavior? Action? Talk? Stories? Written documents?

A description of the methods chosen thereby involves an explanation of how the data gathering techniques are justified by the perspectives being examined, type of data preferred (natural or constructed), and level of analysis. Each of these choices must be then justified by the utility of these methods for answering the main research question.

In writing the methods section of the proposal, it is important to strike a balance between articulating the fundamentals of the method so that people unfamiliar with the method will appreciate the justification, and doing so with sufficient sophistication to demonstrate your understanding of specific procedures. In writing the methods section, it is valuable to incorporate aspects of the methods literature. This helps readers to see how you are positioning yourself in relation to the established approaches.

Sampling Plan

- What am I sampling? Experience? Events? Transitions? Sites? Specific behaviors?
- What are my inclusion criteria?
- How will I decide who to talk to as the research progresses (i.e., purposive sampling)? How will I decide to sample for topics or for information?
- How many people do I expect to talk to? Or, how many sites do I plan to visit?
- What are the criteria for knowing when to stop collecting or generating data?
- What are my recruitment techniques? How will I access people and places?

Sampling in qualitative research often goes beyond sampling individual people. When we sample in qualitative research, we are interested in gaining access to various sources of data that will provide us with information about people, places, and activities. One of the strengths of qualitative research is that it provides a means for examining complex interactive phenomena and situations or processes that occur over time. As a result, sampling in qualitative research can be much broader than the individual case analysis that we usually associate with getting the right "N."

For example, when we carry out an ethnographic observation study, we may be more interested in "sampling" events that occur (e.g., families participating in a company picnic), activities within the community (e.g., observing parent-child interactions in minor sports), or mundane, routine interactions within the home (e.g., family mealtimes). Although participants become in a sense the subjects of our research, we are more interested in understanding the situation that brings them together. In observation studies, sampling is about identifying sites and situations that allow us to observe, and then negotiating access to be part of those situations. When articulating a sampling plan in an observation study, it is important to:

- Describe in detail the setting or situation you are interested in by clearly outlining who is involved in these settings and when, where, and how these events occur

- Outline how you will negotiate entry and whether there are key persons who will facilitate this
- Identify within these settings what your focus of observation will be—in other words, are you sampling within these settings in order to understand a particular phenomenon?

Alternatively, when we are interested in examining written texts or looking at cultural artifacts, then sampling becomes a matter of justifying the selection of those texts or artifacts. For example, carrying out an analysis of parenting magazines in order to understand dominant discourses associated with discipline would involve sampling decisions about (a) the types of magazines to be consulted (which titles?); (b) the time frame for those magazines (one year? the past 5 years?); (c) the aspects of the magazines that will be examined (only stories about discipline? all columns? letters to the editor? etc.). In this type of research, sampling involves an articulation of decisions that will focus the analysis on key aspects of the phenomenon of interest.

In studies that involve interviews or focus groups, it is important to develop a sampling strategy that outlines in detail the selection of specific participants for the study. Epistemology plays an important role here. In qualitative studies that follow a set of positivistic principles, it may be important to consider issues of representativeness and generalizability. Given the underlying belief that there is an objective reality that can be represented through empirical research, it is important to draw on the principles of random sampling that provide a basis for arguing that the views of the participants reflect a broader population.

More typically, however, qualitative researchers use the principles of purposive sampling in their research. As the name would imply, researchers develop a sampling strategy that involves contacting participants who are experienced in the phenomenon of interest. Rather than being guided by the principles of representativeness, the researcher is instead guided by the pragmatic concerns of identifying and accessing people who can help to understand a particular type of experience. One of the first steps in developing a proposal is to define clearly who is eligible to participate in the study. Specifically,

- What are the personal characteristics required for participation? (e.g., age, sex, ethnicity)
- What kind of social or phenomenological experience must they have had?
- Are there characteristics or experiences that would exclude them from participating in the study?

One way to approach this in family research is to define the kinds of families we are interested in and then develop a recruitment strategy that allows us to contact these types of families. For example, if we were interested in trying to understand the meaning of adoption for grandparents in the adoptive family, we might begin by identifying community-based adoption services or support groups that would help us to access that population. We might also consider putting in a request for volunteers in an adoptive parent newsletter. These are strategic and targeted approaches that are part of purposive sampling. Given that a primary reason for using purposive sampling is to gain access to individuals with unique characteristics, snowball sampling is often used as a companion to this type of sampling. This involves asking participants to facilitate the recruitment effort by recommending others who might fit with the criterion for participation.

When we use the language of "sampling"—even its qualitative forms—we continue in some ways in the tradition of positivistic thinking about science. To "sample" or "recruit" someone into a study is to uphold the notion of objectifying his or her experience as the subject matter of the study. By contrast, in feminist or social constructionist research, there is more emphasis on coconstructing research conversations, seeking out and forming relationships with people who have insight into the phenomenon, or providing an opportunity for marginalized groups to voice their experience through research. One of the ways the language of sampling shifts here is to talk about "participants" or even "collaborators" in the research, rather than "subjects." For example, in a phenomenological study of African American grandmothers providing primary care to their grandchildren, Gibson (2002) wrote from "a Black womanist/feminist perspective" (p. 343) and preferred to call the grandmothers "consultants" rather than subjects in recognition of the collaborative partnership between the researcher and the women participating in the study. Hence, in a number of paradigm traditions (e.g., critical, constructionist, postmodern), the language of "sampling" may lose its relevance. Instead, there may be a greater emphasis on opening conversations, establishing relationships, being referred to key people, participating in their realities, or having an opportunity to listen to and honor stories.

In an emergent design, the ideas of theoretical sampling are particularly important. Although theoretical sampling is part of the language of grounded theory, it is central to the process of carrying out inductive inquiry more generally. As we engage with participants and begin to form ideas about the meaning of their experience, we use our emerging concepts and ideas as a way to explore further the phenomenon of interest. Theoretical sampling is a way of organizing our questions so that we can deepen our understanding of the phenomenon. We sample for ideas, and direct our inquiry based on what we have come to understand in our prior conversations with participants. Theoretical sampling can involve sampling people insofar as our emerging conceptualizations direct us to contact or speak with persons who might have a very specific type of experience. It may also involve sampling for the negative case—people who obviously hold a different view or who may have a set of experiences that would serve as a point of contrast. Theoretical sampling continues until we are satisfied that our understanding of the phenomenon is saturated and limited new information emerges.

The final aspect of outlining the sampling strategy for the proposal is to indicate something about the number of people who will be sampled. This is probably one of the most difficult and contentious aspects of qualitative research design. A common but often misguided criticism of qualitative research studies is that the "N" is too low. This criticism is usually based on a set of positivist assumptions that may not be appropriate for a constructionist or postmodern approach. Nevertheless, the criticism is prevalent and the repercussion is that qualitative researchers are sometimes preoccupied with getting a sufficient N in order to ward off criticism. There is little consensus in the qualitative literature about what constitutes an adequate sample size; however, there are criteria put forward that can help in making an assessment of adequacy:

- Theoretical saturation—after repeated conversations with participants, have I reached the point where I understand their experience as fully as possible?
- Have I sampled a sufficient range of individuals to allow me to understand both the nature of their patterned experience and the variation that exists in their experience?
- There is a tradeoff between interviewing a larger number of people and exploring the phenomenon in greater depth with a smaller number of people. As Kvale (1996) argued, there is a quantitative presupposition in qualitative research that upholds a positivist message: The more interviews, the more scientific it is. Kvale maintains that interview quality is more important than quantity.

Size Matters: The Small Sample Size Problem in Qualitative Research

One of the most common comments that qualitative researchers receive in a refereed journal review is that the sample size is too small for there to be any confidence in the results. On a number of occasions I have received feedback to the effect that "these are highly interesting results but with such a small sample size we have no way of knowing whether these results are at all representative." The million dollar question is, how many?

Consider the following bits of advice:

McCracken (1988b): when doing long, in-depth interviews, 8 should be sufficient to achieve a good understanding of the experience. Going much beyond 8 is potentially a waste of resources.

Spradley (1980): as an anthropologist interested in conducting interviews with cultural members, the preference was for repeated interviews (approx. 6) with 25 to 30 participants.

Kvale (1996): observes that "in current interview studies, the number of interviews tend to be around 15 ± 10. This number may be due to a combination of time and resources available for the investigation and of the law of diminishing returns" (p. 102).

Johnson (2002): the right number is "enough." "Enough interviews must be conducted so that the interviewer feels he or she has learned all there is to be learned from the interviews and has checked out those understandings by reinterviewing the most trusted and most knowledgeable informants" (p.113).

In my own interview studies, I have had various samples ranging from 32 men in a fatherhood study to 27 families in a study of gender and time to 74 couples in a study of the transition to adoptive parenthood. The "enough" point—or the point at which I have begun to feel theoretical saturation—has usually occurred when I have conducted between 20 and 25 interviews. The decision to go beyond this number has been a combination of factors—sometimes it was to complete interviews with all participants who have volunteered; sometimes it was going just the extra bit to make sure my developing interpretive ideas were sound. In the adoptive parenthood study that included interviews with 74 couples, I wanted to have sufficient sample size to conduct some quantitative analysis of the data.

The Unit of Analysis in Human Development and Family Research

- What is the phenomenon I am trying to understand?
- Whose perspective is critical to my effort to understand this?
- Am I interested in individual experience and perceptions? Relational dynamics? Family processes?

One of the unique features of studying developmental transitions in relation to family dynamics is that there are many possibilities for how we decide on our "unit of analysis." Most qualitative research, for example, focuses on the perspectives of individuals who are asked to describe their own experience of growth and development and their perceptions of family relationships and influences. Using the individual as the unit of analysis provides an important means for understanding how mothers and fathers talk about parenting in different ways or how individuals from different generations might talk about values in both similar and different ways. In family research there are also opportunities to examine couple dynamics, intergenerational relationships, and family processes and interactions. As a result, one of the important decisions to be made when designing the research is whether to study individual perspectives, shared meanings within a relationship, or family dynamics.

Studying Couples and Relationships

Using the couple as a unit of analysis serves as an important means for understanding the relational aspects of family dynamics. For example, in a study that focused on "father responsiveness" in the context of a heterosexual marriage relationships, Matta and Knudson-Martin (2006) sought to make the "relational processes visible" (p. 25) by asking couples to talk about how they make decisions together, communicate with one another, and organize their everyday lives. Although their focus was on fatherhood, the couple interviews provided a means to understand how fatherhood was experienced within the context of the relational system.

In my own research with childless infertile couples (Daly, 1988, 1992b, 1992c, 1999) and dual-earner couples (Daly, 2001, 2002), I was intentional about interviewing couples together in order to gain an appreciation for how they perceived their experience in both similar and different ways but also as a means to observe how they jointly constructed their reality together. In other words, these interviews of heterosexual couples provided a means to see gender in action, the management of emotion, and the negotiation of various roles and responsibilities in relationships. For example, in a couple interview I did as part of the dual-earner study, there was growing tension between Jennifer and Terry as Jennifer talked about her resentment at having to choose between her children and a career she loved (which she saw as a problem that women experienced more intensely than men). As the interviewer, I could feel the tension rising between the two of them with Jennifer becoming more angry and Terry more defensive. In order to ward off any attribution of blame to Terry or any negative attribution to them as a couple, Jennifer went on to externalize the problem:

Terry: So the resentment you were referring to was referring to me?

Jennifer: No, no more kind of general, like why can't we do both (i.e., work and parent)?

Terry: Oh, I see, social.

Jennifer: Social.

Terry: From society, OK.

By externalizing the explanation of resentment to society, Terry and Jennifer safely removed any attribution of blame and restored balance between themselves. I provide this example because it offers some insight into how they interactively managed this tension, but it was also an illustration of one of the challenges of doing couple research—which is the tendency of couples to present a unified set of perspectives. As a way of trying to balance this in this study, I did both individual and conjoint interviews. When I conducted the couple interview (after the individual interviews), it was not uncommon for couples to question whether the joint interview was a "test" of their consistency of how they told their stories. Although that was not my intention, it was testimony to the presence of strong social norms associated with couplehood: their need to be consistent, together, in their stories and equal contributors of their shared reality. This was not always the case—and there were couples who were more comfortable than other couples in expressing disagreement and talking about conflict in their relationship—but it was, nevertheless, indicative of the powerful norms that were operating here.

One way of minimizing the effects the interviewer has on how couples present themselves is to have them engage in a videotaped discussion of their relationship. For example, using a purposive sample of 40 same-sex couples (20 male, 20 female), Rostosky et al. (2004) asked couples to have a 30-minute conversation between themselves about their relationship, their commitment to their relationship, and their experiences of family support from members of their family of origin. These videotaped conversations took place in a private counseling room with a set of eight written prompts asking them to discuss various aspects of their relationship. The results provide insight into the ways couples experienced deleterious effects when there was lack of support, how this resulted in experiences of self or partner rejection for some, and provided insight into some of their coping strategies.

Studying Family Experience as a Focus of Analysis

One approach to understanding family experience is to interview members of the same family in order to come to an appreciation of their shared and divergent perspectives. While there are a number of excellent examples where entire nuclear families have been studied, it is more often the case that individuals within families are chosen to offer their perspectives on some aspect of family life. In a study of parents' and children's perceptions of family processes in a multiethnic sample of inner-city families, Madden Derdich, Leonard, and Gunnell (2002) conducted in-depth interviews with 61 previously incarcerated male youths and 33 of their parents. The interviews focused on the ways parents and children perceived the problem, what they saw as either amplifying the problem or helping to resolve it, and how they saw parenting practices in relation to the challenges they were facing. While this research was based on individual interviews, its focus was on perceived family dynamics and processes. Similarly, in a study of dying, Wright (2003) conducted interviews with a person who was dying and, when possible, their family members. Here the goals were to gain a more relational understanding of what families experienced, how they coped, and how they made meaning when a family member was dying.

Chaitin (2003) provides an example of how the "life-story" approach can be used to study the family experience of several generations of Holocaust survivors. Based on 57 interviews that came from 20 survivor families, the research focused on the experiences of at least two and often three generations of survivors in these families in order to understand the long-term adaptive strategies that were used to cope with the traumatic events associated with the Holocaust. By examining the stories of family members from different generations, the researcher could analyze the degree to which, for example, the experience of victimization either prevailed across a particular generation or shifted from one generation to the next. It was also a means for understanding the complexity of adaptive family strategies as indicated by a number of families who demonstrated different but concurrent coping strategies.

In the narrative tradition, Fiese and Bickham (2004) asked both parents to tell their child a story about growing up. A review of stories told in 120 families helped them understand a variety of family dynamics, including how the parents engaged the child in the storytelling tasks and how they brought emphasis to certain themes in the family story, including risk taking, success, or being independent.

Choosing the appropriate unit of analysis in human development and family relations research is influenced by the kinds of questions we ask, the perspectives that are needed, and the processes we wish to understand. Individual interviews can provide good insight into one person's experience of a developmental transition or family event, whereas including couples and multiple members of families can provide insight into relationship dynamics, shared and conflictual viewpoints, and the multiple realities that constitute everyday family life.

Role/Self-Positioning

- What is my relationship to the phenomenon I am trying to understand? Will I be a participant in coconstructing the data, or will I be a disengaged observer?

- What is the nature of the relationships I will set up with the participants in the study? One time? Short term? Repeated over time?
- Am I an insider or an outsider? Am I an insider only to some degree? What are the implications of my having shared or different experiences?
- What values are driving this research?

How we reflect on our own stakes and interests in the research is an ongoing process that begins with the articulation of our broad research question and continues on throughout analysis and interpretation. Two aspects of this process should be outlined in the research proposal. The first involves taking stock of what we bring to the research project. Specifically, this has to do with what Glaser and Strauss (1967) and Strauss and Corbin (1990) originally referred to as "theoretical sensitivity" and later referred to as simply "sensitivity" (Strauss & Corbin, 1998). This is the capacity or quality of the researcher to think in theoretical terms about the emerging data based on personal and professional experience, empirical and theoretical knowledge, and personal insights and understandings. Hence by reviewing our own values, experiences, and understandings as part of shaping the research question, we can demonstrate to the reader how our standpoints influence the direction and, by implication, the outcome of the research. Although self-positioning must be monitored throughout the research process, it is especially important to articulate this standpoint at the proposal stage. It provides a transparency of the researcher's values and interests that contributes to the overall integrity of the research effort.

The second aspect of role positioning that should be outlined in the research proposal is the way the researcher will include this reflexive process in the research plan. There are a number issues that should be addressed in the proposal:

- How will I maintain a posture of sensitivity, and how will I incorporate these personal insights into the research?
- How will I keep track of key decisions as the research progresses?
- How will I work through my own meaning-making process and ensure that I have a record of this?

Mapping out the ways we navigate a research project has taken on a variety of labels in the literature, including writing field notes, memoing, reflexive journaling, and creating an audit trail (Lincoln & Guba, 1985). Each of these is concerned with ensuring that we develop a record of the practical decisions made in the research. They all serve as a systematic basis for tracing the interpretive process and the creation of theoretical and conceptual insights throughout the research process. Although it is not possible at this stage of the research to indicate the content of these decisions, it is important to outline the procedures the researcher will use in structuring this reflexive process.

Plan for Data Analysis

- What exactly are the data?
- How does the study's methodology direct the analysis? Am I using an appropriate language for the methodology?
- What is the goal of the analysis? Theory? Description? Narrative? Case study? Substantive or formal theory?
- Who will transcribe recorded accounts?
- Who will conduct the analysis? On my own? Shared with participants? With other researchers?
- Will I be using any software packages to assist in the analysis?
- Will I be using strategies to establish the trustworthiness of the data? For example, will I be checking out interpretations with participants?

Outlining the plan for analysis can be one of the most difficult aspects of a research proposal because it is, at this stage of the research, projected and hypothetical. Nevertheless, having a plan for data analysis can help to structure and organize the inquiry and at the same time communicate to readers what to expect.

One of the first tasks in outlining the plan for data analysis is to indicate what the data are. When we talk about transcribing the data for analysis, the assumption is often made that the data reflect our participants' voices and as a result, the emphasis is placed on what *they* say. Implicitly, then, the word *data* comes loaded with objectivist assumptions. While this may be of primary interest, it is also important to recognize how those data are coconstructed through question and answer and conversation. In this regard, the data are an emergent product of those interactive episodes. Of course, the way we talk about the creation of data is a function of our paradigm beliefs. In the plan for analysis, it is important that these beliefs be considered and discussed because they influence our approach to the data analysis.

Of critical importance in outlining the plan for analysis is to draw on the language and procedures of the chosen methodology. For example, if your plan is to conduct a narrative analysis of people's stories, you would need to highlight the kinds of analysis you will be using that are part of the narrative tradition. Accordingly, you might talk about how you will identify narrative structures (such as plot, sequence of events, protagonists), examine dominant and subjugated stories, or carry out an analysis of the narrative styles used in the telling. These descriptions of analytical strategies help to focus the research and provide direction for the inquiry. Similarly, if your purpose is to provide an ethnographic account, then it is important to use the language of ethnography to outline your analysis. Specifically, if you are providing "thick description," set out how you will go about focusing this analysis. What is the nature of the experience or social situation you will be describing? Who are the particular individuals, family groups, or organizations you will be focusing on in this description? What aspects of culture will be examined in this analysis? Will you be identifying cultural themes?

The way we describe the analysis in a research proposal must be consistent with the appropriate outcomes for the methodology to be used. For example, in a grounded theory study, the primary outcome for that type of analysis is to generate a substantive theory. In order to arrive at a substantive theory, it is necessary to follow the analytic procedures of "constant comparative analysis" that involve the creation of categories, properties, and dimensions; the identification of a core category; and possibly using procedural guidelines such as open, axial, and selective coding (Strauss & Corbin, 1998). Hence, when describing the analysis procedures, it is important that there be an internal consistency between methodological outcome and analytic procedures.

Data also undergo a number of transformations that have implications for how the analysis is conducted. Critical in this regard is the transcription of data. Often the task of transcription is given to professionals outside of the research team. There is a difference between transcribing data oneself (as the researcher) and having others transcribe the data. As we will discuss in Chapter 9 on analysis, the way punctuation is assigned or the way phrases are constructed can have an impact on the interpretation of meaning in the data. It is important that this decision about who will do the transcription be included in the research plan. Similarly, if data analysis software is to be used in the study, then it is also important to identify the type of software to be used and a brief justification for its use.

When describing the analysis, it is also important to be attentive to who will be conducting it. A common default position is to presume that the researcher will be the sole analyst of the research data. Given the variations in the way the researcher is positioned in various paradigm traditions, it is important to be explicit about this. There are many possibilities here, from the researcher conducting the analysis of the data independently, to engaging research participants in the process of making sense of their own and others' experiences, to engaging in collaborative or team-based models of analysis that involve multiple viewpoints and interpretations. In student research proposals, it would be useful to talk about how an advisor, committee members, or other colleagues might be engaged in the process of analysis.

Finally, the plan for analysis should include reference to any strategies that might be used to support the trustworthiness of the data. In some paradigm traditions, a trustworthiness strategy is not a meaningful exercise as it is based on the traditional ideas of reliability and validity, which are in turn contingent on assumptions of the researcher accurately representing an external, objective reality. As will be discussed in Chapter 10, however, there are a number of alternative frameworks that researchers use to establish the credibility of their research effort, and these should be summarized as part of the research plan.

Overview of the Research Plan: Practical Considerations

- What is my timetable for the research?
- What resources are required to conduct the research?
- What will I include in the ethics protocol?

This final component of the research proposal is focused on outlining a workable research plan within the time and resource constraints of the project. The timetable is typically something that needs to be negotiated with either advisors or collaborators. It needs to be a flexible document because of the number of unexpected contingencies that can arise, but also a document that identifies and has respect for realistic deadlines that help to keep the project moving at a reasonable pace. All projects—big or small—require resources of some kind. In order to determine whether the project is doable within the available money, it is important to be realistic about costs and outline these in detail. For a thesis project, these might include travel to interviews or observation sites, recording equipment (including batteries!), photocopying, recording tapes, transcription, paper and cartridges for printing hundreds of pages of transcripts and any additional research or administrative support required for the project. The research ethics protocol can be developed when there is a clear sense of the direction of the project and the specific procedures to be followed (see Chapter 10 for a discussion of ethics issues).

8

Positioning the Self

Role Considerations and the Practices of Reflexivity

The personality of the artist passes into the narration itself, flowing round and round the persons and the action like a vital sea. . . . The dramatic form is reached when the vitality which has flowed and eddied round each person fills every person with such vital force that he or she assumes a proper and intangible esthetic life. The personality of the artist, at first a cry or a cadence or a mood and then a fluid and lambent narrative, finally refines itself out of existence, impersonalises itself, so to speak. The esthetic image in the dramatic form is life purified in and reprojected from the human imagination. The mystery of esthetic like that of material creation is accomplished. The artist, like the God of the creation, remains within or behind or beyond or above his handiwork, invisible, refined out of existence, indifferent, paring his fingernails.

(James Joyce, 1964, p. 219)

Joyce provides a provocative portrait of the place of the artist in the production of imaginative work. At the center of this description is a paradox between the artist's being present in every character and at the same time lurking beyond the narrative as a distant observer. This paradox, which is central to the process of creating a story from imagination, is also central to the process of creating qualitative accounts of observed realities. When we do qualitative research, we begin with intangible ideas and imaginations, we engage with participants and we bring to them our "reprojected" ideas in the process of understanding their lives, and we creatively produce accounts of those experiences in a way that often leaves us somewhat invisible—"beyond or above" our own "handiwork."

In qualitative research, when we invoke an awareness of the ways our own personalities and experience pass into the constructed products of our research, we are engaged in a process of reflexivity. A simple definition of *reflexivity* is: the ways in which a researcher critically monitors and understands the role of the self in the research endeavor. Reflexivity serves a heuristic function for the research for it is through an internal search that the researcher discovers the nature and meaning of experience and develops methods and procedures for carrying the investigation and analysis to a deeper level (Moustakas, 1990).

Although reflexivity has come to hold a central position in all forms of qualitative methods, it is still often invisible in the final reports of research. Faced with the challenge of publishing a journal article in a 25-page format within a set of vague postpositivist expectations, researchers often strip away the reflexive commentary in order to present a research article that will appear convincing and robust when reviewed. As a result, there is an underlying tension in qualitative research: be reflexive throughout the process but hold this tightly when it comes time to publish. Although there are a number of publishing fora that allow for the inclusion of reflexive insights, this remains a tension in the construction of qualitative reports.

As qualitative research has become more accepted and methodologies more clearly articulated, it is important that we move toward a greater alignment of principles and practice. The principles and merits of reflexivity within interpretive, critical, and postmodern paradigms are well established; the practices, from the start of the project to the final write-up, may be less apparent. As Mauthner and Doucet (2003) have clearly articulated, there is widespread acknowledgment that being reflexive is important in the process of creating meanings in qualitative research; nevertheless, there is little emphasis on the difficulties, practicalities, and methods of doing it.

Dimensions of Reflexive Practice

At the broadest level, reflexive practice is concerned with examining and monitoring the role that we play in shaping the research outcome. There are a number of dimensions to reflexive practice that can help us to think about this role.

Research Results Are Mediated

There is no such thing as innocent research (Järviluoma, Moisala, & Vilkko, 2003). In this regard, all outcomes of the research endeavor are mediated in some way. In the tradition of qualitative research, the researcher is the instrument through which research results are produced (Lincoln & Guba, 1985). Reflexivity, therefore, becomes the means by which we scrutinize the mediating role of the self in the production of research results.

Focus on Experience

Feminist critiques of traditional science (e.g., Allen, 2000; Harding, 1991; Oakley, 1981; Reinharz, 1992) highlighted the fallacy of separating the researcher and researched in social science research activity. In an effort to bring women's experience to the foreground in a patriarchal landscape, they argued that women must start their inquiry by attending to their own experience. Rather than rendering the researcher invisible or upholding the pretence that their own views and experience didn't matter, feminist scholars argued for the importance of including personal experience as a way of legitimating what were often women's private, unnoticed, or invisible subjective experiences as a woman. In order to understand how subjective experience was shaping the research process, women were encouraged to reflect on feelings as well as thoughts (Kleinman & Copp, 1993) and to consider the ways personal knowledge and experience affected their understanding of other women's experience. These feminist understandings served as a basis for including subjective experience in all forms of qualitative research.

More generally, reflexivity begins with the principle of including personal and professional experience in the research endeavor. It recognizes that the self cannot be excluded from the research process and that accumulated life experiences color all aspects of the research process from the selection of focus, to the shaping of questions, to the interpretation of data.

When we study human development and family relationships, we are always, at some level, insiders in relation to the topic under study. Our own experiences of growth, transition, and family relationships shape the way our attention is drawn to particular topics, the way we puzzle about them, and ultimately the way we make sense of what is going on. In all of the qualitative projects I have been involved in, my own personal experiences of family and development have served as the beginning point for my reflexive practice. Experiences of involuntary childlessness, adoption, father involvement, work and family tensions, being a man in a family, and negotiating time schedules in a dual-earner family have all served as a primary resource in my thinking about these experiences as research foci.

Identity Issues

Whenever we are carrying out interviews or are involved in observations, we are socially situated. In keeping with the principles of symbolic interactionist identity theory, who we are and how we are seen in the situation is a product of the interplay between our own motives and the attributions that are made about us under the changing conditions of the situation. Therefore, in any research situation, we present ourselves in a way we wish to be seen, and at the same time are attentive to the way others are seeing us in that situation. Reflexivity is concerned with the ways we manage our identities in research settings. Although there is a tradition that emphasizes the importance of presenting and managing the professional researcher role in these settings, many other identities are either presented by us or attributed to us in research settings. We may present or be seen to be presenting ourselves in a variety of ways: in family roles and identities; as the passionate listener; as friend; or as an advocate for a shared cause. To be reflexive is to monitor how we are presenting ourselves and how we are perceived in these social research settings.

Hence, when we conduct research, our research identity is not fixed in terms of a preconceived idea about what it means to be a researcher; rather it is in flux and emerges as the conditions of the research situation unfold. In this regard, who we are as a researcher is something that is interactively created in the research setting. Through reflexive practice, we record and monitor this changing identity.

Reflexivity and Physical Presence in the Field

Research and analysis are often thought of as activities that take place in people's heads without the benefit of an attached body. When we enter into field sites to observe activity or engage with a participant in an interview, we bring along our bodies, appearance, and a variety of behavioral cues. How we physically position ourselves in relation to participants can also be an indication of the ways that we produce and perform power relationships in the field (Järviluoma et al., 2003). How we dress, where we sit or stand, and how we posture ourselves (e.g., arms crossed, looking inquisitive, being stiff or nervous, etc.) can make a difference in how relationships with participants are established. Often these physical moves are not conscious or rational but rather reflect our tendency to "act with our bodies before we think or speak" (Järviluoma et al., 2003, p. 31). Being reflexive means realizing the importance of our full body presence as a way of understanding our roles and relationships.

Relationship Between the Researcher and the Researched

In a traditional positivistic orientation to research practice, the link between the researcher and the researched was most likely to be construed as a formal, rule-bound, unidirectional, and professional association. There is a clear differentiation of roles between the researcher and "subjects," with the process involving a one-way flow of information that is manifested as "gathering data" and "extracting data." Social constructionist, critical, and postmodern approaches have reframed this association and have placed a greater emphasis on the relationship between researchers and participants in the research. Instead of an emphasis on separate, neatly defined roles, there is an awareness of the ways in which researchers and participants may have shared, intersubjective experiences; participate in a common cultural environment; and, through their interaction, act as coparticipants in the production of situated knowledge.

When we are reflexive about these relationships, we can be attentive to how our research ideas are socially produced through interviews or observations. Interviews, like any form of social interaction, are likely to bring forward certain kinds of information or experiences while at the same time repressing others. Through the process of reflexivity, we can scrutinize how the research situation is conducive to the production and communication of certain kinds of knowledge and experience. In the words of Ellis and Berger (2003), the interview process becomes

> less a conduit of information from informants to researchers that represents how things are, and more a sea swell of meaning-making in which researchers connect their own experiences to those of others and provide stories that open up the conversations about how we live and cope. (p. 161)

There are times, too, when the research conversation can have a transforming effect on both the researched and the researcher. It can have the effect of a social "awakening" that can be experienced as disturbing and even traumatic (Mitchell & Radford, 1996).

Reflexive practice provides the means for understanding how our own experiences and stories interact with those of our participants. Although the sharing of personal information by an interviewer can be construed as a "tactic" to encourage the respondent to "open up," it is also the case that the researcher is motivated by the desire to reciprocate with the participants and share personal details, feelings, and "private" experiences (Ellis & Berger, 2003).

Clinicians who conduct qualitative research are also in a position of having to monitor carefully the way relationships are managed. Research and therapy interviews call for different positioning of the researcher, and they follow different paths of inquiry. As Burck (2005) indicates, "doing curiosity" without having to carry the therapeutic responsibility for change gives rise to "conversations of a different order" that can open up new areas of understanding while at the same time still allowing participants to discover significant connections for themselves.

Epistemological Positioning

The way we position the self in any research project is contingent on our epistemological beliefs. In Chapter 2, we conceptualized epistemology as a continuum between an objectivist and subjectivist stance. In the practice of science, objectivity has always been a matter to contend with. The credibility of research products is still often tied to questions of objectivity. Whereas positivist oriented research upholds this as an ideal, constructionist or critical research has problematized this practice.

In traditional, positivist research, the methodological directive was to position the researcher's self outside of the participant's experiential domain. Researcher bias was seen as the primary problem and as a result, there was an emphasis on finding ways to create distance between the researcher and participants. Classic double blind experiments serve as one means of separating the researcher from participants and maintaining a sense of blindness about the subjects and the conditions under which the data were collected. The effort to minimize "experimenter effects" and to address the "problem of bias" can result in a number of practical challenges. As Parker (1994) has argued, these efforts often end up as "unworkable correctives" that are undermined by "seepage" of information in patterns of relationships among researchers and subjects, heightened controls and therefore artificiality of the research situation, and the inevitable use of deception with subjects in order to ensure researcher and participant "blindness."

In the qualitative research tradition, objectivity and the problem of bias have been approached from a number of perspectives. In positivist oriented research, a number of strategies have been used to try to minimize the damaging effects of bias. For example, covert ethnographic research that has tried to get at naturalistically occurring behavior and activities insists on keeping the researcher's self at a distance from the naturally occurring activities of the field. The practice of reflexivity has also been used as a way to identify researcher biases on the assumption that identification and awareness of bias is a means by which to put that bias on the shelf so it does not interfere with or encumber the process of observing what is "really" happening with participants.

For qualitative researchers who uphold an objectivist epistemology, there is some consensus that the integrity of the research is enhanced not by creating distance from participants, but by the degree to which they are able to get closer to phenomena under study. Wolff (1964), for example, suggests that the best method for achieving "objectivity" is not for researchers to distance themselves, but to "surrender" to phenomena they wish to understand. This involves "total involvement, suspension of received notions, pertinence of everything, identification and the risk of being hurt" (p. 236). Only when researchers are close enough can phenomena reveal themselves. Then researchers are "being adequate to the object" (p. 236). Likewise, Blumer (1969) emphasizes the importance of the researcher "taking the role of the acting unit whose behavior he is studying" in order to get accurate data. To try to collect data from a distance is to risk "the worst kind of subjectivism" (p. 86) or the "fallacy of objectivism" (Denzin, 1978, p. 10). From this perspective, the assessment of validity is contingent on how closely the researcher can understand the account and its context in terms of who produced it, for whom, and why (Hammersley & Atkinson, 1983). Although the researcher is now accounted for in the relationship, the emphasis here is still on representing the participants' reality. As a result, this form of positioning is consistent with a postpositivist approach to research.

In the middle of the continuum between subjectivism and objectivism are strategies that seek to keep in play the principle of objectivity while placing the self more evidently in the research procedures. Keller (1985) makes a distinction between "static objectivity" and "dynamic objectivity." Whereas static objectivity is concerned with a search for knowledge that radically severs subject from object, "dynamic objectivity aims at a form of knowledge that grants to the world around us its independent integrity but does so in a way that remains cognizant of, indeed, relies on, our connectivity with that world" (p. 117). Dynamic objectivity is reflexive and keeps the researcher's self squarely inside the research process. This idea is consistent with what it means to be both subjective and objective in qualitative research. It does not mean removing the self, but on the contrary, immersing the self.

A subjectivist epistemology places a strong emphasis on making the researcher's voice fully apparent in research accounts. One of the most obvious examples of this is the use of autoethnography as a way of foregrounding the researchers' own experience as they seek to make sense of the culture of which they are a part (see Chapter 5). More broadly in ethnography, there has been increasing emphasis placed on the field researcher as author who produces texts that are laden with the author's meanings. As Atkinson (1992, p. 17) has argued, in spite of the traditional direction given to fieldworkers to "remember" and to record things as "accurately" as possible, they should be aware that there is no "complete" record to be made and "no neutral medium" for its production. Rather, field notes are already encoded with interpretive qualities that reconstruct versions of the social world (Atkinson, 1992). Reflexivity serves as the means by which researchers make sense of and construe their own experiential account of culture.

In participatory action research, subjectivity also comes to the foreground as researchers must be vigilant about the ways their own values, interests, and stakes shape the process of social transformation in the research. Reflexivity in participatory action research, or for that matter any other form of critical research, is a matter of reflecting self-consciously on the ways we contribute to the process of change by studying and influencing social practices. Researchers not only monitor and make apparent their subjective experience, but their political and ideological beliefs as well. In this approach, the distinction between "researcher" and "practitioner" is blurred:

> Practitioners regard themselves explicitly as engaged in action that makes history, and they are likely to regard research as a process of learning from action and history—a process conducted within action and history, not standing outside it in the role of recorder or commentator, or above it in the role of conductor or controller. (Kemmis & McTaggart, 2003, pp. 354–355)

Issues of Voice

Postmodernism places an emphasis on the diversity of experience and highlights the way dominant representations of reality have tended to blur the full spectrum of people's experiences. In postmodern approaches, multivocality is a principle that serves as a means to bring forward multiple perspectives and divergent experience. There is no interest in highlighting the authoritative voice or the correct version of reality. Rather, there is an interest in keeping all voices in play, regardless of the possibility that these may be in tension or contradictory. To be reflexive in postmodern qualitative research is to be keenly attentive to matters of voice. For researchers, this is a matter of weighing their own voice in the cacophony of opinions, ideas, and perceptions expressed by other participating voices in the research.

As Hertz (1997) outlined, there are a number of challenges that researchers face when they set out to present multiple voices. First, there are questions about how to present one's own voice as the author of the text; second, there are decisions about how to present the voices of participants in the text being written; and third, there are additional challenges when the researcher's self is also the subject of inquiry. Researchers still primarily use written texts as the medium for presenting these multiple voices. Although there is no simple formula for how to meet these challenges, the guiding principle is to present these voices (including one's own) with a concern for preserving the integrity, intent, and diversity of the messages, without overworking the participants' stories into a sanitized or "right" version of reality. We seek to maintain the distinctiveness of different voices and to keep in play some of the inevitable tensions and contradictions that arise in the understanding of complex social reality. As part of this, it is important to get beyond what Richardson (2003) has referred to as "acute and chronic passivity" in the way that voice is presented—either through the passive-voiced author or the passive "subjects" (p. 501).

Richardson (2003) has outlined a number of ways in which postmodern researchers can effectively bring forward voices through alternative means. These include use of dramatic textual performances, poetry, layered accounts, or readers' theater. Even writing in the usual form is not about "getting the story right," but rather about "getting it" with all its different contours and nuances (p. 511). Whatever the form of presentation, the researcher's self is always present and as a result, qualitative researchers are always learning about their topics and about themselves. In this regard, reflexivity not only fosters a deeper understanding of the voices of others, but a deeper understanding of one's own voice.

At a very practical level, each of us is faced with the decision of how to present our understanding of self and others in relation to the topic at hand. Although our goal may be to present in a fair and reasonable way the many voices that are part of our research, we may not always be successful in "giving all sides their due." For Gergen and Gergen (2003), one of the pitfalls of writing up qualitative results is that the voices of respondents may be overrun by the researcher's narration: "Typically the investigator functions as the ultimate author of the work (or the coordinator of the voices) and thus serves as the ultimate arbiter of inclusion, emphasis and integration" (p. 581). At the other extreme, researchers can adopt the position that they are presenting the respondents' voice and they have successfully and accurately captured and presented their stories. This is rooted in an assumption that "subjects' utterances are seen as transparent passageways into their experiences and selves" (Mauthner & Doucet, 2003, p. 423). Using critical reflexive practice, Mauthner and Doucet came to an awareness that people's accounts of their lives are not completely transparent, do involve ambiguous and selective representations, and are always incomplete. As a result, the authors suggest two strategies that arise from these reflexive insights. First, they are careful to explain how their own theories are developed out of the interaction between respondents' accounts and their interpretations of those accounts. Second, they pay more attention to the conditions and constraints under which the jointly constructed accounts are produced.

Issues of voice are even more complex in qualitative research that is conducted by a team. Using a postmodern standpoint, Bryan, Negretti, Christensen, and Stokes (2002) carried out a collaborative research project as part of a university course and, in the process, engaged in a form of team reflexivity. In other words, through focus groups and interviews that involved themselves as team members, they explored the collaborative experience of working through some of the team challenges, including hierarchies, authorship, and conflict. This served as a mechanism to make each of their voices—including perspectives, preferences, and concerns—transparent in the research process. Hence, while we tend to think of reflexivity as an individual endeavor in qualitative research, this project brings to the foreground some of the unique challenges associated with collaborative work.

Reflexivity Is Interpretive Practice

Reflexivity is at the heart of qualitative inquiry. Researchers are engaged, at all stages of inquiry, in a process of interpretation and meaning making that necessarily includes their own biography and social position. As a result, research questions are products of an interpretive process. Qualitative researchers enter into relationships with participants, engage in complex social settings, and seek to understand the meanings of their responses. Understanding participants' responses and realities necessarily includes our own realities and interpretive understandings of their experiences.

Reflexivity: Practices and Pitfalls

- Research involves a process of systematic inquiry; it is the means by which we document the assumptions, decisions, and interpretations that constitute the process of inquiry.
- Reflexivity involves the cultivation of good recording habits; designate a notebook, a handheld recorder, or open a file that will serve as a destination to store your unfolding ideas.
- Writing is a form of thinking; therefore the process of writing down reflexive ideas is a way of deepening the inner dialogue and engaging in the process of thinking and discovery.
- Random thoughts need not be fit into the overall picture at the time; you can fit them in later or ignore them if no longer relevant.
- Many insights only come along once; try to capture these when they do appear.
- Don't edit reflexive insights; follow intuitions and outrageous possibilities.
- Being fully reflexive means paying attention to thoughts, ideas, possible interpretations, emotions, and values.
- Reflexivity is a way of capturing how we arrived at our understandings and explanations; it is a means of documenting the logic behind the interpretive process.

Why Do We "Do" Reflexivity?

At the root of reflexive practice is an inherent assumption that this is virtuous activity. As Lynch (2000) has argued, there is now an established tradition within qualitative methods texts that not only advocates for the importance of reflexivity, but in fact extols it as an epistemological, moral, and political virtue. This is manifested in a variety of ways:

- By examining our own experiences and prejudices, we can be in a better position to address and control our personal bias.
- By scrutinizing our political standpoint, we can lay our values and interests on the table in order to prepare readers for what is to come.
- Through a process of self-critical examination, we can reduce the distortions of our own thinking and interpretations.

In all of these approaches, there is an underlying concern with getting at the truth and using reflexivity as a way of minimizing distortion and bias. Ontologically, this approach to reflexivity upholds a form of objectivism—we scrutinize the researcher's self as a way to keep it separate from the reality "out there" (i.e., objective reality) that we are trying to understand. Using reflexivity in this way is concerned with enhancing objectivity and is therefore consistent with positivist or postpositivist principles. In some of my own writings about reflexivity (Daly, 1997), I came to the awareness that I was using reflexivity in this way: I talked about personal experiences and perspectives and presented the awareness as a kind of guarantee to the reader that I would not let these get in the way of representing participants' stories.

Consistent with objectivist principles, Maxwell (2005) talks about the importance of scrutinizing researcher subjectivity as a means to understand bias. The emphasis here is on researchers' examining the ways their own values and expectations influence both the conduct and conclusions of the study in order to avoid any unwelcome consequences. These biases, unless scrutinized and managed, are viewed as a threat to the validity of the study. Although it is acknowledged that removing the influence of the researcher is impossible, there is a focus on limiting the negative effects of such bias and using an understanding of it to determine how the bias might affect the validity of the inferences that are drawn from the interview. The emphasis here is on scrutinizing bias in order to bring forward participants' accounts as accurately as possible.

In contrast to the idea of reflexivity as virtue is the idea that reflexivity is an unavoidable feature of the way all research actions are performed, made sense of, and produced as reports. This is rooted in a belief that it is impossible not to be reflexive in all aspects of research activity. As Stanley and Wise

(1983) argued some time ago, "One's self can't be left behind, it can only be omitted from discussion and written accounts of the research process. But it is an omission, a failure to discuss something which has been present in the research itself" (p. 262). The self is embedded in all forms of interpretation and meaning construction and is part of the embodied practices through which persons singly and together, prospectively and retrospectively, produce accounts of experience (Lynch, 2000). From this assumption, reflexivity works in different ways:

- It demonstrates the situated nature of knowledge construction.
- It exposes uncertainties and "messy contingencies."
- It is attentive to the conditions under which accounts are produced.

At a very practical level, reflexivity also serves as a means by which we can monitor how we are managing our relationships with participants. Specifically, by reflecting on what we do and say, we can assess and make adjustments about the following:

- The level of reciprocity in the research relationship: Is there a give and take? Am I sharing experiences and giving back while at the same time really listening to what is being said?
- A better understanding of our own interviewing style and the implications for how this shapes the outcome of the interview (e.g., do I minimize my own involvement or am I imposing my values or sharing excessively what I have learned or experienced?).
- By monitoring our personal involvement we can see how our empathy and sharing of experience can encourage talk but also see how our own emotions and experiences shape and/or limit how participants respond. Am I inappropriately leading the participant to specific answers (Rubin & Rubin, 2005)?
- Judgment is a normal part of any relationship. We continuously make judgments about what people do and what they say. The judgments we make in an interview can create discomfort, anger, or embarrassment—or empathy, compassion, or support. It is important to interpret what these emerging feelings might say about our understanding of the topic.
- Reflexive practice is also a way to be mindful of blind spots that may be limiting our ability to see (or hear) experiences that are beyond our familiar repertoire.

Reflexivity in Narrative Analysis

Mary Gergen (2004) was interested in the relative flexibility and fluidity of narratives. In other words, she was interested in the ways and conditions under which people chose to change the narrated accounts of their lives in the interview setting. The underlying assumption of this view is that narratives are coconstructions in the research setting that are shaped by the identity of the inquirer, the questions asked, the temporal–spatial characteristics of the interview, and the relationships among these various elements. The same story told at a cocktail party, a therapy session, or a funeral would have a different shape and story line. In narrative analysis, therefore, reflexivity is concerned with an examination of how we as researchers coconstruct the narrative through our own participation. To this end, we can be reflexive about the following:

- How do our silences, smiles, and frowns shape the way the story is told?
- How do our age, race/ethnicity, and/or gender lead to embellishments of some themes and suppression of others?
- How do our own experiences lead us to contribute to the story?

Gergen acknowledges that being reflective about our own role in the production of narrative accounts leads to some troubling questions about how we write up our narrative analyses. Specifically, she asks, "If we do acknowledge that narratives are not simply about others, can we still value them? Should we still do narrative analysis?" The answer is yes, but it means writing up our work in different ways:

- We acknowledge that we "collaborate" with participants in the collection of narratives
- We don't extricate ourselves from the jointly produced materials
- We are inspired to write reports in ways that demonstrate our "multiplicities, as speakers, writers, and analysts" (p. 281).

Reflexivity in Family Research

When qualitative researchers enter into the family domain, they temporarily become part of the family system. They are typically welcomed into the home, and although they may be treated with caution, they nevertheless become part of the network of interacting personalities. Lareau (2002), in her intensive observation studies of families in their homes (approximately 20 visits per family), reports that family dynamics do change when the researcher arrives—especially at the beginning. Specifically, while they were likely to be on their good behavior for the first couple of visits, yelling and cursing often resumed by the third visit.

One of the ways we can be reflexive in family situations is to consider how we shape our roles according to varying circumstances. There are many possibilities here, including passive observer, interactive inquirer, friend, detached inquirer, or participant in the sharing of family stories and experiences. The stance we adopt is a function of both our research interest and personal abilities that shape the course of our position as it changes and evolves in the research context. Being attentive to stance means being reflexive about our role as we attempt to manage our own place in the family dynamics.

When doing qualitative research with couples and families, there is always the potential for power alliances or being triangulated into relationships. When we interview people about personal aspects of their lives, it is not uncommon for them to invite some subtle acknowledgment and/or affirmation of their experiences, life-meaning, and/or feelings. Through our reactions of agreement, support, and interest on the one hand, or indifference or disapproval on the other hand, we give our participants relationship cues that communicate acceptance or rejection or withdrawal or support. In my interviews with infertile couples, I occasionally found myself in the midst of a potentially dangerous alliance that was difficult to avoid. In the following example, a husband and wife were having widely different experiences in the way they were coping with infertility and were having difficulty understanding each other's experience. As a result the wife turned to me to try to understand:

Wife: He doesn't know exactly how I feel and I find that hard to understand, because he is my husband and this is his problem too. He wants a child too. He just seems to be able to accept it so much easier without asking questions.

Husband: Well you just have to accept it, no?

Wife: Well I agree with him, you have to accept it because I have no choice. Like what am I going to do? I can't go on crying all my life. But what I can't understand is, "How can it be so much easier for him to accept than me?" How? (turning to me inquisitively)

For me to provide an answer to this question would be to form an alliance with the wife. By providing advice or an explanation, I would be working with her to explain him. After some initial squirming, I avoided being placed in the role of being both the expert and her ally by simply reflecting the same question back to her. In other words, I asked her why she thought it was easier for him to accept it, to which she responded with a long explanation about his family background. This technique was effective insofar as it served the respondent's need to understand her husband's behavior. More importantly, from my standpoint, it allowed me to manage the intimate space in a way that kept me in a more neutral role and the husband engaged in the interview.

This example highlights some of the complexities of gender mixed with the intricacies of participating in the dynamics of the family system. Reflecting on these positions provides an opportunity to monitor the ways we are both co-opted into the family and the ways we navigate our own role as researcher. Warren (2002) offers a similar experience while conducting research with female mental patients and their husbands. In this case, each wife and husband knew that the other was being interviewed, putting the interviewer in the middle of some awkward triadic relationships as each spouse sought to gather information about the other from the interviewer. On the surface, these raised questions about secrecy and loyalty; at a deeper level, they raised fundamental questions about ethics and confidentiality. Reflexivity about your role becomes critical to having clear guidelines for how to manage these kinds of difficult requests.

Reflexivity and Social Positioning

To be reflexive about social position is to be attentive to our own status characteristics such as race/ethnicity, class, age, sexual orientation, disability, and gender. Reflexivity about our social position is ongoing as we encounter different people throughout a project who have varying characteristics and backgrounds. Reflexivity about our own social positioning is necessary as a means to invoke a critical reflection on the ways we bring to the research our own position of privilege, our vulnerabilities, and ideological commitments (Allen, 2000). It is a means to raise our consciousness of the ways privilege and oppression operate in family life (in our own and in the lives of those we study) in order to be sensitive about how we generate knowledge that will be a catalyst for social change (Allen, 2000).

As part of this, it is important to recognize that all categories are internally diverse and do not come with easy formulas for how to conduct our role as researcher. For example, Kong, Mahoney, and Plummer (2002) have outlined the importance of moving from thinking of "homosexuality" as an objective, essentialist category to thinking about a de-essentialized experience that involves many different kinds of sensibilities and subjectively constructed names for that experience (e.g., queer, gay, lesbian, transsexual). Participants routinely have affiliations with many categories and as a result it is best to avoid making presumptions about participants based on membership in any one category (Schwalbe & Wolkomir, 2002). Furthermore, there is an "intersectionality" among categories such as gender, race, class, and sexual orientation that requires an attentiveness to their overlapping effects (Allen & Piercy, 2005). Reflexivity calls for us to consider how we might rigidly place ourselves in certain kinds of categories and to consider the ways our own sense of self changes within the research experience.

Although there has been an increasing emphasis placed on the importance of entering into nonhierarchical relationships with participants, there are always elements of power that are part of research relationships. These may be subtle or obvious—but there are always dynamics of status, control, and power that operate in these relationships. This has been referred to as the "baseline threat" that is built into any intensive interview situation insofar as agreement to participate in an interview, regardless of how friendly or conversational, involves giving up some personal control and risks having one's public persona altered in some way (Schwalbe & Wolkomir, 2002). Moreover, the dynamics are changeable and subject to situational fluctuations that require an ongoing vigilance about who we are in the situation and the power we hold.

Gender and Sexual Orientation

In research on families, gender plays a key role in how we shape our inquiry and interpret what participants tell us. As Järviluoma et al. (2003) have argued, research is not solely an activity of the brain, but is conducted by a person who has his or her own experience in the gendered world, operates within a gendered environment, has a sexual orientation, and ongoingly participates in the construction of gender in everyday life as well as in research. As a result of the pervasive role that gender plays in the research process, it is difficult to generalize about the ways the researcher's gender can influence the research interview (Johnson, 2002). Critical in this regard is to examine the nature of the research question. In my own research on the gendered nature of scheduling in families, I interviewed both women and men as part of the study. As it became increasingly evident in the interviews that women continued to play a dominant managerial role in the orchestration of family schedules, I, as a male, had to contend with some of my own struggles, questions, and—yes—defensiveness about not being in control of various decisions and dynamics. As a participant in these same kinds of family experiences, I needed to consider how my roles first as a son, then as a husband and father, shaped how I understood and responded to the experiences that were being conveyed to me. There were of course a range of responses, and I found myself aligning my own experience with some men's more than others'. At other times I was appreciative of the detailed descriptions wives were able to bring to their everyday routines. There were times when I was somewhat aghast at how pronounced the power differences were in these relationships; at other times I admired the fair and creative balance they seemed to have achieved. This was an area of family experience where women have traditionally exerted a great deal of power, and as a result, it was important for me to reflect on my experience as I conducted the interviews and puzzled through my interpretations of what I was hearing.

When we conduct interviews of members of the opposite sex, different challenges emerge as a result of social position. In an overview of research on men interviewing women, Reinharz and Chase (2002) point to examples where women were less likely to volunteer information about personal experiences when interviewed by a man; male interviewers had to be more mindful of where interviews were conducted in order to ensure women's safety; and men had to be deliberate about downplaying gender, desexualizing the interview in order to put women at ease. When conducting an in-home study of female seniors, Wenger (2002) reports that male interviewers were perceived as threatening and could not be trusted, resulting in higher refusal rates. Somewhat different challenges are reported by women interviewing men. As a female interviewer of divorced fathers, Arendell (1997) described how men were not only skeptical about her ability to understand and represent their experience as men, but they were often aggressively resistant in the interview, with dominance displays and assertions of superiority. Similarly, Wolkomir (see Schwalbe & Wolkomir, 2002) described the challenge of being a heterosexual woman interviewing gay men about their religious beliefs. In these kinds of situations, reflexivity serves as a means to strategize ways to manage the dynamics of control in the situation (Schwalbe & Wolkomir, 2002).

Oswald (2002) examined the way urban gay, lesbian, and queer adults who were raised in rural areas returned to their families and communities of origin to attend heterosexual family weddings. Writing from an insider perspective, Oswald traces what it means to negotiate their sense of self when returning to rural settings in relation to visibility/invisibility, closeness/distance, and comfort/discomfort during these weddings.

Class

In terms of class, a number of qualitative researchers have provided accounts of the importance of monitoring the effects of class differences on the research process. Sword (1999), for example, in her interviews with pregnant women on social assistance, talked about how conspicuous she felt in the way that she initially dressed as a white, middle-aged professional woman with economic and social resources. After some initial awkwardness, she was deliberate about dressing down as a way of reducing the class differences.

In contrast with Sword's experience of having to be mindful of the social class difference, Edwards (2004) writes from the perspective of one who had a class experience similar to participant's. In an analysis of working-class women living in two rural trailer park communities, she provides insight into the meanings women assign to the invisible labor of family identity management. She writes from the perspective of a white woman from a working-class family who lived in trailer park housing as a child and reports on the way her own experience influenced her analysis of the ways families monitor boundaries and manage impressions within the community and beyond.

Age

When researchers interview children, it is important they be reflexive when considering the dynamics of power that exist between an adult interviewer and a younger child. This imbalance is rooted in a number of structured conditions that make it difficult to reduce the status differential. According to Eder and Fingerson (2002), for example, researchers can never have equal status with children because of differences in cognitive, physical, and social development; the fact that children are always the "researched" and never the "researchers"; and children's lower social status resulting from a tradition of expecting children to respect and obey adults. Furthermore, as Nespor (1998) has argued, our understanding of children's perception of the research experience is quite limited. One way of understanding our own role in research with children is to ask children to be researchers themselves—asking questions of each other and taking the lead in the exploration of their own experience. This kind of practice, while at times disconcerting for the researcher, who must relinquish control, provides the opportunity to abandon adult-oriented perspectives that may be quite outside the everyday experience of kids (Nespor, 1998). Reflexive practice serves as a means for heightening awareness of adult assumptions and power imbalances. This awareness can serve as a basis for addressing these in the interview and finding ways to reciprocate and provide support to children and youth in the interview context.

Conducting studies with older people also introduces some unique challenges. Being reflexive about this means paying attention to our own age and the age differential in relation to those we are engaging in the research process. Although there may be a number of special challenges associated with interviewing seniors who might have cognitive or sensory impairments, it is also likely that they are "just like us but they've been alive longer" Wenger (2002). Nevertheless, reflexivity about age provides an opportunity to reflect on your own potentially ageist assumptions about the group you are researching. In a description of her research with older adults with Alzheimer's disease, Dupuis (1999) talks about the importance of "controlling in" rather than "controlling out" her emotions when trying to understand what were often difficult stories coming from her participants living in a long-term care facility. She describes her experience:

> At times I felt enraged and frustrated at the injustices being done to the residents and their family members. I felt terrified, helpless and the need to escape when one of my participants swung at me several times when I would not let him out the door he so desperately wanted to go through in his search for home. I frequently felt deep sadness and was often discouraged. (p. 50)

Race/Ethnicity

Through interviews, oral histories, and thick description, qualitative research has provided a means to understand experiences of personal and institutional racism. In the tradition of ethnography, qualitative research has also served as a means for seeing the experience of race, ethnicity, and culture more clearly. Being reflexive about our own subjectivity in relation to ethnic and racial representation becomes critical. In North America and Western Europe, however, being "white" is still often the unreflected-upon standard from which all other racial identities vary (Dunbar, Rodriguez, & Parker, 2002). Accordingly, researcher reflexivity must take into account these hegemonic forces. For example, Grahame (2003) examines how Asian immigrant women manage the demands of family, job training, and paid work in their new society where many work practices and family policies are built on the experiences of primarily middle-class white women. This research invokes a critical, reflexive awareness at several levels, including individual experience, institutional organization, and social policy.

Reflexivity on social positioning in all of these areas ultimately begs the question of the degree to which it is necessary for the researcher to share the same background characteristics of the participants. In other words, to what degree should men interview men, Latinos interview Latinos, or black women interview other black women? The answer is not straightforward. Morse (2002) tackles the question in relation to interviewing people who are ill, and her response is instructive. She argues that researchers who have training in the health care professions and those who have general social science backgrounds can each bring different agendas, theories, and perspectives to the research endeavor. Being open to different researcher backgrounds and perspectives provides a means for capturing the complex character of what it means to be ill (Morse, 2002).

On the other hand, there are many examples where the gap in social positioning is so great, or the power dynamics so unbalanced, that it is necessary to find a means to align the researcher's background more closely with the participants' experience. For example, in studies where there are extremely sensitive gendered experiences that include issues of misused power or abuse, it may be essential to have same-sex interviewers (Reinharz & Chase, 2002). In studies of racial or ethnic experience, researchers who do not share the same background need to be attentive to the ways their own worldview may lead to unsuccessful research interviews. Rossman and Rallis (2003) provide the example of an Anglophone student conducting research in a Hispanic community. The researcher asked narrative questions using a linear assumption about time, but the participants understood their own lives according to an assumption of important affective episodes that didn't necessarily follow an orderly sequence. Reflexivity serves as a means for scrutinizing these underlying assumptions and making any necessary modifications in the data collection effort.

Self-Positioning: How Do I Do This?

Sometimes our own social position characteristics (gender, race/ethnicity, class) are so deeply embedded and taken for granted that it is difficult to "see" how they are shaping our research roles and activity. Through a process of reflexivity, we invoke a deliberate awareness of these experiences. One way to start this process is to reflect on "epiphany" moments in our own experience where we are acutely aware of our social positioning. Open a file on this and begin by describing those experiences that come to mind. These might include occasions when you felt vulnerability, power, awkwardness, affirmation, conflict, or an experience of clear self-awareness. Think and write about what these imply for an understanding of your standpoint and perspective.

Balancing Vulnerability and Researcher Presence

Reflexivity serves as a means for monitoring our own subjectivity throughout the research process. When we write up the results of our qualitative research, there is always the question about the degree to which we include aspects of our reflexive accounts in these final products. Finding the right balance means attending to your epistemological beliefs and, at a more practical level, navigating your way through a number of potential criticisms. For example, given our rootedness in objectivist scientific practices, there is the potential that including too much of your own story can be criticized as a form of "emotional exhibitionism" (Kleinman, 1991). This may be accompanied by a feeling of vulnerability that comes with having your own experiences placed into the public forum. In some of my own research, I have provided disclosures about aspects of my own life, including involuntary childlessness and adoptive parenting. While I was never criticized for including this information, I was aware that I was sharing personal information in a very public way. By contrast, for researchers who do autoethnography, this is an intentional way of communicating the nuance of subjective experience. At the other end of the spectrum is the practice of not including any of our reflexive thoughts in the final written account of our research. Yet when we silence our own voice and strip out all reflexive thoughts and experiences, we risk presenting a one-sided form of objectivism where we render ourselves invisible. Friedrichs (1981) has referred to this practice in the write-up of research results as involving the "disembodied intellect" whose only role is to present analytic products that are devoid of any researcher subjectivity.

Conscious inclusion of our own biographical experiences and values can also play an important role in getting beyond the "universalizing impulse" in research in order to generate more inclusive studies of families and their complex diversities (Allen, 2000). When we reflect critically on the ambiguities and complexities of our own family experience, we can become vulnerable participants in the telling of the research story. At the same time, however, the interlacing of our own story with those of participants can become more credible and powerful in the telling (see, e.g., Allen, 2000; Miller, 1993).

9

Analytical Strategies

What Is Analysis in Qualitative Research?

A classic definition of analysis in qualitative research is that the "analyst seeks to provide an explicit rendering of the structure, order and patterns found among a group of participants" (Lofland, 1971, p. 7). Usually when we think about analysis in research, we think about it as a stage in the process. It occurs somewhere between the data collection phase and the write-up of the discussion. Under this narrow definition, analysis is about what we do with data once collected: it is concerned with how we bring conceptual order to observed experience. When using emergent designs, however, a stronger emphasis is placed on analysis as an activity concurrent with data collection. For example, in grounded theory studies, the analytic process can be thought of as a braid with data collection, analysis, and interpretation as the braided strands. There are two assumptions that underlie this approach. First, there is an assumption that analysis rests solely with the researcher. Second, there is an assumption that analysis begins when we start collection of data. In this chapter, I approach the discussion of analysis with a broadening of these assumptions.

Analysis Occurs Throughout the Research Process

Although there is typically a period in the research process where analysis is the main focus of activity, it is also important to think about analysis as something that occurs throughout the research endeavor. Analysis occurs at all stages of the research, from the articulation of the research problem to the discussion of implications for theory and practice. If we think about analysis as having to do with processes of selection, interpretation, and decision making, then when we make choices about who to talk to and the kinds of questions we want to ask, we are being analytic by virtue of setting a course for the research. Exclusion of some aspects of reality and inclusion of others at an early stage in a project profoundly shape the course of analysis in a project. When we transcribe data from verbal to written formats, we make decisions about sentence structure, pauses, intonation, and meaning. These micro-level decisions are also part of the analytic process. Analysis, at all stages of the project, involves being self-conscious and explicit about the way that we make decisions and give direction to the research process.

Analysis Is an Interactive Process Shaped by Participants and Researchers

In the spirit of a coconstructionist framework, it is important that we take into account the analytic interplay between the researcher and participants. When we engage with participants in an interview or focus group setting, it is important to recognize that our participants are also analytic. They interpret our questions (sometimes in quite different ways), are selective in what they choose to tell us, and, in their response to questions, are quite deliberate about organizing portrayals of their own experience. Their decisions shape the course of our analytic efforts. This is essentially an interactive process. As Kvale (1996) indicates, participants often begin with a description of their lived world, but in the course of the interaction with researchers, may come up with new meanings, interpretations, and connections in their own life world. When researchers offer on-the-spot interpretations of what participants are saying, the participants may in turn offer different explanations or "correctives" to the interpretations being made by the researcher. It is in this regard that the interactions that occur in an interview or an observational episode are part of collaborative meaning-making episodes that include many participants and many layers of interpretation and analysis. As part of this, there are times when researchers deliberately engage participants in a process of thinking through particular themes or interpretations (Rapley, 2004). Rather than gathering data from participants and then analyzing it, researchers can engage participants as partners in the knowledge production effort.

Analysis Is Thinking and Writing

Laurel Richardson (2003) talks about writing as a method of inquiry. While we often think of the final write-up of a project as a mode of telling about the social world, it is also a pervasive activity throughout a project that serves as a method of discovery and analysis. Through the process of writing at various stages in the project, we work through how we are thinking about our topic of inquiry and our relationship to it. From this perspective, writing is the means by which we make our analytic process manifest and available for review. According to Richardson, it is through writing that we word and reword the world we are studying. Writing is a research practice, not simply a research product, through which we express our analytic insights and constructions of lived experience.

Analysis Is a Process of Selection, Interpretation, and Abstraction

One of the reasons we do social scientific research is to come to a different understanding of the social world. In the absence of analysis, we would have largely undifferentiated descriptions of lived experience. Analyzing social reality is a process of thoughtful reflection whereby the researcher serves as a catalyst in the creation of an ordered, conceptual portrayal of the reality at hand. At the very least, in descriptive-oriented studies, this analytic process involves the selection of certain kinds of reality to study and present. Implicitly, this is a meaning-making process that involves the construction of that reality. In the same way that the photographer brings us snapshots of reality, the researcher brings to the reader meaningfully created windows on social reality. Moreover, in studies where the aim is to interpret these realities and generate explanation, this involves a process of abstraction that is a kind of "double hermeneutic" that involves the "dialectical interplay" between the subjective meaning of people's experiences described using everyday language and the researcher's reconstructions of that reality using emerging concepts and interpretations (Rothe, 1993). For the social scientist, it means articulating a conceptual (i.e., abstracting) language in an effort to order and understand everyday language and experience. For Schutz (1971), this involves creating "second order constructs," which are the "constructs of the constructs made by the actors on the social scene" (p. 6). Hence, although participants are contributors to the analytic process, it is typically the case that the researcher has the final word through analysis.

These assumptions, when taken together, create a portrayal of analysis that is "switched on" at the beginning of the project and that is shaped by decisions at all stages of the research; interactive influences of participants; and the active meaning-making process of coding, interpretation, and writing.

Analysis for What?

Given the range of epistemological assumptions and the diversity of methodologies, it is important to recognize that analysis has many purposes. At the most general level, we can consider several important distinctions that can guide our thinking about analysis:

Nomothetic and Idiographic

In the philosophy of science, there are two broad purposes for scientific analysis. Basing its name on the Latin root *nomos,* which means laws, consistencies, or regularities, nomothetic science is concerned with the analysis of social reality in order to identify patterns and uniformities (Crotty, 1998). By contrast, the Latin root *idios* can be translated to mean individual or idiosyncratic aspects of reality. Idiographic science is therefore concerned with the analysis of the individual in order to understand that which is unique and is concerned with the variability of individual behavior. When we conduct qualitative research, we can do either idiographic or nomothetic research, or some combination of the two. For example, when we conduct case study research, we are primarily interested in understanding the unique ways that individuals in families navigate relationships and make choices about their own lives. In nomothetic research, we might be more inclined to interview many people and seek to understand some of the patterned ways or shared meanings that people have in their lives. For example, in grounded theory studies, the goal of research is to create categories that reflect some of these common experiences. As a result, there is often a tension in qualitative research between examining and maintaining the integrity of the individual case in research, and the tendency toward fragmentation of the case in order to identify themes, patterns, and uniformities. Both provide valuable information—and they can be used compatibly in research projects.

Emic and Etic

When we conduct qualitative research, there is a tension that exists between the insider accounts of those who are experiencing the phenomenon (i.e., emic) and the outsider perspectives of the researcher or observer who is examining that experience (i.e., etic). The way we as researchers align ourselves with these perspectives has profound implications for how we conduct analysis.

The emic perspective most closely aligns with an idiographic approach, which is a case-based position that focuses on the specifics and constraints of everyday life (Denzin & Lincoln, 2003). Furthermore, an emic perspective also seeks to understand the multiple ways in which cultural insiders view the reality of which they are a part in order to understand why people think and act in the different ways they do (Fetterman, 1998). An etic perspective, by contrast, places a greater emphasis on the ways in which preexisting theory or empirical findings can shape how researchers orient their own inquiry and make sense of the results.

The tension between emic and etic perspectives has been particularly salient in ethnographic research. It has highlighted the representational challenges associated with having an outsider ethnographer with an etic perspective observe and portray the beliefs and practices of everyday cultural life as they are experienced within (the emic perspective). There are a number of ways that researchers have approached this tension between insider and outsider accounts. Morse and Richards (2002), for example, argue that ethnography is best conducted by researchers (i.e., using an etic perspective) who are not part of the cultural group being studied because they can see more clearly the beliefs, practices, and values of participants by virtue of being outside that group. At the same time, there has been a critical dialogue within ethnography that has questioned the "production of texts that gave the researcher-as-author the power to represent the subject's story" (Denzin & Lincoln, 2003, p. 21). From this perspective, the etic viewpoint is problematized. A third position would argue that both emic and etic positions are markers along a continuum of different analytic styles (Fetterman, 1998). In this regard, the argument is that both emic and etic are necessary for good analysis, whereby the qualitative researcher starts with the cultural native's emic point of view but then seeks to make sense of those data in relation to the etic tools of scientific theory and prior research.

When we ask the question, "Analysis for what?" the distinction between emic and etic raises a fundamental question about how we think about the products of our research efforts and the degree to which they represent outsider and/or insider perspectives. How we think about the products of our analysis is contingent on our epistemological beliefs. If our beliefs are rooted in a positivist or postpositivist paradigm, then a leaning toward an etic perspective is consistent with those beliefs. If, on the other hand, our approach is social constructionist or postmodern, then there is a blurring of the boundaries between etic and emic whereby research accounts are viewed as "interpretations of interpretations" (Geertz, 1973, 1983) or second-order stories (Daly, 1997). In this regard, insider and outsider views are necessarily confounded as they interactively contribute to the construction of analytic outcomes.

Description Versus Explanation

Although the boundary between description and explanation is not a clear one, there is a good deal of divergence among qualitative approaches with respect to the degree to which researchers are expected to produce theory (explanation) or description as analytic outcomes. Grounded theory methodology has been most explicit with respect to the importance of generating theoretical explanation as an outcome of analysis. In their original work, Glaser and Strauss (1967) argue that theory generation is a necessary component of a grounded theory approach. Theory is inductively generated through a process of comparative analysis of grounded data. Theory is by nature a form of explanation that goes beyond description and involves the construction of categories, properties, and their relationships. The goal of ongoing theorizing activity within grounded theory is to generate empirical generalizations that can both delimit and broaden the theory so that it is "more generally applicable and has greater explanatory and predictive power" (Glaser & Strauss, 1967, p. 24). Although theoretical explanation has been viewed as a necessary element of grounded theory work (LaRossa, 2005), it would appear that theoretical explanation is often missing in the final products of grounded theory research (see Daly, 1997).

By contrast, ethnographic and phenomenological approaches have placed a greater emphasis on description. For example, within the ethnographic tradition, "thick description" (Geertz, 1973) has stood out as the primary analytical aim. In phenomenology, the goal of the research is to examine a phenomenon among participants by paying attention to "first hand experiences that that they can describe as they actually took place" (Giorgi & Giorgi, 2003, p. 27). In both of these traditions, the primary goal is to capture as closely as possible the descriptions of lived experience in a particular context.

Although these methodologies place different emphasis on the importance of description and explanation, it is prudent to think of this as a matter of degree. For example, it is not possible to present anything that even approaches "pure description," for all accounts of reality that are put forward in research reports involve a number of analytical features. It is necessary to be attentive to the conditions under which the descriptive accounts were produced; it is important to provide commentary on how and why some accounts are brought forward and others not; and it is necessary to be attentive to the ways certain themes or topics are chosen as part of the representation of descriptive accounts. Similarly, it is difficult to think about "pure explanation" in qualitative research without the benefit of rich descriptive accounts that ground and give vitality to the inductive theories.

When embarking on the analysis of data, it may also be useful to make the distinction between analysis and interpretation. Like description and explanation, we can differentiate the conceptual meanings they hold; however, it is difficult to separate them when engaged in the process of doing analytic/interpretive work. Definitions of analysis focus on the process of identifying or separating something into component parts. Dictionary definitions use key phrases such as "examining the constitution," "showing the essence," or "ascertaining the constituents" (*Concise Oxford Dictionary of Current English [Oxford Dictionary]*, 1990). Interpretation focuses on the process by which we make meaning of a component part. Here, the dictionary definitions emphasize "to understand," "bringing out," or "explaining the meaning of" (*Oxford Dictionary*, 1990). Hence, when we examine data, we are engaged in a recursive process of analysis and interpretation whereby we go back and forth between trying to see the component parts and the meanings that these have for understanding the broader phenomenon (see Figure 9.1).

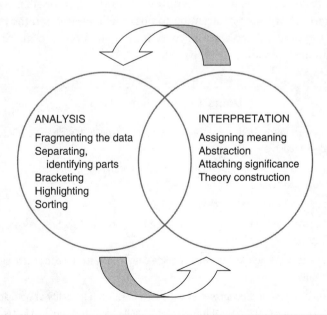

Figure 9.1   The Interplay Between Analysis and Interpretation

Transcription as Part of Analysis

Researchers sometimes make reference to a stack of transcripts or a folder filled with field notes as their "raw data." The implication is that these are unprocessed or unanalyzed segments of experience. The "accurate" production of transcripts is therefore rooted in a realist ontology (Poland, 2002). This in turn is built on the assumption that the interview itself is a representation of a social reality that is experienced and expressed by participants. Based on a realist assumption, the way transcriptions are done can raise important questions about reliability and validity of the data (Kvale, 1996). These are assessed on the basis of whether the verbatim transcript is seen as "a faithful reproduction of the oral record, with the latter being taken as the indisputable record of the interview" (Poland, 2002, p. 635).

It is important to recognize, however, that field notes and transcriptions are in fact "textual products" (Atkinson, 1992, p. 5). This involves a process of construction beginning with the practical transactions and activities of data collection, the literary activities of writing field notes, and drawing on literary and grammatical conventions when transforming verbal accounts into textual accounts. Transcription itself is a type of representation that involves selection and reduction (Riessman, 1993). It also involves many decisions not only about what was said, but how it was said (Poland, 2002). Hence in contrast to a realist approach to transcription, a postmodern or social constructionist approach would pay attention to both the interview and the transcript as a "co-authored conversation in context . . . that is open to multiple alternative readings" (Poland, 2002, p. 635).

Doing Transcription: Setup

1. Ensure that respondent ID, date, and time of interview are clearly outlined as a header on each page.

2. Set margins so there is approximately one third of the page open on the right-hand side for open coding.

3. Number all lines of text for easy reference.

4. Be consistent in the transcription of nonverbal expressions (laughing, crying, pauses, hesitations, etc.).

5. Be sure to make note of statements made with a sarcastic tone, or expressed with insincerity.

6. Set up a system of pseudonyms in order to protect confidentiality of participants—keep a glossary of these substitutions in a separate file that is kept in a locked place.

7. When using the services of transcribers, it is important that they be made aware of their ethical obligation to maintain confidentiality.

Like the process of analysis itself, it may be helpful to think about transcription as a process that involves different considerations at various stages. In the early stages of any data collection effort, there are good reasons to do some first transcriptions on your own. Sitting down to listen carefully to a taped interview provides you with the opportunity to reexperience the interview at a slow pace. Engaging in this process, as difficult and as onerous as it may seem, is an opportunity to maximize attentiveness to what was said. It is important at the outset of this activity to have a structure for building on preliminary insights gained in the interview. Memoing during these first transcriptions is an excellent way to capture first interpretations of what is happening with the participant.

Doing your own transcribing at these early stages serves a number of purposes:

- Opportunity to develop a system of dealing with pauses, expressions of emotion, lack of clarity in the tape, and commentary on what might have been happening at the time in terms of interruptions or outside influences
- Appreciation for the challenges associated with turning talk into text—for example, decisions about where to put punctuation in spoken words and the implication for reading the text, how to handle tone of voice or phrases that are strongly emphasized, how to handle situations that may be "tongue in cheek," how to deal with overlapping talk
- Greater appreciation of how questions shape responses and the importance of looking at the data transcript as a dialogue

Once you have done several transcripts—and if the research budget allows—it is valuable to have someone help with the transcription. Keep in mind when enlisting the services of a transcriber that it takes approximately 4 or 5 hours to transcribe one hour of tape (although this will vary depending on the level of detail required—e.g., more time would be required for conversation analysis). When making the transition from doing it yourself to having someone else do it, the following may be helpful:

- Sit down with the transcriber and review the transcription techniques you used: What techniques did you use to deal with pauses, expressions, and grammatical conventions?
- Once the transcriber has done one transcription, it is useful to listen to the tape and review the transcript. You might then request modifications in style or technique, based on this review.

In the final stages of the research, you may wish to be more selective about what is transcribed. This is a utilitarian stage of data collection that can be more focused on transcribing the areas most directly relevant to the emerging analysis. In grounded theory work, for example, transcription may focus on areas that contribute to theoretical saturation of categories or further development of the substantive theory. This involves selective coding in order to work toward the saturation of categories. Although it may be optimal to have the entire set of interviews transcribed, this may not be practical. This approach is an efficiency strategy that is contingent on having reached a level of confidence in the theory generation process. It does, however, require clear and specific directions about what parts of the interview should be transcribed.

Choice Points: How Much Detail to Provide?

Transcription, the transformation from oral to written text, always involves some level of selectivity. Macnaghten and Myers (2004) offer some choice points: The key is not which is right, but being consistent in how the transcripts are done.

- Using conventional spelling versus using spelling to indicate pronunciation (e.g., "So, I said to him..." versus "Sooooo, I said to him...")
- Indicating pauses versus leaving them out in favor of running text
- Including utterances (e.g., "uh-huh") or repetitive words versus ignoring these

In making these decisions, more is not necessarily better: "using a transcript that is more detailed than one needs is like giving a few unnecessary decimal places on one's statistics" (Macnaghten & Myers, 2004, p. 74).

Analytic Approaches in Various Methodologies

Every methodology, by virtue of its underlying assumptions and theoretical principles, approaches the analysis of data in a different way. As a result, there may be a different focus for analysis or a different language for analysis in each of the methodologies. Although there are some distinctive features in each of these methodologies, it is also the case that each of them has variation within its own traditions. For example, given the long history of ethnography and its development in a number of different disciplines, the number of analytic approaches is quite large. In grounded theory, there is not just one approach to analysis; due in part to a disagreement between the originators, there are several. In the discussion that follows, I have tried to capture some of the key components of each approach. Nevertheless, it is important to remember that these analytic approaches within methodologies are varied and at times contested.

At the same time, however, there are many similarities across methodologies and the intention is not to place rigid boundaries around any one of these approaches. In practice, there are many parallels between analytic approaches, and some methods are used in conjunction with each other. For example, Kvale (1996) talks about looking for the narrative structure in phenomenological research. Charmaz and Mitchell (2001) have explored the ways grounded theory methods can be used in ethnography. In a study of family dynamics in relation to childhood disability, Kelly (2005) uses a combination of ethnographic observations at a medical clinic, narrative interviews, and grounded theory analytic techniques. Hence there is both variability within these analytic approaches and permeability in the boundaries among these approaches.

One of the common features of all methodologies is the emphasis placed on doing analysis and interpretation as data collection proceeds. This is the intertwined "braid" of collection, analysis, and interpretation that is central to carrying out research that has an emergent and inductive orientation. This avoids what Kvale (1995) referred to as the 1,000-page problem that occurs when analysis waits until all of the data are collected. Analysis that is concurrent with data collection helps to focus the data collection effort and move toward analytic accounts that are full and saturated.

Some of the distinctive features of analysis for various methodologies follow.

Phenomenology

The starting point for any phenomenological analysis is the description of lived experience that is provided by the participant. Most important, the analyst's job is to see the world through participants' eyes. In more specific terms, phenomenological analysis is interested in "elucidating both that which appears and the manner in which it appears . . . it attempts to describe in detail the content and structure of the subjects' consciousness, to grasp the qualitative diversity of their experiences and to explicate their essential meanings" (Kvale, 1996, p. 53). This is a process of maintaining "fidelity to the phenomena" as they are experienced by participants (Kvale, 1996). To this end, there are several steps in phenomenological analysis (as outlined by Giorgi & Giorgi, 2003):

Attend to the Phenomenon Being Studied. Analysis begins with the descriptions provided by participants. The researcher reads and rereads transcriptions of the interview or written accounts of experience in order to see and appreciate the subjective experience of the participant. At this stage, the researcher adopts a stance of deliberate naiveté in order to see the experience as the participant would see it.

The Constitution of Parts. Descriptions of experiential reality given in a phenomenological interview are often long and detailed; it is therefore useful to break down these accounts into meaningful parts. The researcher pulls apart the holistic account into meaning units that are formed by careful rereading of the description. This involves identifying "experiential structures that make up the experience" (van Maanen, 1990). It is a process of meaning condensation whereby the researcher marks off "natural" meaning units from complicated passages and then explicates their main themes (Kvale, 1996). At a practical level, this means focusing on the primary research question and eliminating digressions in the data.

Transforming Meanings in Data From Implicit to Explicit. Although rooted in description of lived experience, it is "ultimately meanings that phenomenological analysis seeks to discover" (Giorgi & Giorgi, 2003, p. 33). Researchers transform "raw data" into meaningful segments by a process of converting what are implicit or unarticulated meanings in lived experience so they explicitly render visible the meanings that play a role in the experience of the participant (Giorgi & Giorgi, 2003). This is essentially an interpretive process that involves the identification of themes and the assignment of thematic labels (Smith & Osborn, 2003). This transformation process of making meanings explicit involves not only highlighting the meaning that arises from the concrete experience, but also generalizing that meaning by identifying that it is an example of something and then showing what it is an example of.

Articulating the Structure of Experience. Analysis at this level involves reviewing the identified meaning units across cases in order to highlight the typically essential units. This is a procedure of creating typologies and underlying meaning structures that are based on the recognition of common constituent elements. This is a process that involves connecting similar themes and clustering them together under broader conceptual labels. Usually in an analysis of this type, there would be variability in the experience of participants that would result in not just a single structure, but several. The overall aim is to identify the underlying essence of the phenomena being studied. In this regard, rather than focusing only on the particulars of individual experience, there is an effort to understand the essential elements of that experience by comparing across cases. In a study of 103 caregivers living with a family member with Alzheimer's disease, researchers conducted a phenomenological analysis by identifying 38 preliminary structural elements in the data, followed by a refinement to 8 structural elements, and concluding with a synthesis statement about the nature of the experience (Holkup, Butcher, & Buckwalter, 2000). Typologies provide another strategy for organizing findings that show similarities, differences, and overlaps between and within classes of phenomena and are valuable for sorting through complex human behaviors in a variety of settings (Gilgun, 20005b).

Narrative

In narrative analysis, the central focus is on the way individuals tell the story of their own experience. Accordingly, we are interested in the content of the story itself—the events and activities that are included in the story—and the way the account or the narrative is constructed. When doing narrative analysis, it is important that we keep in mind that a story is a part of a person's life and not simply a representation of some other life. In other words, narratives are constitutive of a person's life, for it is through the telling of the story that meaning of life is communicated and identity is presented. In the study of human development and family relationships, narrative analysis is a means by which we can understand the life course itself. According to Daiute and Lightfoot (2004), narrating is inherently developmental and as a result, analysis of narratives can serve to examine the following:

- How does the story organize the experiences of one's life?
- What are the time and space frames that emerge as important in the organization of the story and the person's life?
- How do flashbacks and foreshadows enter into the present telling of the story?
- How does the story encompass other people, events, motivations, and judgments?
- What kinds of values and morals are included in the story?
- What are the internal and interpersonal conflicts that are experienced?

In keeping with this developmental focus, narratives also serve as a means for analyzing and understanding identities. Bamberg (2004), for example, suggests that the construction of story content is the construction of identity for the storytelling subject. In this regard, narrative analysis is also concerned with matters of positioning. When individuals story their lives, they are agentic and must always make choices about how they position themselves in relation to a wide range of competing and potentially contradictory discourses. As a result, the way the story is told in relation to various discourses becomes a matter of self-marking or positioning. Narrative analysis thereby becomes a matter of examining the identities of storytellers by looking at how "they actively and agentively position themselves in talk—in particular with and in their stories—[with] an assumption the orderliness of story talk is situationally and interactively accomplished" (Bamberg, 2004, p. 137). Through this type of narrative analysis, stories are not simply tales of preexisting identities; they are actively constructed positions that are shaped by the demands and choices available in any interactive situation.

Narrative analysis is also critical for understanding the relationship between individual stories and family stories. According to Pratt and Fiese (2004), the stories of individuals and families are intertwined across the life course and as a result, they can provide insight into both individual development and family systems of change. Accordingly, narrative analysis can contribute to an understanding of this relationship in three ways (Pratt & Fiese, 2004). First, storytelling can be understood as an act through which children learn to become competent narrators of their own lives. Second, stories can be analyzed according to the message that provides lessons about values and cultural mores. Finally, stories can be analyzed for the ways they support the creation of personal identity that evolves over time within the context of the family.

When our focus of attention is on family stories, there are a number of analytical strategies that can be used. According to McAdams (2004), there are two different kinds of family stories that can be analyzed. The first type is stories told by family members in the presence of one another that may or may not be about family events but that serve to connect family members across generations and create a sense of family history and identity. These stories can be analyzed according to the standpoint of practice (How was the story told?) and the standpoint of representation (What was the story about? What were the main themes in the story?). The second type of family stories that are told about family may or may not include other family members as audience to the story. These are stories about family that are generated in order to make sense of turning points in one's own life or to account for and make sense of one's identity in relation to family experience.

Narratives can also be analyzed according to their temporal structure. Gergen and Gergen (1984) identify three types of stories that are concerned with the relationship between the self and the processes of transformation:

Progressive: In these stories, the protagonist tells a story of progress and growth that involves an increasing sense of integration and cohesion. These are stories of success, coming of age, and healthy transitions in development. They typically show an awareness of how change is occurring in relation to other people and events.

Stable: These are stories where there is little evidence of transformation. Events that do occur are not perceived to be significant or life altering. Rather, they are included in the story as events and episodes of interest but that have little impact on identity or the assessment on one's own development.

Regressive: These are often stories of adversity that involve "coming undone" or unraveling. These experiences lead to emotional anguish, loss, and in severe situations suicide or attempted suicide. These stories are often archetypal and contain common themes of decline, regression, and disintegration.

Narrative analysis, then, provides a means for gaining insight into the way people story their own lives. It provides a means for examining both the process by which people create and reconstruct that story and the kinds of events and experiences they identify is being salient in that construction. When doing narrative analysis, we must always pay attention to the relationship between how the story has been told and how the story has been received by the listener. In qualitative research, we are one of those listeners, and we play an important role in the way we interpret the narrative account that is provided. Hence, when analyzing stories, we can think of the analysis of narrative being divided into two phases: descriptive and interpretive (Murray, 2003):

Descriptive. The focus of analysis here is to provide an overview of the plot by examining both the content and structure of the story. In terms of content, this involves highlighting characters and their relationships, describing settings, and providing an overview of key events. The analysis of structure involves examining the temporal sequence of the story according to a beginning, middle, and end; the identification of subplots that may exist within the main narrative; and the identification of key turning points or epiphanies in the story line. The analysis of structure also involves looking at the way the story is embedded in the context of relationships, family experience, or broader social and cultural events. We might also analyze a set of stories for gender differences in the way women and men tell the story, use language, or emphasize different kinds of experiences. Riessman (1993) suggests that when we analyze for the structure of the story, there are a number of questions we can ask:

- How is the story organized?
- Why does the informant tell the story in the way she chose to tell it?
- How did the audience for the story (potentially just you as the researcher) influence the way the story was told?
- What is taken for granted by speaker and listener?
- How is this story situated in social, cultural, or institutional discourses?
- Who has or is given power in (or through) the story?

- Whose voice is prominent in the final product?
- Are there different "poetic structures" in the narratives? For example, do participants use different vocabularies or construct the story in different ways?

Interpretive. As researchers, we are in a position both to elicit and to interpret narratives from participants. As a result, it is important that we pay attention to our own assumptions, beliefs, and similar stories when we listen to stories from our participants. In contrast to the traditional distinction between active storyteller and passive audience, interpretation of narratives occurs at the interface between the narrator's intention and the reader's meaning making of the story. Narrative interpretation is a hermeneutic process that involves the correlation of participant and researcher meanings. As part of this interpretive process, the researcher may examine ways the story can be understood within a variety of theoretical frameworks in an effort to understand, for example, the meaning of a particular experience such as loss, providing care, or being in a love relationship. At a more abstract level, stories can be interpreted in relation to theoretical accounts of the meaning of emotions, patterned relationships, or family dynamics. Of critical importance in the interpretive analysis of narratives is to consider the degree to which multiple interpretations of the same story are possible. Specifically, "How open is the text to other readings?" (Riessman, 1993, p. 61).

Although narrative analysis in the qualitative tradition has focused on the descriptive and interpretive aspects of the story, other researchers have focused on ways to score and code the thematic content of family narratives (Fiese & Spagnola, 2005). While these approaches take a quantitative orientation to analysis, they may serve as a useful companion to qualitative narrative analysis.

Ethnography

The analysis of ethnographic data seeks to provide detailed description and interpretation of the way individuals or groups conduct themselves within the context of culture. The term thick description (Geertz, 1973) places the emphasis on providing detailed accounts of these cultural experiences. The primary emphasis is to describe and analyze the specific and particular aspects of a social setting that is grounded in the local. Accordingly, ethnographic analysis involves providing detailed accounts of when, where, and how events occur in the situation. Spradley (1980) refers to this stage of analysis as the "grand tour" where the researcher orients the reader to the main features of the culture or subculture under study. This "tour" involves being a narrator of the cultural story through writing about what you have observed and seen.

Ethnographic analysis involves both the provision of descriptive accounts of what was observed and interpretive commentaries on the meanings of the cultural experiences. Interpretations become the means by which researchers make comparisons with other cultural groups and provide commentary on the meanings that their observations hold. These descriptive accounts involve the interpretation of "what is going on," which can occur in relation to a number of focal areas:

Key Events. These are social activities that occur within the culture or sub-culture that can be analyzed for meaning. These can be celebrations, key meetings in an organization, ritual, or unexpected occurrences. In families, they are memorable events (weddings, funerals), transitions (launching children, retirement), or difficult turning points (separation, accident, illness). Why are these events significant? In what ways do these events help us to understand the values and practices of the individuals being studied? Who are the key actors in these events and why and how are their roles important?

Patterns. The identification of activity or behavioral patterns involves a process of comparison among participants in the culture. This can include routine activities that are similar across participants and can also include common meanings that they bring to their experience. What are the common cultural meanings that people bring to objects, places, or situations? When examining ethnographic data for patterns, researchers can look for themes or construct typologies that reflect different patterns of activities (Lofland, 1971). Similarly, they can create various types of classification systems or taxonomies that have the function of naming and displaying data in a way that shows relationships among components of the data.

Space and Time. One of the strengths of an ethnographic approach is that it examines social and cultural practices in situ. As a result, analysis needs to be attentive to an examination of where and how events and activities occur. Specifically, what are the characteristics of the physical place where these events occur? Are there unique features of this space and place? Maps that provide visual representations of homes, communities, or organizations can serve as a useful tool in the analysis of activity (Fetterman, 1998). Analyzing for temporal experience is also valuable. What is the sequencing of events? How important was time in these activities? Was there a past, present, or future orientation to the activities? How do activities or beliefs change over time?

Cultural Meanings and Themes. Although ethnographic analysis is concerned with the identification and description of specific parts within a culture, it is also concerned with the systems of meaning within a culture that have to do with collective beliefs, practices, values, symbols, and world-views. These are the cultural themes that are recurrent, have a high degree of generality, and reflect shared assumptions about the nature of commonly held experience (Spradley, 1980). These cultural themes can be explicit and taken for granted (as indicated through rules, public norms, or announcements) or tacit (whereby people do not express them easily but nevertheless understand the implicit and unspoken meanings). For example, in some of my own research with fathers, although men made reference to working in a company that had an explicit family-friendly creed, they also referred to a tacit cultural norm: There was some danger for men who took advantage of flexibility strategies in the workplace because of a set of values and practices that primarily supported women in relation to these initiatives.

When our emphasis in ethnographic analysis is on families, there are a number ways that we can analyze for family experience:

Family as Context. When our focus is on individual actors within families, then families become a means by which we make sense of those individual lives within context. For example, if we are interested in understanding the activities and experiences of an aging parent who has moved into a son or daughter's home, then we can examine the ways that both the aging parent and the son or daughter's family must adapt to this transition. If our focus is on the meaning of the transition for the aging parent, then the family is a primary context for understanding this change.

Family in Context. When the family itself is the primary level of analysis, ethnographic analysis is interested in understanding the patterns of activity that go on in families within the context of a broader cultural system. For example, if we were to examine how families act in a religious organization setting, we could look at how their activities and behaviors as a family are shaped by the norms and practices of the religious organization. Specifically, we could look at the interactions between parents and children in the context of the religious organization in order to determine how parents seek to influence children and how children endeavor to influence parents. We might also examine other kinds of intergenerational influences that shape ongoing participation in that religious culture.

Grounded Theory

Grounded theory, like *participant observation,* is an oxymoronic term. In our everyday language, we think of something that is "grounded" as being rooted, concrete, visible, and tangible. By contrast, "theory" is anything but grounded: abstract, ephemeral, hypothetical, and transsituational. Hence, when we talk about grounded theory analysis, it is important that we be mindful of this underlying contradiction or tension. At the root of grounded theory analysis is the dynamic interplay between observations grounded in experience and conceptualizations abstracted from those observations. Metaphorically, this process of analysis is like lengthening the spine in a yoga exercise: at the same time you lengthen the spine by allowing the tailbone to drop closer to the ground, you are also allowing your spine to extend through the top of your head. Grounded theory analysis is like this: simultaneous stretching down through to the ground and up through the head.

Epistemologically, this "stretching" involves a recursive cycle of inductive and deductive reasoning. Although grounded theory typically places an emphasis on the inductive creation of theory from observation, it also involves the deductive testing of various ideas that either existed prior to the research or emerged as part of the research. This is consistent with the original version of grounded theory (Glaser & Strauss, 1967), which talked about the primacy of generating theory while at the same time using existing or emerging ideas as a basis for theory verification. When we carry out grounded theory interviews using the principles of theoretical sampling, we begin to develop a stock of knowledge about the research questions that we then feed back to our participants as a way of verifying our understanding of the phenomenon (Johnson, 2002).

Although not a part of some of the original grounded theory writings, abduction also plays an important role in grounded theory analysis. As discussed in Chapter 3, abduction is a form of reasoning that involves a process of inference to the best explanation that links together theories, observation, and interpretation. In abductive reasoning, the focus is not on finding the correct explanation, but rather on using a variety of theories and ideas to generate insights and interpretations that provide the most meaningful way of making sense of the data (Dey, 2004). Furthermore, when using the processes of induction, deduction, and abduction in grounded theory research, it is also important to consider paradigm positioning as objectivist, constructivist, and postmodern assumptions will lead to different kinds of analytic approaches (see Chapters 3 and 5 for a review of these).

In grounded theory analysis, there are two fundamental principles that shape the overall approach to analysis: the importance of emergent design and the importance of theory as an outcome.

The Importance of Emergent Design for Understanding Grounded Theory Analysis. In an effort to be fully attentive to understanding the way participants describe their experience, grounded theory approaches typically begin with limited structure and an open-ended approach to questioning and data collection. Embedded in this approach is an assumption that we can learn the right questions to ask by listening to what participants have to tell us. Although we always approach our inquiry with theoretical sensitivities that come from prior theory, research, and experience, we enter into the data collection phase with an effort to suspend preconceived ideas and remain open to new meanings, interpretations, and understandings.

At the root of an emergent design is the methodological principle of theoretical sampling. Theoretical sampling is a means for making analytic decisions throughout the research project. Theoretical sampling involves making choices about who to talk to next, what kinds of questions to ask, and where to look for meaningful information that will contribute to our understanding of the phenomenon at hand. In this regard, theoretical sampling is inherently analytical insofar as it involves assessments of what we understand at any point in time and decisions about how to deepen that understanding through subsequent data collection efforts. In grounded theory, analysis and interpretation cannot wait until all of the data are collected; rather, it must occur in the earliest stages of data collection. Fundamental to grounded theory analysis is that the researcher concurrently collects, codes, and analyzes data in order to decide what data to collect next and where to find them.

The management of an emergent design is contingent on making excellent notes throughout the process as a way of tracking decisions, recording insights, and generating theoretical ideas. In grounded theory research, these are known as memos and can serve both to shape the direction of the inquiry and serve as a record of the key methodological decisions that have been made in the research process (see text box on different kinds of memos).

Theory Is the Goal of Grounded Theory Research. In the same way that ethnography places thick description as the primary analytical outcome of the research, grounded theory methodology has theory as the main outcome. Generating theory is essentially a nomothetic process. In order to understand how something works under specific circumstances, it is necessary to identify the patterns through comparative analysis. Grounded theory is built on the premise of constant comparative analysis, which involves comparing new segments of data with other segments of data and existing interpretations. Through the process of comparison and the identification of similar elements and processes across cases, themes, patterns, and categories are created that reflect uniformities in the data. These are the basis upon which theoretical explanation is generated. In grounded theory analysis, the construction of a theory that helps to explain the specific topic at hand is referred to as substantive theory. This is an explanation that is built from a set of grounded categories that are systematically interrelated and that serve to explain who, what, where, when, how, why, and with what consequences a specific phenomenon occurs (Strauss & Corbin, 1998). In the study of families, substantive theories would be at the level of explaining marriage adjustment during retirement, adult children returning home to live with parents, or the parenting experience of fathers of children with special needs.

Substantive theory serves as the basis for generating a more abstract form of theory that is known as formal theory. Formal theories are explanations constructed from the specifics of a substantive theory that, when compared with the similarities of other substantive domains, have the power to provide a more generic and abstract form of explanation. Formal theory is therefore more versatile and can be used to explain abstract features of social action and behavior. For example, in the study of families one could construct a formal theory of care by examining how care is understood in a variety of substantive domains that involve the provision of care including parents of young children, adult children to their aging parents, or siblings providing care to each other. A formal theory would build an explanation of care that included the common and essential elements of caregiving across those substantive domains.

Types of Memos

Memo writing is a means to actively record the process of conducting a grounded theory study. There are many different types of memos. Strauss (1987) provides an excellent account of different kinds of memos illustrated with examples from his hospital research. In summary form, here are some of the different kinds of memos you might write as a way of thinking through your analysis:

Textual Memos: These are descriptions of how we are thinking about a code we have assigned to a data segment, or how we have assigned names and meanings to data. Strauss (1987) also refers to these as preliminary and orienting memos and encourages researchers to stop coding in order to capture interpretive ideas that emerge along the way. This is a way to capture early hunches and interpretations.

Observational Memos: Given the emphasis placed on talk in interviews and transcriptions, it is important to write memos that help to preserve context. These memos focus on what our other senses are telling us in the research—what we have seen, felt, tasted, or experienced while doing the research. This is a good place to pay attention to intuitions too!

Conceptual/Theoretical Memos: As the question, "What is going on here?" rings through our heads, it is important to write about the development of a category or how one or

(Continued)

(Continued)

more concepts are directing us to think about a category as being important. As Richardson (2003) has indicated, writing is thinking, and sometimes just starting the process of writing out our hunches helps us with the process of developing our ideas. These memos are crucial in theory development as they allow us to puzzle about category relationships and possible pathways for integrating the theory.

Operational Memos: These are memos that are very practical. They might have to do with remembering to ask a new question that arose in a previous interview. These may also be about sampling strategies, how I might go about trying to achieve saturation on a category, or thoughts about who I might talk to next. These are memos primarily having to do with methodological procedure.

Reflexive Memos: This is a broad category and it potentially cuts across all others. These are essentially observations of ourselves—our voice, our impact, and our changing roles throughout the research process. Through these memos, we pay attention to our arising values, feelings, mistakes, embarrassments, and personal insights and reflect on the implications for how we are making sense of the data.

Stages of Grounded Theory Analysis

Analysis in grounded theory occurs in a number of different stages:

Stage I: Open Coding and the Creation of Concepts

Once the first verbal data have been transcribed it is necessary to begin immediately with the process of data analysis. Open coding is a way of opening up the data in order to explore what it means. Line-by-line analysis does not necessarily mean giving a label to every single line of text, but rather providing labels to those data segments that can be marked off in a meaningful way (After all, a line of text is arbitrary, depending on where you set the margins!). Like any other process that is early in the stages of discovery, it is important to "try out" various codes or labels without worrying too much about "getting it right." Assigning a code to data is a matter of choosing a word or creating a phrase that serves to indicate the meaning of a segment of data. This is essentially a creative process whereby we allow our reading of the data to invoke or provoke a set of meaningful labels. The names we use are also somewhat arbitrary in so far as other researchers might use other labels depending on their background and interpretations (Strauss & Corbin, 1998). In the early stages it is best not to be too choosy but to bring a word to something that stands out for us as being potentially meaningful or important. Sometimes we bring a name to this data episode; other times we might borrow a word from the participant that seems to stand out as having particular importance. For example, in our interviews with single parent families about how they managed time, we coded one segment "learning to be late" after one woman used this term to describe the time stress of getting her young children ready; in another segment where a woman described her minute-by-minute micro-schedule for getting to work on time, we brought to it the term "fragile." In the first example of coding we borrowed from the language of the participant; in the second we imported a term that we thought was apt.

Questions to Help in Coding Data (from Charmaz, 2003a)

- What is going on here?
- What are people saying or doing?
- What is being taken for granted?
- How does the context shape what is happening here?
- What is the nature of the process?
- Under what conditions did this process develop?
- What is contributing to change in this process?

Coding, then, is essentially a process of naming segments of data. Strauss (1959), based on an interpretation of John Dewey's work, argues that naming is central to any human's cognition of the world. To name is to provide an indication of an object, event, or action that can then serve as a basis for identification and classification. To assign a name to an event or an action is to indicate that it is part of a class of events that inherently involve locating, placing, and marking of boundaries. Open coding of a transcript involves exploring many possibilities for the data by assigning names to indicators that we see when we read through the data.

As our analysis deepens through the process of coding transcripts, we begin to see similarities in our participants' descriptions of events and activities. These common indicators give rise to labels that we call concepts. A concept is a label or name that we create that arises from repeated indications in the data that we then group together as a concept (LaRossa, 2005). Concepts are the basic building blocks of theory, and they involve grouping together under a common heading similar events, happenings, or objects that the researcher identifies as being significant in the data (Strauss & Corbin, 1998). Concepts that emerged early on in the coding of our interviews about time included stress, couple time, over-scheduled, or need for down time.

During the open coding stage of analysis, the primary focus is on breaking down or fragmenting the data into manageable segments and opening the search for common codes that can be brought together as concepts with shared characteristics. In the days before computers, transcripts would be coded and physically cut up and placed in piles according to the common characteristics of the codes. I think of this as the traditional shoebox method whereby similar instances in the data are coded and classified together in separate "boxes" so that the researcher can begin to see the patterns across the data. Most software analysis programs begin with a process of creating electronic "shoeboxes."

The Power of Naming

Consider the power of naming in other contexts:

1. Usually when we think about names, we think about how they shape identity. The power of the name is most evident when people change names as a result of family events (like marriage or adoption). The change in name can precipitate a new way of looking at self and shifts the interactions with this person.

2. Changes in role designation that are attached to a name also are powerful in changing how we think about a person. When a lesbian or gay couple decide to have a child, the way they create parenting names for themselves is important for how they think about their roles and how they wish to be seen.

3. Naming plays an important role in diagnosis and can help people to deal with illness. Naming helps to identify the problem and can help to overcome the anxiety associated with uncertainty. For example, when we can name a disease, we know better what to do or how to approach it.

4. Naming in therapy is also helpful in enabling us to move forward with the process of change. Labeling emotions or putting a name to recurring and troubling events in relationships provides a pathway for change.

Naming in all of these different forms serves a number of key functions. Naming brings clarity to complex and troubling matters, it offers a means by which to move from uncertainty to certainty, it helps us to see a phenomenon in a different and more focused way, it provides a kind of "phenomenological address" for the experience that is useful in locating it among similar kinds of experience, and it functions to provide guidelines for social action.

A name assigned to a segment of data functions in similar ways. It helps us to "see" the experience in a more focused way, and it provides the phenomenological address or a means to position the experience in relation to other meaningful events. Naming can also help us to move forward with our thinking about complex phenomena.

Stage II: Creating Categories

Concepts that are created in the process of coding are eventually brought together at a higher level of abstraction known as categories. The formation of categories usually occurs only after there has been enough coding to begin to see broader themes in the data. Although the distinction between a code and a category has been the subject of some confusion (see LaRossa, 2005), the creation of categories is an essential part of the theorizing activity. Categories involve bringing together not only concepts that have similarities, but concepts that are "putatively dissimilar but still allied" (LaRossa, 2005, p. 843). Bringing together similar and dissimilar but allied concepts creates an emphasis on internal continuities and variability. This range of variability within a category is known as identifying the properties of a category, which in turn may have different dimensions. Properties are the characteristics or attributes of a category, whereas dimensions reflect a continuum or a range within a property (Strauss & Corbin, 1998).

For example, in my own research on dual-earner families' perceptions of family time, participants gave a number of indications in the data that they were "investing time for the sake of the children" (concept) or thinking about "spending time" (concept) in order to "create memories" (concept) for the children. These repeated indications gave rise to the category of "banking family time." The idea of "banking" moved these concepts to a higher level of abstraction. There were a number of properties that were associated with this category, including the idea that family time was commodified like money, it had a future orientation like investments, and that there was an expectation of dividends that would accrue over time (see Daly, 2001).

This stage of analysis involves the processes of abstraction and, increasingly, synthesis. The construction of categories serves as the primary means by which we begin to organize and synthesize the data into meaningful groupings. It is also the means by which we begin the process of reducing complex experiential data into more manageable segments.

At this stage of analysis, however, there may be many categories. This is often the stage of greatest complexity in a qualitative research project. It may be useful at this stage to begin to map on a large sheet of paper the kinds of categories and related codes that are emerging. This is sometimes experienced as a valley of despair where there are too many codes, categories, and properties and not enough understanding of how it all fits together. Nevertheless, it is important to stay with the complexity at this stage in order to stay open to a number of theoretical possibilities. Furthermore, as categories begin to take shape, it is important to consider how subsequent interviews can help to saturate our understanding and interpretations of the properties and dimensions associated with these categories.

To Count or Not to Count: How to Respond to the Question!

I have received countless reviews for papers submitted to journals that ask for some indication of the frequency that underlies the presentation of a theme or category. Usually the question is something like, "Wouldn't it be useful information to know how many people were thinking in this way?"

Counting qualitative codes can provide useful information when there is a research design that supports this activity. Specifically, counting makes sense when (a) there is a structured interview that includes the same questions for all participants and (b) the sample is randomly chosen. Both of these components are necessary in order to have a meaningful interpretation of the frequencies.

Counting qualitative codes is not appropriate when researchers follow the principles of emergent design and theoretical sampling. In these studies, the frequency of response is directly related to the frequency of the question. If we are strategically asking the question in some interviews and not others as a way of building theory, then frequency tells us little about the importance of the category. Furthermore, when we use theoretical sampling, we are sampling for kinds of experiences, or specific activities, or lingering puzzles in our theory development. Again, these are inconsistent and uneven activities that readily skew the meaning of frequencies.

Having said all of that, the nomothetic principles underlying a grounded theory approach are implicitly quantitative. One of the reasons why we might create a category is that there are a number of concepts and indicators that are frequently present in the data and that therefore point to its importance and salience. Similarly, the selection of a core category is in part related to the frequency with which it appears in the data. However, assigning numbers to these categories can be misleading. Rather, the focus needs to stay on the way the presented categories reflect the shared and patterned experience of participants.

Stage III: Making Linkages in the Data

In Stages I and II of analysis, the emphasis is on dissecting experience by breaking it down into meaningful parts. When we map these out on a sheet of paper, we may see many parts but have a limited understanding of how they fit together. In order to create a theoretical explanation, however, it is not enough to show what the parts are, it is necessary to build an explanation about how the parts work together. This stage of analysis has been referred to as axial coding, and its purpose is to reassemble data that were fractured during open coding (Strauss & Corbin, 1998).

Axial coding involves looking at relationships within a category and between categories. Category constructions are still somewhat fluid at this stage of analysis. We may have created several categories that are quite similar to one another, and one possibility would be to collapse these together into a more abstract category that would have different properties and dimensions. This then becomes a process of internal axial coding within the category where the aim is to articulate how component parts contribute to the meaningful coherence of the category. This may include paying attention to a variety of characteristics associated with the category, including process, strategies, causes, contexts, contingencies, consequences, covariances, and conditions (Strauss & Corbin, 1990). The key to building these categories is to identify the core "axis" upon which the category is built. This occurs through comparison with other categories and then making linkages between categories when there is a logic to bring them together under one categorical umbrella.

As categories increasingly take shape through the process of axial coding, it is important to work toward theoretical saturation of each category. A category is saturated when no new information emerges to help deepen the meaning of the category. This is always a matter of degree since it is always possible to rework a category or add new ways of thinking about it or some aspect of it. In practical terms, saturation is "a matter of reaching the point in the research where collecting additional data seems counterproductive; the 'new' that is uncovered does not add that much more to the explanation at the time" (Strauss & Corbin, 1998, p. 136).

Axial coding also occurs among and between the many categories that have been created. The goal here is to examine how these categories are related and connected to one another. Part of this exercise is to scrutinize the extent to which categories can stand on their own as a cluster of meanings and the extent to which they overlap with, or are connected in some way to, other categories. Writing memos about these relationships among categories can serve to reduce the number of categories but also elaborate the relationships that exist among the categories.

For example, in my study of infertile couples who were seeking to adopt, I created several categories that in some way related to the experience of loss: loss of fertility and the biological capacity to reproduce, loss of the anticipated and desired role of being a biological parent, and loss of control over their own individual and family development. The common axis here was loss; rather than treating these as three separate categories, they could be treated as one category that focused on loss with several properties: loss of control over body, loss of social status, and loss of future developmental experience. As these theoretical ideas evolved, they later came to have linkages with the properties of a formal theory of ambiguous loss as put forth by Pauline Boss (1999).

Stage IV: Creating the Theoretical Story Line

To generate a substantive theory is to tell a story about the stories our participants have told us. In this regard, grounded theories are like a second order story (Daly, 1997) insofar as they involve creating a narrative from the analysis we have conducted. At this stage of the analysis, not only do we put the fragments back together, but we are selective about how to tell the story, which involves highlighting key elements and salient features (i.e., deciding on our main categories); creating a context for the story; and offering explanation of relationships, processes, and experiences. Like the creation of any good story, generating substantive theory involves choices about what to include and what to exclude. Sometimes the most disconcerting part of creating the theoretical story line is deciding what parts of our data to ignore and leave out of the final theoretical account (you can always come back to them for a different type of analysis).

Selective coding is the term coined by Strauss and Corbin (1990, 1998) to describe the process of integrating and refining the theory. Although some qualitative research studies report a listing of main themes, this falls short of the creation of an integrated theory. To theorize is to place an emphasis not only on what the categories are, but on how they are related to one another. At this stage of analysis, abduction can play an important role in generating an explanation that integrates the key categories that have emerged from the data.

Selective coding begins with the identification of the core or central category. This is like finding the narrative spine for the substantive theory. Accordingly, the central category has the power to pull together a number of categories in order to generate the central explanation. Usually the core category is one that stands out from all the other categories. It has the following characteristics (Strauss, 1987):

- It has centrality, and is "at the heart of the analysis" (p. 36).
- All major categories are related to it in some way.
- It appears frequently and is grounded in the data through a variety of indicators and concepts.
- Through the articulation of properties and dimensions, it allows for maximum variability in the data.
- It is sufficiently abstract to subsume many of the interpretive ideas being brought forward, while at the same time having the potential to build toward a more general formal theory.

Sometimes the core category is not present in the existing array of categories and as a result a new one must be formed that can serve to integrate the theory. This may be a modification of an existing category or it may be the creation of a superseding category from existing concepts that helps to provide a theoretical explanation of relationships among various categories.

One of the techniques that may be helpful in trying to find this integrating core is to think imaginatively about metaphors that might be useful in bringing the data together. The essence of a metaphor is to experience and understand one thing in terms of another (Richardson, 2003): What does this phenomenon remind me of? What are similar kinds of stories that might help me see this more clearly? For example, in a study of the challenges associated with having a fertility problem, Sandelowski (1993) used the metaphorical term *mazing* as a core category to integrate her theoretical account of going through medical treatments and pursuing options through reproductive technologies. Like the stressed lab rat that runs through the maze and faces endless dead ends and convoluted corridors, individuals who encounter a fertility problem encounter similar kinds of challenges. Mazing served as a useful metaphor for integrating the many components of the infertility experience.

In a study of father–mother relationships in 40 married couples with young children, Matta and Knudson-Martin (2006) give a good example in their refereed journal article of how to describe succinctly the process of grounded theory analysis. In three short paragraphs they provide examples of how they moved from open to selective coding: (1) open coding: data organized and labeled to reflect what they were hearing, including "father ignores mother influence" or "father encourages mother's feedback and influence"; (2) axial coding was done to identify and define categories—as a result, the way that fathers experienced the mother's influence, or the way that fathers read signals coming from their wives took shape as a category they called "atunement"; (3) in the final stage of selective coding and the development of theory, "responsivity" emerged as a core category that served as the basis of their theorizing about how responsivity arises within couple processes with attention given to the factors that shape these processes (e.g., perceptions of power, work schedules, sensitivity to signals).

How Do We Know a Good Substantive Theory When We See One?

- Linked closely to the data: faithful to everyday reality
- Saturated: Categories have a range of properties that show similarities as well as variability—this might also include reference to the negative case (see Strauss & Corbin, 1998, p. 159)
- Plausible: The theory is plausible in relation to everyday reality—that is, it passes the phenomenological test
- Involves explanation: The account goes beyond description and is labeled as a theoretical explanation

(Continued)

(Continued)

- Integrated: Category linkages are clear and understandable
- Parsimony: Elegance is achieved through simplicity; the theory is focused and brings clarity out of complexity
- Delimited: Tells a story about some aspect of reality
- Generative and not definitive: Raises new questions and puzzles
- Not overly simplified: Includes contradictions and keeps the "messiness" of life in play (i.e., avoids sanitized theory)
- Available for linkages to formal theory: There is potential to theorize about generic social action

The Diamond Approach: A Theory Development Model for Qualitative Data Analysis

The analytic procedures involved in a grounded theory approach, and indeed in many other approaches to analysis, can be conceptualized as a diamond (see Figure 9.2). At the bottom of the diamond, we begin with a pointed question. Through the process of inquiry, we open many strands of data. As we fracture the data through the process of open coding, we work toward maximizing the number of possibilities or lines of analysis in the data (Stage I). It is at this stage that it is easy to get lost in the complexity of the data. There are too many points of light! Our purpose in these early stages of analysis is to stay open to the many possibilities for how we might code our data. This is consistent with being attentive to the range of possible experience, suspending preconceived ideas, and staying open to many analytical possibilities.

In any project, however, there comes a time when it is too difficult to keep everything in play, and we must begin the process of refinement of data and the creation of categories that can help to narrow the range of analytical possibilities (Stage II). When we cluster data into meaningful categories, we begin the process of data selection and reduction. Although this may happen somewhat unevenly (i.e., categories are created at different times), there is often a phase in the analysis where we actively examine the range of our codes in order to group them to build meaningful categories.

As our categories begin to coalesce, we are also interested in the ways newly formed categories are linked to each other. Using axial coding (Stage III), we work to explore the relationships among the categories. In the same way that Stage I involved fracturing experience into manageable parts, Stage III

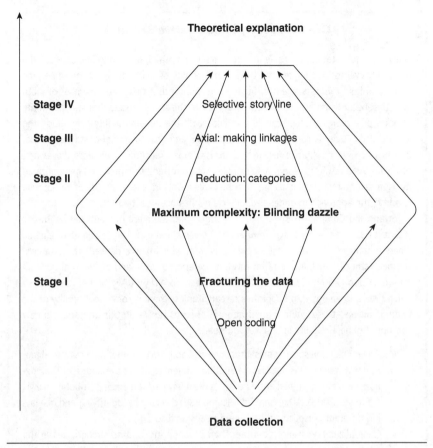

Figure 9.2   The Diamond Model of Analysis

involves looking at how these parts are connected in the everyday unity of experience. In this regard, these linkages are part of a process of reconstructing the lives that were previously deconstructed so that we might understand that experience in a different light.

In Stage IV, the final stage of analysis, we move toward a plateau on the diamond that reduces the complexity of the middle stages while at the same time allowing selected points of light to shine through. This condensed layer is the theoretical explanation that is brought forward. It involves generating the central story line that will provide insight into the phenomenon at hand in a way that is engaging, concise, and reflective of the key aspects of the experience being studied.

Generalizability in Qualitative Research

One of the gold standards of scientific research is maintaining a strong link between the representativeness of samples and the generalizability of the findings. At the same time that we uphold this as a scientific ideal, we recognize that there are a number of problems that occur when we put this into practice: "In the social process that starts with the creation of a representative sample and ends with the generalizability of findings, the researchers' activity is constantly driven by biases and organizational obstacles" (Gobo, 2004, p.436). In qualitative research, there is a broad recognition of these biases and obstacles. As a result, representative samples are not often attempted and generalizability is frequently dismissed as an unachievable goal. In the tradition of qualitative research, the approach to generalizability claims has been cautious.

Straus and Corbin (1998), for example, argue that the merit of a substantive theory is that it has explanatory power in relation to given situations such as stigma or chronic illness within the bounds of the populations from which it was derived. This is a constrained form of generalization that has been referred to as a kind of "internal generalization." Gobo (2004) raises this important question: "Why do we bother to invest so much time and energy into qualitative research unless there is some applicability of the findings beyond these internal applications?" The answer lies in thinking about a new concept of generalizability in qualitative research:

- An emphasis on social representativeness (Gobo, 2004) rather than statistical representativeness. This involves generating inferences about the nature of the phenomenon being studied, rather than its prevalence or statistical distribution (Lewis & Ritchie, 2003). Accordingly, it encompasses diversity by identifying and displaying different perspectives, behaviors, needs, and so on.
- Generalizability is analytic rather than probabilistic, and its strength lies in the application of the results: that is, the extent to which the data illuminate the social and individual processes of new settings (Gilgun, 2001, 2005b). Are the findings useful when applied to understanding new settings?
- Its purpose is to identify the regularities of a phenomenon or the general structures of experience. It contributes to an appreciation of generic concepts (Prus, 1987; see also Chapter 3 in this volume). These are analytic outcomes that help us to understand better the fundamental principles of social action and human behavior.
- It is concerned with the "transferability" of results (Lincoln & Guba, 1985). By describing fully the processes and conditions under which the data were generated, decisions can be made by people in other similar situations as to whether the descriptions or explanations are an adequate fit to that new situation.

Analysis in qualitative research comes in many different forms. We started this chapter with a classic definition of analysis that focused on the "explicit rendering" of the patterns found among a group of participants. Much of what we do in qualitative inquiry fits within this definition. Yet in the work of conducting our own analytic work, it is important to think about the ways in which analytical decisions occur throughout all stages of the research, the ways our participants directly influence and shape the course of analysis, and the way our chosen methodological approaches give a unique character to the analysis endeavor.

10

Integrity Practices

The Ethics, Credibility, and Politics of Conducting Qualitative Research

Near the beginning of the book, I introduced the idea that integrity is an important measure of quality in qualitative research. Integrity can be defined as a process of trying to achieve the qualities of soundness and consistency among values, beliefs, and methodological strategies. Given the central importance of the researcher's self as an engaged, feeling, and interpreting participant in all aspects of the research process, integrity serves as an overriding standard that brings together the ethical character of the researcher, respect for the welfare and best interests of participants, and the quality of the research product. Integrity therefore serves as a basis for examining ethical guidelines, practices to ensure credibility of our research process and results, and finally, a discussion of how to present the written reports of our research in a way that is authentic, convincing, and transparent.

Ethical Guidelines

When we do qualitative research with individuals and families, we engage in a process of scrutinizing private experience with the intention of making that experience publicly understandable. To do this responsibly is a profound ethical challenge. Although therapy and research rest on fundamentally different assumptions and follow different pathways, the underlying ethical sensibilities are quite similar. Research interviews, like therapeutic interviews, have the potential to generate positive insight and behavioral change while at the same time carrying the potential for damaging outcomes.

At the core of our qualitative research practice are a number of ethical values and practices that govern our conduct. As Kvale (1996) has argued, conducting research with human beings is a moral as well as a scientific enterprise. As such, ethical choices are made throughout all aspects of the research, including how we recruit participants; establish and maintain respectful relationships with them; and how data are collected, managed, analyzed, and reported. At all of these stages, we make a multitude of decisions. Rarely are there specific ethical rules for how we make these decisions; rather we must draw on ethical principles in determining how best to act with integrity. In essence, this means acting in ways that not only protect participants from harm but seek to respect their values and dignity and to preserve and enhance their sense of well-being and integrity.

Although there is some variation in the way institutions and organizations outline their protocols for research ethics, there are a number of key underlying themes that are essential when conducting qualitative research.

Informed Consent

The ethical standard of informed consent is built on the assumption that participants need to be given complete information about the purpose of the study, how it will be conducted, and whether there are any risks to their well-being—all before they agree to participate in the study. Specifically, they must be informed about the following:

- The voluntary nature of their participation and that they can withdraw at any time
- Who is conducting the study (including the persons they will encounter and the organizations that are supporting and/or funding the research)
- The purpose of the study
- How the results will be used
- The specific expectations for their contribution: how much time is involved, where the research activity will occur, how many times they will be asked to be involved
- How many participants are in the study
- Whether the exchange will be recorded and transcribed
- How data will be stored and presented in order to protect confidentiality
- An indication of when and how data will be disposed of
- Researchers' professional code of conduct, which requires that they must report instances of abuse

- In consenting to participate in this study, participants need to know they are in no way obligated to continue to participate in the future (i.e., they are free to withdraw from the study at any time even after they have given consent or participated in an interview, with no penalties of any kind)
- Outline of the risks and benefits of the study
- How participants will learn the results of the study
- Who they can contact if they have other questions about the research

These conditions for consent can be provided verbally or in a written form. After reviewing these conditions, it is important to invite participants to ask additional questions about the study in order to ensure that they have an opportunity to express concerns or bring forward queries about any aspect of the research.

In qualitative research practice, informed consent is an ideal that we strive to achieve, but our success in meeting this ideal is always a matter of degree. The principles of emergent design and the use of unstructured or semistructured questionnaire formats are by definition somewhat unpredictable in the direction they will take. Inductive, qualitative research is designed for discovery, and as a result the uncertainty of course and outcome makes it very difficult to inform participants fully at the outset about the content of the research. As family therapists who do qualitative research remind us, questions of any kind are by nature "interventive" (Burck, 2005) and as a result, the way answers are created in the research situation can result in surprising and unanticipated disclosures.

This raises important questions about how and when we get informed consent from participants when doing qualitative research. For example, one of the standard requirements on most institutional ethics protocols is to provide a questionnaire. This is problematic in an emergent design. While examples of questions may be given, a rationale for the absence of questions is usually necessary. Implicit in this request to an ethics review committee is the message, "Trust me." Accordingly, we must take this trust very seriously as the research unfolds: through reflexive practice and through monitoring and checking with our participants to ensure that they are informed as the research unfolds. Hence, whereas more-structured research designs seek to get full consent before the research is carried out, in emergent designs it may be necessary to get consent at different time points. One strategy here is to follow standard practice where we inform participants about the study prior to the data collection phases but then follow that up by revisiting the consent after the interview or observation has been conducted. This would help to ensure that participants are consenting fully to participate based on what was said rather than what they were about to say. Although this is already covered in most protocols by the statement that participants are "free to withdraw at anytime," revisiting the consent is an explicit and proactive strategy that brings participants closer to being fully informed. At a broader level, this shifts our thinking about consent as a single-point-in-time event to a component of the research relationship.

Informed consent is also a matter of our being transparent about personal assumptions, theoretical vantage points, and political agendas when we conduct research. Although all research is inherently political because it carries with it a bundle of values, perspectives, and aims, not all research is explicit about these components. Therefore when we engage participants in the aims of our research, it is important that we be open about purposes and interests. Once again, we do this at various stages in the research process—at the outset to inform our participants about what we hope to accomplish by doing the research, and throughout as we respond to their questions about how the data will be used.

Reflexivity and Ethics: Feminist Perspectives

Although ethical rules and guidelines play an important role in the way we carry out our research, these are never absolute and rarely do they cover all of the situational contingencies we are likely to encounter. As a result, it is important for researchers to invoke reflexive, contextualized reasoning that includes feelings and emotions where the self is placed within ethical negotiations (Birch, Miller, Mauthner & Jessop, 2002). Ethical quandaries emerge in the process of managing our research relationships, and as a result it is necessary to consider reflexively the values and interests at stake and work to ensure, in an open and negotiated way, that there is respect and protection for all parties. This involves adopting an ethic of care as a central component of professional research practice. A feminist ethic of care serves as a basis for deciding how to deal with conflict, disagreement, and ambivalence rather than attempting to eliminate it (Edwards & Mauthner, 2002). Specifically, an ethic of care serves as a means for understanding the moral dilemmas that do emerge in the research process and formulating meaningful strategies for moving through them. Questions such as the following serve as a means for making decisions with an ethic of care (Edwards & Mauthner, 2002):

- Who are the people affected by the ethical dilemma?
- How does the context influence the way that the dilemma is being experienced personally and socially?
- What are the needs of those most involved and how are they interrelated?
- Who am I (as researcher) identifying with?
- What is the balance of personal and social power among those involved?
- How can we best communicate the ethical dilemmas to those most involved, give them room to raise their own views, and negotiate with and between them?

Research focusing on mothers and poverty by Dodson and Schmalzbauer (2005) provides valuable insight into the ethical challenges that researchers encounter when dealing with sensitive topics. When working with marginalized populations, researchers not only have to contend with the power imbalance that exists between a university-educated researcher and someone living in poverty, but they must contend with participants' self-protective practices, the fear that accompanies facing power, and the possibility that the researcher is perceived as part of the "enemy." For the researcher, the ethical challenge is one of learning how to build knowledge with participants without disrupting their ways of protecting themselves and their families (Dodson & Schmalzbauer, 2005).

Protecting Participants Through Confidentiality and Anonymity

When we work with human participants, it is essential that we protect their identity by carefully removing, and in some cases masking, specific details that might in some way reveal who they are. This can be challenging when we do case studies or do research with participants in the same community as our home university. Especially when in smaller communities, we need to be vigilant about ensuring that identifying information is removed. A standard procedure in my own research is to follow this practice, which is communicated to participants:

> All information that you provide in questionnaires or interviews/focus groups will be kept confidential. Specifically, documents will be identified with a number only; all names will be removed; documents will be kept in a locked filing cabinet; and no names or identifying information will be used when reporting the results of the study. If we use your exact words in a quote, we will make every effort to ensure that no one will be able to identify you.

Simply removing information that would reveal an identity may not be enough. In some cases it may be necessary to change certain background information such as occupational status or the ages of the children in order to protect participants from being identified. A footnote indicating that this has been done is appropriate. Even when we follow these kinds of procedures, absolute guarantees of anonymity cannot be promised; participants must be made aware of this risk.

One of the unique challenges of doing research with couples or families is setting up a design that establishes a level of confidentiality within the family. When doing interviews with members of a couple, for example, it is quite easy to get into a situation where we are drawn into a discussion of the couple's reality with knowledge that comes from an interview with the other partner. It is very important here to be careful about respecting the confidentiality of the information that was provided to us by one of the partners and to make sure that it is not disclosed in the interview with the other partner. In these situations, it is very important to keep the focus on the social experience of the partner you are talking with. In cases such as these, it would be important to be clear that they can access their own interview transcript, but not that of their partner. This kind of situation also has implications for informed consent. If, for example, one of the goals in the study is to compare and contrast family members' constructions of the same reality, then we need their informed consent to conduct this analysis and to present the results in a way that may be identifiable by partners. When we present the nuances of gender dynamics within a particular couple, they may be able to identify themselves in the data. It is important that they provide their consent at the outset for this type of analysis.

Accountability

When we take on the ethical responsibility of ensuring that the rights of our participants are protected, we are accountable for any missteps that might compromise those rights. This involves not only anticipating what the implications might be for individual participants, but it means giving consideration to the implications of the research for their families and the community of which they are a part. It is essential that our protection of participants extend to these broader levels of accountability.

At the root of this accountability is the way we as researchers deal with our responsibility of "representing the other" in our research. How we represent participants in our research reports is contingent on our epistemological positioning—the way we either objectively portray participants or offer a coconstructed view of the research account. While at some level in qualitative research we represent the other to some degree, ethically we need to be mindful of the dangers of "othering" (Burck, 2005), where we presume with certainty to account for how our participants are thinking or feeling. Our ethical responsibility here is not to try to avoid any kind of othering, but rather, to be transparent about how the accounts were produced, inviting participants to contribute to and comment on the way their experience is being presented and to include their multiple and potentially contradictory interpretations of the same experience. As Gilgun (2005b) points out in a reflection on being a woman who represents the views of violent men, there are no easy answers to these questions. Rather, what is required is an ongoing diligence to examine the relationship between her own reflexive position and the views of these men.

This accountability is central to the way we responsibly establish and maintain research relationships. At a primary level, this is about acting ethically and respectfully toward our research participants; at another level, it is concerned with many other research relationships that are involved in the processes of knowledge production. For Doucet and Mauthner (2002), "knowing responsibly" involves an accountability to a number of other "unmentioned relationships" including our relationship to the readers of our work, those who might use and apply our work, and the knowledge communities that influence our work (e.g., epistemological, theoretical, disciplinary). This is a more complex web of relationships that gives rise to potential conflicts of interest and ethical dilemmas. Acting and knowing responsibly in these relationships means taking reflexivity seriously in a way that includes reflecting on social, political, and institutional locations as well as being transparent and accountable about our ontological and epistemological values (Doucet & Mauthner, 2002).

Accountability is not only about protecting our participants, but also ensuring that the time we expect of them is put to good use. Many participants are willing to devote time to research if they think it will make a difference. At the most basic level, this means clarifying for ourselves and our participants what the immediate benefits of the research might be. Specifically, how will this knowledge be used in a way that will benefit them and other participants who share in the same experience? At a professional level, part of our accountability is making every effort possible to ensure that our research is published and when appropriate, brought to the media or service providers for use in practical and applied ways.

When we do research with individuals and families, we also carry with us a professional code of conduct that involves the protection of participants from harm. As Lewis (2003) has outlined, one of the thorniest ethical issues we can encounter is when we have assured our participants of confidentiality but then become aware in the course of the research that either the participant or a member of the family is being harmed or at risk of harm. There are a number of ways the researcher may deal with this:

- In some cases (e.g., child abuse), there are legislative and professional requirements that these be reported to the appropriate authorities. If this happens, you should seek counsel within your institution.

- When not mandated by legislation but where there is an indication of harm the researcher can:
  - Encourage the participant to seek help or report it himself or herself
  - Support the participant in seeking help by providing contact information or a referral
  - Offer to talk to someone on his or her behalf in order to facilitate a connection with a service

In dealing with these kinds of situations, it is important that researchers have an opportunity to debrief and get support and direction from colleagues and other professionals who can help them to navigate through this emotionally difficult terrain.

In the same way that it is important to be attentive to situations of harm among participants, it is important as part of accountability to be attentive to our own safety when conducting research:

- Let people know where you are conducting interviews
- Carry a cell phone for emergencies
- When conducting interviews in a participant's home, do so in the public spaces in the home
- When there are concerns about safety, carry out interviews in offices or other public places
- Consider working with a partner

This can also include situations where we may hear things in interviews that trigger strong emotional responses from our own past history. In such cases, it is important to find a colleague or counselor who can help us work through our responses.

Accountability and Dealing With Sensitive Topics

When we do research on family experiences and relationships, it is easy to enter into topics that are quite sensitive and give rise to lots of feelings. Sometimes we know ahead of time that we are dealing with a sensitive topic; at other times, issues arise somewhat unexpectedly that may carry with them strong emotions or feelings of ambivalence. Students often ask how to deal with the expression of strong emotions in an interview. In addition, research on sensitive topics raises a number of ethical quandaries. Rosenblatt (1995a), for example, in his research on farm families who had lost a family member due to a farm accident, comments on the ethical challenges that arise in relation to recruiting people who are bereaved, the ethics of causing additional pain through the interview, and conundrums arising from the disclosure of secrets in the research process.

When I interviewed couples about their experience of infertility, there were many emotions expressed—often accompanied by tears. As an insider to this experience, I could understand the intensity of the pain they were experiencing and, while it was difficult, I was quite willing to stay with them in their expression of these feelings as a central part of their overall experience. These were important, if not some of the most important, things they wished to communicate to me, and rarely did they choose to stop the interview or wish to change the subject to safer ground. Often at the end of the interview, participants would express their gratitude for my willingness to listen respectfully and witness their anguish. Like many forms of telling, this had a cathartic effect for them. Strong emotions were an important part of understanding their reality.

One of the tendencies when we encounter emotional moments in interviews is to question whether we have crossed a boundary and perhaps probed too deeply or crossed over into a therapeutic mode. We certainly do not want to go into an emotional terrain where people might feel regret later on. As a result, we may be tempted to change the subject or move the topic to safer ground. We need to question whether it is a matter of our own discomfort or whether in fact we are infringing on another's private experience. While there is no simple answer to this, it is important to realize that emotions are a normal part of talking about family experience and that we provide the opportunity for these to be expressed in the interview. If you are unsure about whether to stay with an emotional topic, it may be helpful simply to check in with participants to see if they are OK to continue on that line of discussion or, alternatively, to give them the option of switching to another line of discussion, or possibly to terminate the interview. Furthermore, if participants appear to be particularly vulnerable in relation to a disclosure, it may be an appropriate time to check in with them about their comfort and consent to use the information in the research. Sometimes participants ask us to turn off the tape recorder in order to tell us something that they do not wish to have recorded. Unless explicit permission is given to use this information, this should be treated as sensitizing information only and should not be referred to as data.

It is also important when doing research with individuals and families that we be mindful of our primary role as researchers and not counselors or therapists. While having an opportunity to tell one's story in research may have a cathartic effect, it is important that as researchers we be vigilant about our professional boundaries. Maintaining this boundary can be a difficult task, because the research interview and the therapeutic interview are structured in similar ways: They both include "high levels of disclosure accompanied by profound and potentially disruptive insights and emotional release" (Mitchell & Radford, 1996, p. 53). Furthermore, the research interview may give rise to more unanticipated disclosures, at a faster rate, than counseling interviews (Mitchell & Radford, 1996).

Maintaining the boundary between these means staying with the research question, listening to their story, and providing empathy when appropriate, but at the same time refraining from offering advice, making moral judgments, or offering solutions to problems that have been brought forward. In the spirit of reciprocity and relationship, however, we should be ready to suggest resources or professional services that they could pursue and to respond to questions about the research so they can put themselves in the context of other participants' experiences.

Credibility Issues

In the world of modern art, it is not unusual for expensive, abstract pieces of art to be controversial. What is construed as brilliant by some is seen as meaningless by others. As a result, the determination of value of the piece is shaped as much by the process of critical and interpretive commentary as it is by the artwork itself. To speak about credibility issues in qualitative research is to pay attention to the ways in which we construct and evaluate the meaning and importance of our research products.

In a discussion of the history of qualitative methods, Vidich and Lyman (2003) suggest that when we ask artists about their method of creation, the answer is always a matter of ex post facto reconstruction. The method of doing art, as a creative endeavor, can be understood only by looking back at the way events, moods, or accidents affected the outcome. In social science, we face a similar challenge. In spite of insisting on clearly articulated methodologies and methods as maps for doing research, and in spite of the emphasis in more positivist-oriented research on ensuring that research is replicable, the practice of doing research is often more like art. We have the clearest idea of what our method is, or was, when the project is nearing completion. This retrospective construction of method is most obvious in emergent designs where questions and directions are open-ended. In studies like these, method can be understood fully only in retrospect. However, even in studies that seek to be more structured and rigorous at the outset, method is always subject to unanticipated turns and decisions. For example, sampling strategies need to be adjusted because of practical problems of recruitment; surprising or anomalous data precipitate a rethinking of central questions; or different hypotheses or interpretations arise midstream, calling into question our original assumptions.

Credibility, then, is a time-bound concept. In the early stages of any project, credibility is concerned with the way research projects are planned and designed in relation to the guidelines of the relevant methodology. Credibility also involves the assessment of the results as a project draws to a close. Accordingly, the credibility of qualitative research is concerned with two key issues. The first of these focuses on the credibility of procedures. This has to do with the way the method was articulated in the study, the way it reflects the decisions that were made along the way, and the transparency of the strategies and techniques used in the research. The second emphasizes the credibility of the outcome. Here, standards of quality and trustworthiness of the data are paramount.

Credibility of Procedures

Researchers in the qualitative research tradition have discussed a number of ways to ensure that their methodological procedures are understandable and visible. The "audit trail" (Lincoln & Guba, 1985) is one metaphor that has been used to stress the importance of documenting decisions and strategies throughout the research process. When called on to justify why certain decisions were made about design or sampling, an audit trail allows the researcher to work back through operational memos (see Chapter 9) that outline how the decision was made. This is a kind of functional reflexivity (Wilkinson, 1988) that provides an ongoing critical examination of the assumptions, decisions, and procedures that become available for a retrospective analysis of research procedures. Written memos and reflexive journals serve as important means for tracking procedures and communicating these to our audiences. Lurking in the background, and in the spirit of traditional scientific practice, is a concern with the replication of our research processes to provide readers with a full and transparent account of how the research was done. In qualitative research, however, there are limitations on the extent to which an audit trail can fully communicate the kinds of decisions that have been made. For example, as Morse and Richards (2002) point out, although an audit trail can be a useful mechanism for recording operational decisions about a project (methodology and design choices, sample selection, rationale for questions, etc.), it is less effective as a record of the complex decisions that take place in coding and in the creation and interpretation of categories. These involve complex and nuanced decisions about meanings that are not only difficult to track, but onerous to document in detail.

The way qualitative researchers endeavor to present the credibility of procedures is contingent on their epistemological standpoint.

Objectivism

When we adopt an objectivist stance with the goal of accurately representing an observed reality, then credibility is rooted in the scientific notions of methodological rigor, efforts to minimize personal bias, and a concern with validity and reliability. Accordingly, one of the ways we endeavor to minimize bias (thereby ensuring credibility of procedures) is by manufacturing distance between ourselves as researchers and our participants. We do this by using reflexivity to keep our own agendas and biases in check; we ask participants open-ended, nonleading questions in an effort to avoid "influencing" them; and in our analysis, we abide by the principle of "letting the data speak" in a way that minimizes the impact of our own analytic efforts.

Reliability and validity are very much a part of the objectivist standpoint, but these are contested terms within the qualitative research tradition. Given their origins in the natural sciences where the emphasis was on precision of measurement and certainty of results, it is not surprising that in qualitative research, these tenets take on a different meaning. Lewis and

Ritchie (2003), for example, indicate that the terms are useful when we consider their underlying intent. For reliability, the emphasis is placed on the sustainability of the results. In the qualitative research tradition, this sustainability can be demonstrated though a variety of strategies, including the confirmability, trustworthiness, transferability, and dependability of the findings (Lincoln & Guba, 1985). This is in contrast with the traditional emphasis that was placed on replicability as the essential component of reliability, which is problematic in naturalistic observation studies and emergent designs where it is impossible and undesirable to reproduce complex, emergent social phenomena. For this reason, rarely do researchers seek to replicate a qualitative study as a way to demonstrate reliability of findings. More common are efforts within a study (internal reliability) to generate confidence in the interpretation of the data. Based on the principles of interrater reliability, researchers engage other researchers (often graduate students) to analyze and interpret segments of data to see the extent to which they come to the same conclusions about the data (see Rostosky et al., 2004, for an example of "consensual" coding of data within a research team). This is driven by an objectivist principle that seeks to uncover the truth in the data. Again, the underlying concern in this approach is to minimize the "biasing" effects of individual interpretations.

In its traditional positivistic usage, validity is concerned with the integrity of measurement—in other words, "Are we measuring what we claim to be measuring?" In the qualitative research tradition, we are less concerned with the correctness of the measurement and more concerned with whether our claims are "well grounded in the data" (Lewis & Ritchie, 2003, p. 270). This becomes a matter of "fidelity" to the meanings that participants attribute to their lives—do we understand what they are telling us through their words and actions (Gilgun, 2005)?

In qualitative practice, validity is connected to the issues of representation and interpretation. Specifically, validity is demonstrated when the analytic account does a good job of the following: portraying the experience that it set out to describe or explain, using data to support the interpretative assertions, and providing a full and feasible account of the phenomenon being explored.

The determination of reliability and validity in a qualitative account must be attentive to a number of procedural aspects of the research. While it is tempting to focus only on outcome, reliability and validity are contingent on attention to a number of steps in the research design (Lewis & Ritchie, 2003). Specifically, question design, sample selection, transcription procedures, analysis, and interpretation all play a role in shaping the degree to which the results are seen to be sustainable, credible, and grounded in the data.

Subjectivism

As discussed in Chapter 8, reflexivity is concerned with how we account for the self in the research process. This is a matter not only of what we do in the research process, but how we are a catalyst in shaping and creating the research focus and how we interpret and coconstruct a portrayal of a reality in which we have participated. From an interpretivist or subjectivist perspective, we ensure credibility of procedures by being reflexive about how we bring meaning and focus to the research. Validity, from a subjectivist standpoint, is concerned with the ways knowledge is interactively constructed, rather than unidirectionally represented.

In this vein, Kvale (1996, p. 239) talks about the move from "knowledge as observation" (an objectivist position) to "knowledge as conversation" (a subjectivist position). When we replace a conception of knowledge as a mirror of reality with a conception of knowledge as a social construction, then validity becomes a matter of assessing the way knowledge is interactively generated through dialogue, negotiation, and multiple interpretations. Given the important role that the researcher plays in contributing to the generation of this knowledge, validity is linked to the craftsmanship and credibility of the researcher (Kvale, 1996). This includes not only an assessment of how the methods were used, but an assessment of the moral and scientific integrity of the researcher. Again, these can be demonstrated throughout the research process and include indications of the following:

- How personal experiences or theoretical interests led to specific lines of inquiry
- How participants were chosen for inclusion in the study and the way relationships were established and maintained
- How key findings were dialogically generated through interaction with participants
- The extent to which the researcher is able to demonstrate commitment through intensive (and at times prolonged) immersion in the field
- How various meaning-making strategies, including the researcher's own, were incorporated into the analytic process

Credibility of Outcome

In our everyday vernacular, the most prudent pathway to credibility is "to tell the truth." In our daily interactions, we gain a reputation according to the extent to which we are honest and tell the truth. Of course, "telling the truth" is not a simple matter when seen against the backdrop of epistemological debates. Nevertheless, there is virtue in presenting the results of our research in a way that is careful, honest, and transparent. There will of course be many readings and interpretations of the "truth" that we present, and likely a number of plausible ways that we might present this "truth"—but in the end, "telling the truth" does serve to uphold a standard of credibility.

One of the elementary ways we judge the credibility of a product is to assess it for ourselves "on the standard of whether the work communicates or 'says' something to us—that is does it connect with our reality. . . . Does it resonate with our own image of the world?" (Vidich & Lyman, 2003, p. 58). This is a kind of phenomenological validity whereby we use our own lived experience as a basis for assessing the credibility of the work. As Glaser and Strauss (1967) argued, this is a matter of bringing readers into the description in a way that gives them a "vicarious" experience of the phenomenon being studied. Critical here is the extent to which the results presented are "grounded in the data." Reports that capture the detail and nuance of lived experience provide us with the "aha's" of identification that contribute to this phenomenological assessment. When we consider multiple epistemological standpoints, it is important to keep in mind that credibility is not necessarily contingent on the presentation of just one version of reality but may include a collage of different experiences and viewpoints.

One of the ways researchers have attempted to reconcile realist and constructionist approaches to credibility is to emphasize how knowledge is situated (Gergen & Gergen, 2003). Somewhere between the extremes of a universalistic, correspondence theory of truth and the relativistic position that there is nothing beyond the text is the idea that understandings and knowledge are situated within particular communities at particular times operating within a set of specific conditions. Situated knowledge can be used as a standard by which we assess the credibility of outcome. It is a means for communicating to readers how our results emerged from specific questions and inquiries, and it becomes a means to situate and contextualize the results according to time, space, and social meanings.

There are also practices where we turn to our participants for help in assessing the credibility of the outcome. There are many ways we can do this. From a positivistic perspective, we take our analytic results back to them and ask, "Did I get it right?" or, "What's missing in this account?" Alternatively, from a social constructionist or postmodern perspective, we go back to participants not so much to verify our findings, but to get their impressions and open a further dialogue about what has been presented (Johnson, 2002). In this regard, it is not the responsibility of the researcher to have an accurate representation of their reality, though it is important that the researcher makes the results available so the participants can draw their own questions and conclusions about them.

Triangulation is one of the means that researchers have used to deepen the credibility of their findings. Triangulation is based on the premise that we can best understand experience when we take multiple standpoints, use multiple sources of data, and examine phenomena at different levels of analysis. According to Tindall (1994) this can occur in a variety of ways. *Data triangulation* involves collecting accounts from participants who may be at different stages in their experience of a phenomenon, be across different kinds of settings, or who bring different backgrounds and experiences to the research. By maximizing the variability of experience in participants, we may be in a better position to see what their common experience is like. *Investigator triangulation* involves using more than one researcher, who therefore bring different perspectives, raise different questions, and offer different interpretations of what is being said. This can occur at any or all stages of the research process. Having several researchers carry out analysis of the same data can reveal some important commonalities as well as divergent interpretations. Although this can slow down the analysis process, it also serves as a fruitful means of opening up new pathways for making sense of the data. *Theoretical triangulation* involves bringing to the research a number of disciplinary perspectives or theoretical approaches. These sensitizing approaches can provide different ways of conducting the analysis and can open up a variety of interpretive pathways. Finally, *method triangulation* involves using different methods to examine the same phenomenon. In ethnography, for example, this often includes observation episodes, interviews with key informants, and examination of documents or artifacts. It may also include combining quantitative surveys and qualitative interviews. All forms of triangulation have as their purpose to thicken or deepen our understanding of a phenomenon by incorporating multiple perspectives and procedures. From a positivist perspective, this can enhance the confidence that we have in the way we represent reality; from a postmodernist perspective, triangulation can open up multiple and diverse understandings of the same phenomenon.

When we work from a critical paradigm, the credibility of the outcome can be assessed by the extent to which the research has been successful in meeting its goals for social change. From this standpoint, the outcome is not assessed according to the quality of the report, but rather is assessed by the degree to which the research process was successful in changing the way people think and act in their own lives. Credibility is achieved in critical research when the knowledge and understandings that are achieved lead to a reassessment of values, different forms of organization and interaction, and new insights into justice and equality. In short, the credibility of outcome for critically oriented research can be assessed by the degree to which intended empowerment strategies have taken hold. This is an assessment of credibility through pragmatic utility: "Has the research been useful and effective?"

Presenting the Results of Our Research With Integrity

One of the best ways that we can present the results of our qualitative research with integrity is to present the results in a way that "brings to life" the experiences of our participants. As Rosenblatt (2002) has suggested, we all like a good story, and part of what makes for a good research report is fascinating reading. The ingredients are a vivid story, powerful metaphors, and authentic statements of feelings—in short, "narratives good enough to be fiction" (p. 898). This is not to suggest that style should override content in our writings, but rather to suggest that we capitalize on the strengths of qualitative research by capturing the vitality and spirit of lived experience in our research reports. This is research that has "verisimilitude"—the appearance of being real or true (Piercy & Benson, 2005)—and which can be assessed according to its aesthetic merits (Sprenkle & Piercy, 2005).

The research reports we write will be assessed according to a set of evaluative criteria. One of the default criteria used to assess any research report is to rely on the inherited practices of our positivist scientific tradition. In order to ward against the inappropriate use of these criteria, it is necessary for qualitative researchers to be deliberate about communicating with the audience how paradigm assumptions have shaped the course of the research. This involves being clear about our epistemological starting points and our methodological approaches.

Epistemological Integrity. The way we bring the "finishing touches" to our research is contingent on the way we begin. In other words, the form and style of our written reports is rooted in and shaped by our ontological and epistemological starting points. Accordingly, there are different kinds of research reports and different rationales or arguments that we might draw on as a way of presenting our results. Mason (2002), for example, suggests that different epistemological positions invoke different kinds of arguments in our writings. We can argue evidentially by demonstrating clearly how we assembled the evidence and what data constitute evidence for particular arguments. These may be arguments that involve comparison, prediction, or explanation of how something works. We can argue interpretively, narratively, or illustratively by demonstrating that the story we have to tell is meaningful, sensitive, and appropriately nuanced. Our reports can also argue reflexively or multivocally by making the reader aware of the meaningful range of perspectives, experiences, and standpoints the analysis makes possible. The postmodern approach includes a willingness to raise questions, keep contradiction in play, and be open to concurrent but divergent interpretations of the data. Beyond forms of argument highlighted by Mason, we might also consider arguing politically as a way of writing from a critical paradigm perspective. From this perspective, our interpretations of data serve as a means to bring into focus dynamics of age, gender, and social class accompanied by arguments about values, social change, and justice. These different forms of argument are not simply matters of style or rhetorical preference; rather, they are embedded in our foundational assumptions about the nature of reality and our role and relationship to that reality.

One of the questions that arise with respect to the presentation (and integrity) of results has to do with the effectiveness of communicating with our audiences. Piercy and Benson (2005), for example, talk about the importance of using aesthetic forms of data representation in family therapy research as an effective means of communicating with audiences and engaging audiences in an active process of reflecting on the meaning of the data. They draw on the use of storytelling, theater, and demonstration as a way of communicating knowledge and engaging audiences. This is rooted in a belief that researchers (and in particular family researchers) have an obligation to conduct research that has practical value. They provide a number of examples of how researchers have effectively engaged audience members in a reflection of their own experiences, such as their beliefs about gays and lesbians, perceptions of their own power, or understandings of their own relationships. Aesthetic forms of data representation, however, while effective in reaching audiences, are more vulnerable to critiques about whether they are "robust" or in keeping with the positivist criteria of "good" social science. For Piercy and Benson (2005), this form of research activity is not exempt from these criteria. The researcher must still be responsible for producing credible data with accountability to the participants, the scholarly community, and the participating audience members. If anything, they argue, the standards are even more stringent insofar as the products of the research must not only be presented with credibility and accountability, they must also meet a moral standard where empathy, honesty, and social justice prevail.

"Messy" or "Clean" Portrayals of Reality

One of the underlying pressures in all scientific writing is to embrace logic, rationality, and certainty. If we are to know and understand the world, then our thinking needs to be orderly and "clean." Indeed, when we follow the methodological guidelines of many of the qualitative approaches, there is an implicit gravitation toward refinement in analysis that will lead to a succinct and orderly explanation. Yet when we study individuals and families, we are confronted with the "messiness" of their everyday realities. When we are

(Continued)

(Continued)

in the thick of our analysis, we are easily overwhelmed by the complexity of responses and the range of viewpoints and experiences. As we generate themes and categories and seek to offer explanation, we often need to go beyond these variations in order to pull out the nomothetic patterns. In so doing, however, we need to be mindful that we not overly sanitize our arguments (Daly, 2003) in a way that strips negative cases, conflicting viewpoints, contradictions, or ambiguity out of our results. When we recognize that life experience is messy, we may do well, in our portrayals of that experience, to hold onto some of that messiness in our writings. This is not to be confused with bad writing—rather the challenge to write well about complex, nuanced human experience is even greater. As part of this, writings about complex human reality invite readers to bring multiple interpretations to their reading of the research results (Sprenkle & Piercy, 2005).

One of the key challenges arising from questions of epistemological integrity is the way we position ourselves in the writings of our final reports. In most journals, there is an implicit message that an objectivist position is most appropriate—which means keeping first person statements of experience out of the account. This may be attributable in part to the continued dominance of quantitative research in many family and human development journals. In these articles, postpositivist assumptions dictate a standardized format that includes a research problem, theory and literature review, methods, hypotheses, reliability and validity efforts, results, and discussion. In this standard reporting format, credibility is typically determined by the extent to which researcher bias or influence has been kept out of the written account.

Qualitative research reports are not immune to the pressure to publish articles in a standard research format, which includes adopting a third person stance that keeps the researcher's influence safely out of the way. If there is a juncture when epistemological integrity is going to be compromised, it is at the point of wanting to publish our research in good quality journals and feeling like we need to adopt an objectivist position in order to do so. Often this is based more on a perception that the editor of a journal will insist on the traditional style than on the editor's willingness to publish qualitative research in a variety of formats. Rather than compromising our epistemological and methodological principles, the onus is on us as researchers and writers to outline our epistemological assumptions clearly and articulate clearly the rationale behind the format we have chosen. This may be accomplished in part by alerting the editor to our approach in the cover letter sent with the paper.

In projects that involve features such as an emergent design, unstructured interviews, ongoing reflexive decision making, and theoretical sensitivity, it is necessary to include in our accounts first person explanations of how key design decisions were made, how relationships with participants were formed, and how results were both created and interpreted through interaction with participants. In short, it is important to bring our subjective self into the research account in order to communicate, with transparency, how our experiences, ideas, and interpretations contributed to the construction of the research report. Accordingly, it is most appropriate to use the pronoun *I* in our research reports when working in a critical, constructionist, or postmodern paradigm.

The way we include the researcher's self in final reports of research can take many forms. We might envision this as a continuum where on one end the researcher's narrative dominates the account, and on the other end, we give emphasis to our participants' stories but keep a subjective presence as a meaning-making commentator. Autoethnography or thick description arising from immersed participation would appropriately lead to first-person descriptions of the social phenomenon. In these accounts, the researcher's voice is paramount. On the other hand, if our primary purpose is to convey the stories that our participants have told us, we may choose to foreground the stories and the experiences they have shared with us and background our own voice. The researcher account is a matter of describing how these stories were elicited, how they were analyzed and selected for presentation, and how they are being interpreted. In the middle between these extremes is a subjective commentary by the researcher about how explanations came to be coconstructed through interaction in the research interview. In these accounts, there is an emphasis on explaining how ideas emerged and both the researcher and the participant contributed to these shared meaning structures. Making a choice about how to present our subjectivity in research accounts becomes a matter of determining the degree of emphasis on my story, their story, or our story (Ellis & Berger, 2002).

One of the challenges we face in presenting their story, my story, or our story is that researchers and research participants may have different views about what constitutes the "truth" in a research account. As Rosenblatt (2002) has convincingly argued, researchers may approach their research inquiry with a postmodernist assumption that there are many realities to be heard and portrayed in the research report. By contrast, participants often enter into a research project with a modernist presumption that there is a truth to be told and that there are "right answers" to be told to the researcher. Rosenblatt describes his approach:

> Many people I have interviewed seem to me to feel an almost sacred obligation
> to provide the truth. So even if I am in a post-modern and perspectival world

as I read and write social science, the people I interview offer me truth and push me to be like reporters, detectives and others they believe to be seekers of the truth. This naïve realism influences me. Although I can frame what people say to me in terms that are quite foreign to them and quite compelling to me, I often write my social science in ways that honor their realities. I don't want them to read what I have written and wonder where their realities went. I also don't want to abandon their realities because I think part of what I have to offer readers is what the people I interview seem to say is real and true. (p. 895–896)

Methodological Integrity. One of the ways we can improve the success of our publishing efforts in qualitative research is always to use the language of our chosen methodology in our research reports. If we are doing a grounded theory study, it is important to communicate with readers how we used theoretical sensitivity in the shaping of our research question. It is important to use the language of categories or substantive theory to describe the results of our inquiry. When we use methodological language in this way it serves two mutually reinforcing purposes. The first is that it demonstrates our adherence to the underlying principles and procedures of the methodology, and as a result, serves as a basis for assessing the integrity of the research process. Second, it provides the reader with an important set of cues for how to locate the research in the broad landscape of qualitative research methodologies.

In my experience of being a journal reviewer of qualitative papers, I have found it most difficult to assess papers that provide little information about the methodology that was used. For example, some papers will simply state that this was a "qualitative approach" resulting in a report of broad themes. At other times, researchers will borrow an analytic strategy such as open and axial coding from grounded theory but then ignore all other aspects of a grounded theory approach. When adopting the use of broad generalities or cherry-picking components of a methodology, it is nearly impossible, from the reader's standpoint, to understand how and why methodological decisions were made throughout the project. In the absence of this methodological information, it is more difficult to assess the credibility of the results. By contrast, papers that are clearly located in a methodological approach and use the language of the methodology provide the reader with a basis for assessing the integrity of the research process according to the practices and guidelines that have emerged in that methodological tradition.

At a practical level, authors wishing to publish in mainstream journals must also take into account the expectations and formats of the journal itself. In the family domain, Matthews (2005) has outlined a number of practical considerations for authors who wish to optimize their success in publishing qualitative work in key journals. These include valuable descriptions of how to structure the introduction, methods (including sample and description of informants, procedures, analysis), results, and discussion. In the spirit of qualitative inquiry, these suggestions are not intended to be prescriptive, but rather to offer guidelines for enhancing publishing success.

Conclusion

Integrity can be accomplished by traveling many pathways in qualitative research. As Gilgun (1992) once said, it is not for the faint of heart. Given the variety of choices and the onus on the researcher to construct and defend many decisions throughout the research process, there is necessarily a need for informed, transparent, and accountable procedures.

I have likened this process to crossing an unsteady bridge without railings: We must be attentive every step of the way and be sure of our footing in the absence of clear and unambiguous rules and procedures. Like all adventures, however, our successful arrival at the other side is enhanced by the attention and effort invested along the way. While there are many qualitative pathways, they all require engagement of our senses, some vulnerability about our own experience, a scrutiny of values, and a commitment to deepen our collective understanding of developmental experience and the complex world of family life.

References

Acock, A. C., van Dulmen, M. M., Allen, K. R., & Piercy, F. P. (2005). Contemporary and emerging research methods in studying families. In V. Bengston, A. Acock, K. Allen, P. Dilworth-Anderson, & D. Klein (Eds.), *Sourcebook of family theory and research* (pp. 59–89). Thousand Oaks, CA: Sage.

Allen, K. (2000). A conscious and inclusive family studies. *Journal of Marriage and Family, 62,* 4–17.

Allen, K. (2001). Feminist visions for transforming families: Desire and equality then and now. *Journal of Family Issues, 22,* 793–811.

Allen, K., & Piercy, F. P. (2005). Feminist autoethnography. In D. Sprenkle & F. P. Piercy (Eds.), *Research methods in family therapy* (2nd ed., pp. 155–169). New York: Guilford.

Altheide, D. L., & Johnson, J. M. (1994). Criteria for assessing interpretive validity in qualitative research. In N. K. Denzin & Y. S. Lincoln (Eds.), *Handbook of qualitative research* (pp. 485–499). Thousand Oaks, CA: Sage.

Ambert, A., Adler, P. A., Adler, P., & Detzner, D. (1995). Understanding and evaluating qualitative research. *Journal of Marriage and the Family, 57,* 879–893.

Anderson, H. (2005). Myths about not-knowing. *Family Process, 44,* 497–504.

Andrews, M., Sclater, S. D., Squire, C., & Tamboukou, M. (2004). Narrative research. In C. Seale, G. Gobo, J. F. Gubrium, & D. Silverman (Eds.), *Qualitative research practice* (pp. 109–124). Thousand Oaks, CA: Sage.

Arendell, T. (1997). Reflections on the researcher-researched relationship: A woman interviewing men. *Qualitative Sociology, 20,* 341–368.

Atkinson, P. (1992). *Understanding ethnographic texts.* Newbury Park, CA: Sage.

Atkinson, P., & Coffey, A. (2002). Revisiting the relationship between participant observation and interviewing. In J. Gubrium & J. Holstein (Eds.), *Handbook of interview research: Context and method* (pp. 801–814). Thousand Oaks, CA: Sage.

Avis, J. M., & Turner, J. (1996). Feminist lenses in family therapy research: Gender, politics and science. In D. H. Sprenkle & S. M. Moon (Eds.), *Research methods in family therapy* (pp. 145–169). New York: Guilford.

Bakhtin, M. M. (1981). *The dialogic imagination: Four essays by M. M. Bakhtin* (M. Holquist, Ed.). Austin: University of Texas Press.

Bamberg, M. (2004). Positioning with Davie Hogan: Stories, tellings and identities. In C. Daiute & C. Lightfoot (Eds.), *Narrative analysis: Studying the development of individuals in society* (pp. 135–157). Thousand Oaks, CA: Sage.

Baxter, L. A. (1990). Dialectical contradictions in relationship development. *Journal of Social and Personal Relationships, 7,* 69–88.

Baxter, L. A., & Montgomery, B. M. (1996). *Relating: Dialogues and dialectics.* New York: Guilford.

Beck, U., & Beck-Gernsheim, E. (1995). *The normal chaos of love.* Cambridge, UK: Polity Press.

Becker, H. (1964). Problems in the publication of field studies. In A. J. Vidich, J. Bensman, & M. R. Stein (Eds.), *Reflections on community studies* (pp. 267–284). New York: John Wiley.

Becker, H. S., & Geer, B. (1970). Participant observation and interviewing: A comparison. In W. J. Filstead (Ed.), *Qualitative methodology: Firsthand involvement with the social world* (pp. 133–142). Chicago: Markham Publishing.

Bengston, V., Acock, A., Allen, K. R., Dilworth-Anderson, P., & Klein, D. (2005). Theory and theorizing in family research: Puzzle building and puzzle solving. In V. Bengston, A. Acock, K. Allen, P. Dilworth-Anderson, & D. Klein (Eds.), *Sourcebook of family theory and research* (pp. 3–33). Thousand Oaks, CA: Sage.

Benner, P. (Ed.). (1994). *Interpretive phenomenology: Embodiment, caring and ethics in health and illness.* Thousand Oaks, CA: Sage.

Berger, J. (1972). *Ways of seeing.* London: Penguin.

Berger, P., & Luckmann, T. (1966). *The social construction of reality.* Norwich, UK: Penguin.

Bernardes, J. (1986). Multidimensional developmental pathways: A proposal to facilitate the conceptualisation of "family diversity." *Sociological Review, 34,* 590–610.

Birch, M., Miller, T., Mauthner, M., & Jessop, J. (2002). Introduction. In M. Mauthner, M. Birch, J. Jessop, & T. Miller (Eds.), *Ethics in qualitative research* (pp. 1–14). London: Sage.

Blalock, L., Tiller, V., & Monroe, P. (2004). They get you out of courage: Persistent deep poverty among former welfare-reliant women. *Family Relations, 53,* 127–137.

Blumer, H. (1969). *Symbolic interactionism: Perspective and method.* Englewood Cliffs, NJ: Prentice Hall.

Bornat, J. (2004). Oral history. In C. Seale, G. Gobo, J. F. Gubrium, & D. Silverman (Eds.), *Qualitative research practice* (pp. 34–47). Thousand Oaks, CA: Sage.

Boss, P. (1999). *Ambiguous loss: Learning to live with unresolved grief.* Cambridge, MA: Harvard University Press.

Bourdieu, P. (1990). *The logic of practice.* Stanford, CA: Stanford University Press.

Bronfenbrenner, U. (1979). *The ecology of human development.* Cambridge, MA: Harvard University Press.

Bruner, J. (1990). *Acts of meaning.* Cambridge, MA: Harvard University Press.

Bryan, L., Negretti, M., Christensen, F. B., & Stokes, S. (2002). Processing the process: One research team's experience of a collaborative research project. *Contemporary Family Therapy, 24,* 333–353.

Burck, C. (2005). Comparing qualitative research methodologies for systemic research: The use of grounded theory, discourse analysis and narrative analysis. *Journal of Family Therapy, 27,* 237–262.

Burgess, E. W. (1926). The family as a unit of interacting personalities. *Family, 7,* 3–9.

Butler, R. N. (1963). The life review: An interpretation of reminiscence in the aged. *Psychiatry, 26,* 65–73.

Carr, D. (1986). *Time, narrative and history.* Bloomington: Indiana University Press.

Chaitin, J. (2003). "Living" with the past: Coping and patterns in families of Holocaust survivors. *Family Process, 42,* 305–322.

Chambers, E. (2003). Applied ethnography. In N. K. Denzin & Y. S. Lincoln (Eds.), *Collecting and interpreting qualitative materials* (2nd ed., pp. 389–418). Thousand Oaks, CA: Sage.

Charmaz, K. (2002). Qualitative interviewing and grounded theory analysis. In J. Gubrium & J. A. Holstein (Eds.), *Handbook of interview research: Context and method* (pp. 675–694). Thousand Oaks, CA: Sage.

Charmaz, K. (2003a). Grounded theory. In J. A. Smith (Ed.), *Qualitative psychology: A practical guide to research methods* (pp. 81–110). London: Sage.

Charmaz, K. (2003b). Grounded theory: Objectivist and constructivist methods. In N. K. Denzin & Y. S. Lincoln (Eds.), *Strategies of qualitative inquiry* (2nd ed., pp. 249–291). Thousand Oaks, CA: Sage.

Charmaz, K., & Mitchell, R. G. (2001). Grounded theory in ethnography. In P. Atkinson, A. Coffey, S. Delamont, J. Lofland, & L. H. Lofland (Eds.), *Handbook of ethnography* (pp. 160–174). London: Sage.

Cheal, D. (1991). *Family and the state of theory.* Toronto: University of Toronto Press.

Cheal, D. (1993). Unity and difference in postmodern families. *Journal of Family Issues, 14,* 5–19.

Clark, P., Thigpen, S., & Yates, A. M. (2006). Integrating the older/special needs child into the adoptive family. *Journal of Marital and Family Therapy, 32,* 181–194.

Clausen, J. (1998). Life reviews and life stories. In J. Z. Giele & G. H. Elder (Eds.), *Methods of life course research: Qualitative and quantitative approaches* (pp. 189–212). Thousand Oaks, CA: Sage.

The concise Oxford dictionary of current English. (1990). (8th ed.). Oxford, UK: Clarendon.

Coontz, S. (1992). *The way we never were.* New York: Basic Books.

Cresswell, J. (1998). *Qualitative inquiry and research design: Choosing among five traditions.* Thousand Oaks, CA: Sage.

Crotty, M. (1998). *The foundations of social research: Meaning and perspective in the research process.* London: Sage.

Dahl, C. M., & Boss, P. (2005). The use of phenomenology for family therapy research: The search for meaning. In D. Sprenkle & F. P. Piercy (Eds.), *Research methods in family therapy* (2nd ed., pp. 63–84). New York: Guilford.

Daiute, C., & Lightfoot, C. (2004). Theory and craft in narrative inquiry. In C. Daiute & C. Lightfoot (Eds.), *Narrative analysis: Studying the development of individuals in society* (pp. vii–xviii). Thousand Oaks, CA: Sage.

Daly, K. J. (1988). Reshaped parenthood identity: The transition to adoptive parent-hood. *Journal of Contemporary Ethnography, 17,* 40–66.

Daly, K. J. (1989). Anger among prospective adoptive parents: Structural determinants and management strategies. *Clinical Sociology Review, 7,* 80–96.

Daly, K. J. (1992a). The fit between qualitative research and the study of families. In J. Gilgun, K. Daly, & G. Handel, (Eds.), *Qualitative methods in family research* (pp. 3–11). Newbury Park, CA: Sage.

Daly, K. J. (1992b). Interactive resocialization: The case of adoptive parenthood. *Qualitative Sociology, 15,* 395–417.

Daly, K. J. (1992c). Parenthood as problematic: Insider interviews with couples seeking to adopt. In J. Gilgun, K. Daly, & G. Handel (Eds.), *Qualitative methods in family research* (pp. 103–125). Newbury Park, CA: Sage.

Daly, K. J. (1997). Re-placing theory in ethnography: A postmodern view. *Qualitative Inquiry, 3,* 343–365.

Daly, K. J. (1999). Crisis of genealogy: Facing the challenges of infertility. In H. McCubbin, E. A. Thompson, A. I. Thompson, & J. A. Futrell (Eds.), *The dynamics of resilient families* (pp. 1–40). Thousand Oaks, CA: Sage.

Daly, K. J. (2001). Deconstructing family time: From ideology to lived experience. *Journal of Marriage and Family, 63,* 283–294.

Daly, K. J. (2002). Time, gender and the negotiation of family schedules. *Symbolic Interaction, 25,* 323–342.

Daly, K. J. (2003). Family theory versus the theory families live by. *Journal of Marriage and Family, 65,* 771–785.

Daly, K. J., & Dienhart, A. (1998). Navigating the family domain: Qualitative field dilemmas. In S. Grills (Ed.), *Fieldwork settings: Accomplishing ethnographic research* (pp. 97–120). Thousand Oaks, CA: Sage.

Davies, K. (1994). The tensions between process time and clock time in care-work: The example of day nurseries. *Time & Society, 3,* 276–303.

Davis, C. S., & Salkin, K. A. (2005). Sisters and friends: Dialogue and multivocality in a relationship model of sibling disability. *Journal of Contemporary Ethnography, 34,* 206–234.

Delamont, S. (2004). Ethnography and participant observation. In C. Seale, G. Gobo, J. F. Gubrium, & D. Silverman (Eds.), *Qualitative research practice* (pp. 217–229). Thousand Oaks, CA: Sage.

Denzin, N. K. (1978). *The research act: A theoretical introduction to sociological methods* (2nd ed.). New York: McGraw–Hill.

Denzin, N. K. (1989). *Interpretive interactionism.* Newbury Park, CA: Sage.

Denzin, N. K. (1994). The art and politics of interpretation. In N. K. Denzin & Y. S. Lincoln (Eds.), *Handbook of qualitative research* (pp. 500–515). Thousand Oaks, CA: Sage.

Denzin, N. K., & Lincoln, Y. S. (1994). Introduction: Entering the field of qualitative research. In N. K. Denzin & Y. S. Lincoln (Eds.), *Handbook of qualitative research* (pp. 1–17). Thousand Oaks, CA: Sage.

Denzin, N. K., & Lincoln, Y. S. (2003). Introduction: The discipline and practice of qualitative research. In N. K. Denzin & Y. S. Lincoln (Eds.), *The landscape of qualitative research: Theories and issues* (2nd ed., pp. 1–45). Thousand Oaks, CA: Sage.

Dey, I. (2004). Grounded theory. In C. Seale, G. Gobo, J. F. Gubrium, & D. Silverman (Eds.), *Qualitative research practice* (pp. 80–93). Thousand Oaks, CA: Sage.

DeVault, M. (1991). *Feeding the family: The social organization of caring as gendered work*. Chicago: University of Chicago Press.

DeVault, M. (2000). Producing family time: Practices of leisure activity beyond the home. *Qualitative Sociology, 23,* 485–503.

Dillard, A. (1985). *Pilgrim at Tinker Creek*. New York: Harper Perennial. (Original work published 1974)

Djilas, M. (1990). Toward an imperfect world. In C. Fadiman (Ed.), *Living philosophies* (pp. 187—192). Garden City, NY: Doubleday.

Dodson, L., & Dickert, J. (2004). Girls' family labor in low income households: A decade of qualitative research. *Journal of Marriage and Family, 66,* 318–332.

Dodson, L., & Schmalzbauer, L. (2005). Poor mothers and habits of hiding: Participatory methods in poverty research. *Journal of Marriage and Family, 67,* 949–959.

Doherty, W. J., & Beaton, J. (2000). Family therapists, community and civic renewal. *Family Process, 39,* 149–162.

Doherty, W. J., & Carlson, B. Z. (2002). *Putting family first: Successful strategies for reclaiming family life in a hurry-up world*. New York: Henry Holt.

Doucet, A., & Mauthner, N. (2002). Knowing responsibly: Linking ethics, research practice and epistemology. In M. Mauthner, M. Birch, J. Jessop, & T. Miller (Eds.), *Ethics in qualitative research* (pp. 123–145). London: Sage.

Douglas, M., & Isherwood, B. (1996). *The world of goods: Towards an anthropology of consumption*. London: Routledge.

Driver, J. L., & Gottman, J. M. (2004). Daily marital interactions and positive affect during marital conflict among newlywed couples. *Family Process, 43,* 301–314.

Duck, S., Acitelli, L., & Nicholson, J. H. (2000). Family life as an experiential quilt. In R. Milardo & S. Duck (Eds.), *Families as relationships* (pp. 175–189). New York: John Wiley.

Dunbar, C., Rodriguez, D., & Parker, L. (2002). Race, subjectivity, and the interview process. In J. Gubrium & J. Holstein (Eds.), *Handbook of interview research: Context and method* (pp. 279–298). Thousand Oaks, CA: Sage.

Dunbar, N., & Grotevant, H. D. (2004). Adoption narratives: The construction of adoptive identity during adolescence. In M. W. Pratt & B. H. Fiese (Eds.), *Family stories and the life course: Across time and generations* (pp. 135–161). Mahwah, NJ: Lawrence Erlbaum.

Dupuis, S. (1999). Naked truths: Towards a reflexive methodology in leisure research. *Leisure Sciences, 21,* 43–64.

Echevarria-Doan, S., & Tubbs, C. Y. (2005). Let's get grounded: Family therapy research and grounded theory. In D. Sprenkle & F. P. Piercy (Eds.), *Research methods in family therapy* (2nd ed., pp. 41–62). New York: Guilford.

Eder, D., & Fingerson, L. (2002). Interviewing children and adolescents. In J. Gubrium & J. Holstein (Eds.), *Handbook of interview research: Context and method* (pp. 181–201). Thousand Oaks, CA: Sage.

Edwards, B. (1999). *The new drawing on the right side of the brain*. New York: Jeremy P. Tarcher/Putnam.

Edwards, M. L. (2004). We're decent people: Constructing and managing family identity in rural working class communities. *Journal of Marriage and Family, 66,* 515–529.

Edwards, R., & Mauthner, M. (2002). Ethics and feminist research: Theory and practice. In M. Mauthner, M. Birch, J. Jessop, & T. Miller (Eds.), *Ethics in qualitative research* (pp. 14–31). London: Sage.

Eichler, M. (1988). *Families in Canada today*. Toronto: Gage.

Einstein, A. (1990). Living philosophies. In C. Fadiman (Ed.), *Living Philosophies* (pp. 3–6). Garden City, NY: Doubleday.

Elias, N. (1992). *Time: An essay*. Oxford, UK: Basil Blackwell.

Ellis, C., & Berger, L. (2002). Their story/my story/our story: Including the researcher's experience in interview research. In J. Gubrium & J. Holstein (Eds.), *Handbook of interview research: Context and method* (pp. 849–875). Thousand Oaks, CA: Sage.

Ellis, C., & Bochner, A. P. (2003). Autoethnography, personal narrative, reflexivity. In N. K. Denzin & Y. S. Lincoln (Eds.), *Collecting and interpreting qualitative materials* (2nd ed., pp. 199–258). Thousand Oaks, CA: Sage.

Enosh, G., & Buchbinder, E. (2005). The interactive construction of narrative styles in sensitive interviews: The case of domestic violence research. *Qualitative Inquiry, 11,* 588–617.

Erikson, E. (1963). *Childhood and society* (2nd ed.). New York: Norton.

Ezzy, D. (1998). Theorizing narrative identity: Symbolic interactionism and hermeneutics. *Sociological Quarterly, 39,* 239–252.

Farnsworth, E. B. (1996). Reflexivity and qualitative family research: Insider's perspectives in bereaving the loss of a child. In M. Sussman & J. Gilgun (Eds.), *The methods and methodologies of qualitative family research* (pp. 399–415). New York: Haworth.

Ferree, M. M. (1990). Beyond separate spheres: Feminism and family research. *Journal of Marriage and the Family, 52,* 866–884.

Fetterman, D. M. (1998). *Ethnography: Step by step*. Thousand Oaks, CA: Sage.

Fiese, B. H., & Bickham, N. L. (2004). Pin curling grandma's hair in the comfy chair: Parents' stories of growing up and potential links to socialization in preschool years. In M. W. Pratt & B. H. Fiese (Eds.), *Family stories and the life course: Across time and generations* (pp. 259–277). Mahwah, NJ: Lawrence Erlbaum.

Fiese, B. H., & Sameroff, A. J. (1999). The Family Narrative Consortium: A multidimensional approach to narratives. In B. H. Fiese, A. J. Sameroff, H. D. Grotevant, F. S. Wamboldt, S. Dickstein, & D. Fravel (Eds.), The stories that families tell: Narrative coherence, narrative interaction and relationship beliefs. *Monographs of the Society for Research in Child Development, 64*(2), 1–36.

Fiese, B. H., & Spagnola, M. (2005). Narratives in and about families: An examination of coding schemes and a guide for family researchers. *Journal of Family Psychology, 19,* 51–61.

Fiese, B. H., & Wamboldt, F. S. (2003). Coherent accounts of coping with a chronic illness: Convergences and divergences in family measurement using a narrative analysis. *Family Process, 42,* 439–451.

Fontanna, A. (2003). Postmodern trends in interviewing. In J. Gubrium & J. Holstein (Eds.), *Postmodern interviewing* (pp. 51–66). Thousand Oaks, CA: Sage.

Fraenkel, P. (1994). Time and rhythm in couples. *Family Process, 33,* 37–51.

Fraenkel, P. (2006). Engaging families as experts: Collaborative family program development. *Family Process, 45,* 237–257.

Fravel, D., & Boss, P. (1992). An in-depth interview with the parents of missing children. In J. Gilgun, K. Daly, & G. Handel (Eds.), *Qualitative methods in family research* (pp. 126–145). Newbury Park, CA: Sage.

Freire, P. (1972). *Pedagogy of the oppressed.* Harmondsworth, UK: Penguin.

Friedrichs, D. O. (1981). The problem of reconciling divergent perspectives on urban crime: Personal experience, social ideology and scholarly research. *Qualitative Sociology, 4,* 217.

Geertz, C. (1973). *The interpretation of cultures.* New York: Basic Books.

Geertz, C. (1983). *Local knowledge: Further essays in interpretive anthropology.* New York: Basic Books.

Gergen, K. (1985). The social constructionist movement in modern psychology. *American Psychologist, 40,* 266–275.

Gergen, K. J. (1994). Exploring the postmodern: Perils or potentials? *American Psychologist, 49,* 412–416.

Gergen, K. J., & Gergen, M. M. (1984). The social construction of narrative accounts. In K. J. Gergen & M. M. Gergen (Eds.), *Historical social psychology* (pp. 173–190). Hillsdale, NJ: Lawrence Erlbaum.

Gergen, M. M. (2004). Once upon a time: A narratologist's tale. In C. Daiute & C. Lightfoot (Eds.), *Narrative analysis: Studying the development of individuals in society* (pp. 267–285). Thousand Oaks, CA: Sage.

Gergen, M. M., & Gergen, K. J. (2003). Qualitative inquiry: Tensions and transformations. In N. K. Denzin & Y. S. Lincoln (Eds.), *The landscape of qualitative research: Theories and issues* (pp. 575–610). Thousand Oaks, CA: Sage.

Gibson, P. A. (2002). Caregiving role affects family relationships of African American grandmothers as new mothers again: A phenomenological perspective. *Journal of Marital and Family Therapy, 28,* 341–353.

Giddens, A. (1990). *The consequences of modernity.* Stanford, CA: Stanford University Press.

Giele, J. Z., & Elder, G. H. (1998). Life course research: Development of a field. In J. Z. Giele & G. H. Elder (Eds.), *Methods of life course research: Qualitative and quantitative approaches* (pp. 5–27). Thousand Oaks, CA: Sage.

Gilgun, J. (1995). We shared something special: The moral discourse of incest perpetrators. *Journal of Marriage and the Family, 57,* 265–281.

Gilgun, J. (2001). Grounded theory and other inductive research methods. In B. A. Thyer (Ed.), *Social work research methods* (pp. 345–364). Thousand Oaks, CA: Sage.

Gilgun, J. (2005a). Deductive qualitative analysis and family theory building. In V. Bengston, A. Acock, K. Allen, P. Dilworth-Anderson, & D. Klein (Eds.), *Sourcebook of family theory and research* (pp. 83–84). Thousand Oaks, CA: Sage.

Gilgun, J. (2005b). Qualitative research and family psychology. *Journal of Family Psychology, 19,* 40–50.

Giorgi, A., & Giorgi, B. (2003). Phenomenology. In J. A. Smith (Ed.), *Qualitative psychology: A practical guide to research methods* (pp. 25–50). London: Sage.

Glaser, B. (1992). *Basics of grounded theory analysis: Emergence vs. forcing.* Mill Valley, CA: Sociology Press.

Glaser, B., & Strauss, A. L. (1967). *The discovery of grounded theory: Strategies for qualitative research.* New York: Aldine.

Gobo, G. (2004). Sampling, representativeness and generalizability. In C. Seale, G. Gobo, J. F. Gubrium, & D. Silverman (Eds.), *Qualitative research practice* (pp. 435–456). Thousand Oaks, CA: Sage.

Goffman, E. (1959). *The presentation of self in everyday life.* Garden City, NY: Doubleday Anchor.

Goffman, E. (1974). *Frame analysis.* New York: Harper & Row.

Grahame, K. M. (2003). "For the family": Asian immigrant women's triple day. *Journal of Sociology and Social Welfare, 30,* 65–90.

Greer, S. (1969). *The logic of social inquiry.* Chicago: Aldine.

Guba, E., & Lincoln, Y. S. (1994). Competing paradigms in qualitative research. In N. K. Denzin & Y. S. Lincoln (Eds.), *Handbook of qualitative research* (pp. 105–117). Thousand Oaks, CA: Sage.

Gubrium, J. (1993). Introduction: Rethinking family as a social form. *Journal of Family Issues, 14,* 3–4.

Gubrium, J., & Holstein, J. (1990). *What is family?* Mountain View, CA: Mayfield.

Gubrium, J., & Holstein, J. (2003a). Analyzing interpretive practice. In N. K. Denzin & Y. S. Lincoln (Eds.), *Strategies of qualitative inquiry* (2nd ed., pp. 214–248). Thousand Oaks, CA: Sage.

Gubrium, J., & Holstein, J. (2003b). From the individual interview to the interview society. In J. Gubrium & J. Holstein (Eds.), *Postmodern interviewing* (pp. 21–50). Thousand Oaks, CA: Sage.

Gubrium, J., & Holstein, J. (2003c). Postmodern sensibilities. In J. Gubrium & J. Holstein (Eds.), *Postmodern interviewing* (pp. 3–18). Thousand Oaks, CA: Sage.

Gilgun, J. (1992). Definitions, methodologies and methods in qualitative family research. In J. Gilgun, K. Daly, & G. Handel (Eds.), *Qualitative methods in family research* (pp. 22–39). Newbury Park, CA: Sage.

Habermas, J. (1996). *Between facts and norms: Contributions to a discourse theory of law and democracy.* Cambridge: MIT Press.

Haig, B. D. (1996). Grounded theory as scientific method. *Philosophy of Education,* 281–294. Available online at http://www.ed.uiuc.edu/EPS/PES yearbook/95_docs/haig.html

Hammersley, M., & Atkinson, P. (1983). *Ethnography: Principles in practice.* London: Tavistock.

Hammersley, M., & Atkinson, P. (1995). *Ethnography: Principles in practice* (2nd ed.). London: Routledge.

Handel, G. (1996). Family worlds and qualitative family research: Emergence and prospects of whole family methodology. In M. Sussman & J. Gilgun, (Eds.), *The methods and methodologies of qualitative family research* (pp. 335–348). New York: Haworth.

Harding, S. (1987). Introduction: Is there a feminist method? In S. Harding (Ed.), *Feminism and methodology* (pp. 1–14). Bloomington: Indiana University Press.

Harding, S. (1991). *Whose science? Whose knowledge? Thinking from women's lives.* Ithaca, NY: Cornell University Press.

Hertz, R. (1996). Introduction: Ethics, reflexivity and voice. *Qualitative Sociology, 19,* 3–9.

Hertz, R. (1997). Introduction: Reflexivity and voice. In R. Hertz (Ed.), *Reflexivity and voice.* Thousand Oaks, CA: Sage.

Hess, R. D., & Handel, G. (1959). *Family worlds.* Chicago: University of Chicago Press.

Hill, E. (1966). *The language of drawing.* Englewood Cliffs, NJ: Prentice Hall.

Hochschild, A. (1997). *The time bind: When work becomes home and home becomes work.* New York: Henry Holt.

Holkup, P. A., Butcher, H. K., & Buckwalter, K. C. (2000). A phenomenological study of the experience of caring for a family member with Alzheimer's disease living at home. *The Gerontologist, 40,* 288.

Holstein, J. A., & Gubrium, J. F. (1994). Constructing family: Descriptive practice and domestic order. In T. R. Sarbin & J. Kitsuse (Eds.), *Constructing the social.* London: Sage.

Holstein, J. A., & Gubrium, J. F. (1995). Deprivatization and the construction of domestic life. *Journal of Marriage and the Family, 57,* 894–908.

hooks, b. (1992). Representations of whiteness in the black imagination. In b. hooks (Ed.), *Black Looks: Race and representation* (pp. 165–178). Boston: South End.

Hoppes, S. (2005). Meanings and purposes of caring for a family member: An autoethnography. *American Journal of Occupational Therapy, 59,* 262–272.

Jarrett, R. (1993). Focus group interviewing with low income minority populations: A research experience. In D. L. Morgan (Ed.), *Successful focus groups: Advancing the state of the art* (pp. 184–201). Newbury Park, CA: Sage.

Järviluoma, H., Moisala, P., & Vilkko, A. (2003). *Gender and qualitative methods.* London: Sage.

Johnson, J. (2002). In-depth interviewing. In J. Gubrium & J. Holstein (Eds.), *Handbook of interview research: Context and method* (pp. 103–119). Thousand Oaks, CA: Sage.

Joyce, J. (1964). *Portrait of the artist as a young man.* Thetford, Norfolk, UK: Lowe and Brydone Printers.

Katovich, M. A. (1987). Identity, time and situated activity: An interactionist analysis of dyadic transactions. *Symbolic Interaction, 10,* 187–208.

Keller, E. F. (1985). *Reflections on gender and science.* New Haven, CT: Yale University Press.

Kelly, S. E. (2005). In a different light: Examining impairment through parent narratives of a childhood disability. *Journal of Contemporary Ethnography, 34,* 180–205.

Kemmis, S., & McTaggart, R. (2003). Participatory action research. In N. K. Denzin & Y. S. Lincoln (Eds.), *Strategies of qualitative inquiry* (2nd ed., pp. 336–396). Thousand Oaks, CA: Sage.

Kincheloe, J. L., & McLaren, P. (2003). Rethinking critical theory and qualitative research. In N. K. Denzin & Y. S. Lincoln (Eds.), *The landscape of qualitative research: Theories and issues* (pp. 433–488). Thousand Oaks, CA: Sage.

Kleinman, S. (1991). Field-workers' feelings: What we feel, who we are, how we analyze. In W. Shaffir & R. A. Stebbins (Eds.), *Experiencing fieldwork: An inside view of qualitative research* (pp. 184–195), Newbury Park, CA: Sage.

Kleinman, S., & Copp, M. A. (1993). *Emotions and fieldwork.* Newbury Park, CA: Sage.

Knudson-Martin, C., & Mahoney, A. R. (2005). Moving beyond gender: Processes that create relationship equality. *Journal of Marital and Family Therapy, 31,* 235–246.

Kong, T. S., Mahoney, D., & Plummer, K. (2002). Queering the interview. In J. Gubrium & J. Holstein (Eds.), *Handbook of interview research: Context and method* (pp. 239–258). Thousand Oaks, CA: Sage.

Kral, M. J, Burkhardt, K. J., & Kidd, S. (2002). The new research agenda for cultural psychology. *Canadian Psychology, 43,* 154–162.

Kreppner, K. (2005). Analyzing family interaction patterns from videotapes over time. In V. Bengston, A. Acock, K. Allen, P. Dilworth-Anderson, & D. Klein (Eds.), *Sourcebook of family theory and research* (pp. 80–82). Thousand Oaks, CA: Sage.

Krieger, S. (1991). *Social science and the self: Personal essays on an art form.* New Brunswick, NJ: Rutgers University Press.

Kuczynski, L. (Ed.). (2003). *Handbook of dynamics in parent-child relations.* Thousand Oaks, CA: Sage.

Kuczynski, L., & Daly, K. J. (2003). Qualitative methods for inductive (theory generating) research: Psychological and sociological approaches. In L. Kuczynski (Ed.), *Handbook of dynamics in parent-child relations* (pp. 373–392). Thousand Oaks, CA: Sage.

Kuhn, T. (1962). *The structure of scientific revolutions.* Chicago: University of Chicago Press.

Kvale, S. (1977). Dialectics and research on remembering. In N. Datan & H. Reese (Eds.), *Life-span developmental psychology* (pp. 165–190). New York: Academic Press.

Kvale, S. (1995). The social construction of validity. *Qualitative Inquiry, 1,* 19–40.

Kvale, S. (1996). *InterViews: An introduction to qualitative research interviewing.* Thousand Oaks, CA: Sage.

Ladkin, D. (2004). Action research. In C. Seale, G. Gobo, J. F. Gubrium, & D. Silverman (Eds.), *Qualitative research practice* (pp. 536–548). Thousand Oaks, CA: Sage.

Lareau, A. (2002). Invisible inequality: Social class and childrearing in black families and white families. *American Sociological Review, 67,* 747–776.

LaRossa, R. (2005). Grounded theory methods and qualitative family research. *Journal of Marriage and Family, 67,* 837–857.

LaSala, M. C. (2002). Walls and bridges: How coupled gay men and lesbians manage their intergenerational relationships. *Journal of Marital and Family Therapy, 28,* 327–339.

Lather, P. (1986). Research as praxis. *Harvard Educational Review, 56,* 256–277.

Lather, P. (1990). Reinscribing otherwise: The play of values in the practices of the human sciences. In E. Guba (Ed.), *The paradigm dialog* (pp. 315–332). Newbury Park, CA: Sage.

Lather, P. (1991). *Getting smart: Feminist research and pedagogy with/in the post-modern.* New York: Routledge.

Legard, R., Keegan, J., & Ward, K. (2003). In-depth interviews. In J. Ritchie & J. Lewis (Eds.), *Qualitative research practice: A guide for social science students and researchers* (pp. 138–169). London: Sage.

Lewis, J. (2003). Design issues. In J. Ritchie & J. Lewis (Eds.), *Qualitative research practice: A guide for social science students and researchers* (pp. 47–76). London: Sage.

Lewis, J., & Ritchie, J. (2003). Generalising from qualitative research. In J. Ritchie & J. Lewis (Eds.), *Qualitative research practice: A guide for social science students and researchers* (pp. 263–286). London: Sage.

Lincoln, Y. S., & Guba, E. G. (1985). *Naturalistic inquiry.* Newbury Park, CA: Sage.

Lofland, J. (1971). *Analyzing social settings: A guide to qualitative observation and analysis.* Belmont, CA: Wadsworth.

Lollis, S., & Kuczynski. (1997). Beyond one hand clapping: Seeing bidirectionality in parent-child relations. *Journal of Social and Personal Relationships, 14,* 441–461.

Lopata, H. (1971). *Occupation: Housewife.* New York: Oxford University Press.

Lynch, M. (2000). Against reflexivity as an academic source of privileged knowledge. *Theory, Culture & Society, 17,* 26–54.

Lyotard, J.-F. (1984). *The post-modern condition: A report on knowledge.* Minneapolis: University of Minnesota Press.

Macnaghten, P., & Myers, G. (2004). Focus groups. In C. Seale, G. Gobo, J. F. Gubrium, & D. Silverman (Eds.), *Qualitative research practice* (pp. 65–79). Thousand Oaks, CA: Sage.

Madden Derdich, D. A., Leonard, S. A., & Gunnell, G. A. (2002). Parents' and children's perceptions of family processes in inner city families with delinquent youths: A qualitative investigation. *Journal of Marital and Family Therapy, 28,* 355–369.

Madriz, E. (2003). Focus groups in feminist research. In N. K. Denzin & Y. S. Lincoln (Eds.), *Collecting and interpreting qualitative materials* (2nd ed., pp. 363–388). Thousand Oaks, CA: Sage.

Maines, D. (1993). Narrative's moment and sociology's phenomena. *The Sociological Quarterly, 34,* 17–38.

Marcus, G., & Fischer, M. M. J. (1986). *Anthropology as cultural critique.* Chicago: University of Chicago Press.

Marks, L. (2004). Sacred practices in highly religious families: Christian, Jewish, Mormon and Muslim perspectives. *Family Process, 43,* 217–231.

Mason, J. (2002). *Qualitative researching* (2nd ed.). London: Sage.

Masterman, M. (1970). The nature of a paradigm. In I. Lakatos & A. Musgrave (Eds.), *Criticism and the growth of knowledge.* Cambridge, UK: Cambridge University Press.

Matta, D. S., & Knudson-Martin, C. (2006). Father responsivity: Couple processes and the coconstruction of fatherhood. *Family Process, 45,* 19–37.

Matthews, S. (2005). Crafting qualitative research articles on marriages and families. *Journal of Marriage and Family, 67,* 799–808.

Mauthner, N. S., & Doucet, A. (2003). Reflexive accounts and accounts of reflexivity in qualitative data analysis. *Sociology, 37,* 413–431.

Maxwell, J. A. (2005). *Qualitative research design: An interactive approach* (2nd ed.). Thousand Oaks, CA: Sage.

McAdams, D. (2004). Generativity and the narrative ecology of family life. In M. W. Pratt & B. H. Fiese (Eds.), *Family stories and the life course: Across time and generations* (pp. 235–258). Mahwah, NJ: Lawrence Erlbaum.

McBride Murray, V., & Brody, G. H. (2004). Partnering with community stakeholders: Engaging rural African American families in basic research and the strong African American Families Preventative Intervention Program. *Journal of Marital and Family Therapy, 30,* 271–283.

McCall, M. M. (2003). Performance ethnography: A brief history and some advice. In N. K. Denzin & Y. S. Lincoln (Eds.), *Strategies of qualitative inquiry* (2nd ed., pp. 112–133). Thousand Oaks, CA: Sage.

McCracken, G. (1988a). *Culture and consumption: New approaches to the symbolic character of goods and activities.* Bloomington: Indiana University Press.

McCracken, G. (1988b). *The long interview.* Newbury Park, CA: Sage.

Mead, G. H. (1932). *The philosophy of the present.* La Salle, IL: Open Court.

Mead, G. H. (1934). *Mind, self and society.* Chicago: University of Chicago Press.

Mendenhall, T. J., & Doherty, W. J. (2005). Action research methods in family therapy. In D. Sprenkle & F. P. Piercy (Eds.), *Research methods in family therapy* (2nd ed., pp. 100–118). New York: Guilford.

Miller, B. (1993). Families, science and values: Alternative views of parenting effects and adolescent pregnancy. *Journal of Marriage and the Family, 55,* 7–21.

Miller, R. L. (2000). *Researching life stories and family histories.* Thousand Oaks, CA: Sage.

Mitchell, T., & Radford, J. L. (1996). Rethinking research relationships in qualitative research. *Canadian Journal of Community Mental Health, 15,* 49–60.

Montgomery, K. S. (2002). Planned adolescent pregnancy: What they wanted. *Journal of Pediatric Health Care, 16,* 282–289.

Morgan, D. L. (1988). *Focus groups as qualitative research.* Newbury Park, CA: Sage.

Morgan, D. L. (1999). Risk and family practices: Accounting for change and fluidity in family life. In E. B. Silva & C. Smart (Eds.), *The new family* (pp. 13–30). London: Sage.

Morgan, D. L. (2002). Focus group interviewing. In J. Gubrium & J. Holstein (Eds.), *Handbook of interview research: Context and method* (pp. 141–159). Thousand Oaks, CA: Sage.

Morse, J. (1994). Designing funded qualitative research. In N. K. Denzin & Y. S. Lincoln (Eds.), *Handbook of qualitative research* (pp. 220–235). Thousand Oaks, CA: Sage.

Morse, J. (2002). Interviewing the ill. In J. Gubrium & J. Holstein (Eds.), *Handbook of interview research: Context and method* (pp. 317–328). Thousand Oaks, CA: Sage.

Morse, J. (2004). Preparing and evaluating qualitative research proposals. In C. Seale, G. Gobo, J. F. Gubrium, & D. Silverman (Eds.), *Qualitative research practice* (pp. 493–503). Thousand Oaks, CA: Sage.

Morse, J., & Richards, L. (2002). *Read me first for a user's guide to qualitative methods.* Thousand Oaks, CA: Sage.

Moustakis, C. (1990). *Heuristic research design, methodology and applications.* Newbury Park, CA: Sage.

Murray, M. (2003). Narrative psychology. In J. A. Smith (Ed.), *Qualitative psychology: A practical guide to research methods* (pp. 111–131). London: Sage.

Nespor, J. (1998). The meanings of research: Kids as subjects and kids as inquirers. *Qualitative Inquiry, 4,* 369–388.

Neugarten, B. L. (1968). Adult personality: Toward a social psychology of the life cycle. In B. L. Neugarten (Ed.), *Middle age and aging: A reader in social psychology* (pp. 137–147). Chicago: University of Chicago Press.

Oakley, A. (1974). *The sociology of housework.* London: Martin Robertson.

Oakley, A. (1981). Interviewing women: A contradiction in terms. In H. Roberts (Ed.), *Doing feminist research* (pp. 30–61). London: Routledge & Kegan Paul.

Olson, M. M., Russell, C. S., Higgins-Kessler, M., & R. Miller. (2002). Emotional processes following disclosure of an extramarital affair. *Journal of Marital and Family Therapy, 28,* 423–434.

Osmond, M. W., & Thorne, B. (1993). Feminist theories: The social construction of gender in families and society. In P. G. Boss, W. Doherty, R. LaRossa, W. Schumm, & S. K. Steinmetz (Eds.), *Sourcebook of family theories and methods* (pp. 591–623). New York: Plenum.

Oswald, R. F. (2002). Who am I in relation to them? Gay, lesbian, and queer people leave the city to attend rural family weddings. *Journal of Family Issues, 23,* 323–348.

Overton, W. F. (1991). Metaphor, recursive systems, and paradox in science and developmental theory. In H. W. Reese (Ed.), *Advances in child development and behavior* (pp. 59–71). New York: Academic Press.

Palkovitz, R. (2002). *Involved fathering and men's adult development: Provisional balances.* Mahwah, NJ: Lawrence Erlbaum.

Parker, I. (1994). Qualitative research. In P. Banister, E. Burman, I. Parker, M. Taylor, & C. Tindall (Eds.), *Qualitative methods in psychology: A research guide* (pp. 1–16). Buckingham, UK: Open University Press.

Parra-Cardona, J. R., Wampler, R. S., & Sharp, E. A. (2006). "Wanting to be a good father": Experiences of adolescent fathers of Mexican descent in a teen fathers program. *Journal of Marital and Family Therapy, 32,* 215–231.

Patton, M. (1997). *Utilization-focused evaluation* (3rd ed.). Thousand Oaks, CA: Sage.

Piercy, F., & Benson, K. (2005). Aesthetic forms of data representation in qualitative family therapy research. *Journal of Marital and Family Therapy, 31,* 107–119.

Piercy, F., & Hertlein, K. M. (2005). Focus groups in family therapy research. In D. Sprenkle & F. P. Piercy (Eds.), *Research methods in family therapy* (2nd ed., pp. 85–99). New York: Guilford.

Poland, B. D. (2002). Transcription quality. In J. Gubrium & J. Holstein (Eds.), *Handbook of interview research: Context and method* (pp. 629–650). Thousand Oaks, CA: Sage.

Popper, K. (1959). *The logic of scientific discovery.* New York: Basic Books.

Pratt, M., & Fiese, B. H. (2004). Families, stories and the life course: An ecological context. In M. W. Pratt & B. H. Fiese (Eds.), *Family stories and the life course: Across time and generations* (pp. 1–24). Mahwah, NJ: Lawrence Erlbaum.

Prus, R. (1987). Generic social processes: Maximizing conceptual development in ethnographic research. *Journal of Contemporary Ethnography, 16,* 250–293.

Prus, R. (1994). Approaching the study of human group life: Symbolic interaction and ethnographic inquiry. In M. L. Dietz, R. Prus, & W. Shaffir (Eds.), *Doing everyday life: Ethnography as human lived experience* (pp. 10–29). Toronto: Copp Clarke Longman.

Prus, R. (1998). Respecting the human condition: Pursuing intersubjectivity in the market place. In S. Grills (Ed.), *Doing ethnographic research: Fieldwork settings* (pp. 21–47). Thousand Oaks, CA: Sage.

Rapley, T. (2004). Interviews. In C. Seale, G. Gobo, J. F. Gubrium, & D. Silverman (Eds.), *Qualitative research practice* (pp. 15–33). Thousand Oaks, CA: Sage.

Reinharz, S. (1992). *Feminist methods in social research.* New York: Oxford University Press.

Reinharz, S., & Chase, S. E. (2002). Interviewing women. In J. Gubrium & J. Holstein (Eds.), *Handbook of interview research: Context and method* (pp. 221–238). Thousand Oaks, CA: Sage.

Richardson, L. (2003). Writing: A method of inquiry. In N. K. Denzin & Y. S. Lincoln (Eds.), *Collecting and interpreting qualitative materials* (2nd ed., pp. 499–541). Thousand Oaks, CA: Sage.

Ricoeur, P. (1981). The narrative function. In P. Ricoeur (Ed.), *Hermeneutics and the human sciences.* Cambridge, UK: Cambridge University Press.

Riessman, C. K. (1993). *Narrative analysis.* Newbury Park, CA: Sage.

Roberto, K., Allen, K., & Bleizner, R. (2001). Older adults' preferences for future care: Formal plans and familial support. *Adult Developmental Science, 5,* 112–120.

Roberts, J. M. (1997). *The Penguin history of the world* (3rd ed.). London: Penguin.

Rosaldo, R. (1989). *Culture and truth: The remaking of social analysis.* Boston: Beacon.

Rosenau, P. M. (1992). *Post-modernism and the social sciences: Insights, inroads and intrusions.* Princeton, NJ: Princeton University Press.

Rosenblatt, P. (1995a). Ethics of qualitative interviewing with grieving families. *Death Studies, 19,* 139–155.

Rosenblatt, P. (1995b). *Multiracial couples: Black and white voices.* Thousand Oaks, CA: Sage.

Rosenblatt, P. (2002). Interviewing at the border of fact and fiction. In J. Gubrium & J. Holstein (Eds.), *Handbook of interview research: Context and method* (pp. 893–909). Thousand Oaks, CA: Sage.

Rosenblatt, P., & Stewart, C. C. (2004). Challenges in cross-cultural marriage: When she is Chinese and he Euro-American. *Sociological Focus, 37,* 43–58.

Rosenthal, G. (2004). Biographical research. In C. Seale, G. Gobo, J. F. Gubrium, & D. Silverman (Eds.), *Qualitative research practice* (pp. 48–64). Thousand Oaks, CA: Sage.

Rossman, B., & Rallis, S. (2003). *Learning in the field: An introduction to qualitative research.* Thousand Oaks, CA: Sage.

Rostosky, S. S., Korfhage, B. A., Duhigg, J. M., Stern, A. J., Bennett, L., & Riggle, E. D. (2004). Same-sex couple perceptions of family support: A consensual qualitative study. *Journal of Marital and Family Therapy, 43,* 43–57.

Rothe, J. (1993). *Qualitative research: A practical guide.* Toronto: RCI Publications.

Roy, K., Tubbs, C. Y., & Burton, L. (2004). Don't have no time: Daily rhythms and the organization of time for low-income families. *Family Relations, 53,* 168–178.

Rubin, H. J., & Rubin, I. S. (2005). *Qualitative interviewing: The art of hearing data* (2nd ed.). Thousand Oaks, CA: Sage.

Saffilios-Rothschild, C. (1969). Family sociology or wives' family sociology? A cross-cultural examination of decision making. *Journal of Marriage and the Family, 31,* 290–301.

Sandelowski, M. (1993). *With child in mind: Studies in the personal encounter with infertility.* Philadelphia: University of Pennsylvania Press.

Sarbin, T. R. (2004). The role of imagination in narrative construction. In C. Daiute & C. Lightfoot (Eds.), *Narrative analysis: Studying the development of individuals in society* (pp. 5–20). Thousand Oaks, CA: Sage.

Sassler, S. (2004). The process of entering into cohabiting unions. *Journal of Marriage and Family, 66,* 491–505.

Savvidou, I., Bozikas, V. P., Hatzigeleki, S., & Karavatos, A. (2003). Narratives about their children by mothers hospitalized on a psychiatric unit. *Family Process, 42,* 391–402.

Schutz, A. (1971). *Collected papers I: The problem of social reality.* The Hague: Martinus Nijhoff.

Schwalbe, M., & Wolkomir, M. (2002). Interviewing men. In J. Gubrium & J. Holstein (Eds.), *Handbook of interview research: Context and method* (pp. 203–219). Thousand Oaks, CA: Sage.

Seale, C., Gobo, G., Gubrium, J., & Silverman, D. (2004). Introduction: Inside qualitative research. In C. Seale, G. Gobo, J. F. Gubrium, & D. Silverman (Eds.), *Qualitative research practice* (pp. 1–11). Thousand Oaks, CA: Sage.

Senter, K. E., & Caldwell, K. (2002). Spirituality and the maintenance of change: A phenomenological study of women who leave abusive relationships. *Contemporary Family Therapy, 24,* 543–564.

Sevón, E. (2005). Timing motherhood: Experiencing and narrating the choice to become a mother. *Feminism & Psychology, 15,* 461–482.

Shank, G., & Cunningham, D. J. (1996). Modeling the six modes of Peircean abduction for educational purposes. Retrieved September 25, 2006, from http://www.cs.indiana.edu/event/maics96/Proceedings/shank.html

Shehan, C. (Ed.). (1999). *Through the eyes of the child: Revisioning children as active agents of family life.* Stamford, CT: JAI.

Shweder, R. A. (1996). Quanta and qualia: What is the "object" of ethnographic method? In R. Jessor, A. Colby, & R. A. Shweder (Eds.), *Ethnography and human development* (pp. 53–71). Chicago: University of Chicago Press.

Singleton, R. A., & Straits, B. C. (2002). Survey interviewing. In J. Gubrium & J. Holstein (Eds.), *Handbook of interview research: Context and method* (pp. 59–82). Thousand Oaks, CA: Sage.

Small, S., & Uttal, L. (2005). Action oriented research: Strategies for engaged scholarship. *Journal of Marriage and Family, 67,* 936–948.

Smith, D. (1993). The standard North American family: SNAF as an ideological code. *Journal of Family Issues, 14,* 50–65.

Smith, J., & Osborn, M. (2003). Interpretive phenomenological analysis. In J. A. Smith (Ed.), *Qualitative psychology: A practical guide to research methods* (pp. 51–80). London: Sage.

Speer, S. A. (2002). What can conversation analysis contribute to feminist methodology? Putting reflexivity into practice. *Discourse & Society, 13,* 783–803.

Spiegleberg, H. (1972). Phenomenology in psychology and psychiatry: A historical introduction. Evanston, IL: Northwestern University Press.

Spradley, J. P. (1980). *Participant observation.* New York: Holt, Rinehart & Winston.

Sprenkle, D., & Piercy, F. P. (2005). Pluralism, diversity and sophistication in family therapy research. In D. Sprenkle & F. P. Piercy (Eds.), *Research methods in family therapy* (2nd ed., pp. 3–18). New York: Guilford.

Stake, R. E. (2003). Case studies. In N. K. Denzin & Y. S. Lincoln (Eds.), *Strategies of qualitative inquiry* (pp. 134–164). Thousand Oaks, CA: Sage.

Stanley, L., & Wise, S. (1983). *Breaking out: Feminist consciousness and feminist research.* London: Routledge & Kegan Paul.

Strauss, A. (1959). *Mirrors and masks: The search for identity.* Glencoe, IL: Free Press.

Strauss, A. (1987). *Qualitative analysis for social scientists.* Cambridge, UK: Cambridge University Press.

Strauss, A., & Corbin, J. (1990). *The basics of grounded theory.* Newbury Park, CA: Sage.

Strauss, A., & Corbin, J. (1998). *The basics of grounded theory* (2nd ed.). Thousand Oaks, CA: Sage.

Stringer, E. T. (1999). *Action research* (2nd ed.). Thousand Oaks, CA: Sage.

Swidler, A. (1986). Culture in action: Symbols and strategies. *American Sociological Review, 51,* 273–286.

Swidler, A. (2001). *Talk of love: How culture matters.* Chicago: University of Chicago Press.

Sword, W. (1999). Accounting for the presence of self: Reflections on doing qualitative research. *Qualitative Health Research, 9,* 270–278.

Tedlock, B. (2003). Ethnography and ethnographic representation. In N. K. Denzin & Y. S. Lincoln (Eds.), *Strategies of qualitative inquiry* (pp. 165–213). Thousand Oaks, CA: Sage.

Thomas, W. I., & Znaniecki, F. (1958). *The Polish Peasant in Europe and America.* New York: Dover. (Original work published 1918)

Thompson, L., & Walker, L. (1995). The place of feminism in family studies. *Journal of Marriage and the Family, 57,* 847–865.

Thorne, B. (1982). Feminist rethinking of the family. In B. Thorne & M. Yalom (Eds.), *Rethinking the family: Some feminist questions* (pp. 1–24). New York: Longman.

Tierney, W. G. (2003). Undaunted courage: Life history and the postmodern challenge. In N. K. Denzin & Y. S. Lincoln (Eds.), *Strategies of qualitative inquiry* (2nd ed., pp. 292–318). Thousand Oaks, CA: Sage.

Tindall, C. (1994). Issues of evaluation. In P. Banister, E. Burman, I. Parker, M. Taylor, & C. Tindall (Eds.), *Qualitative methods in psychology: A research guide* (pp. 142–159). Buckingham, UK: Open University Press.

Tubbs, C. Y., & Burton, L. M. (2005). Bridging research: Using clinical practice to inform clinical practice. In D. Sprenkle & F. P. Piercy (Eds.), *Research methods in family therapy* (2nd ed., pp. 136–154). New York: Guilford.

Tubbs, C. Y., Roy, K., & Burton, L. (2005). Family ties: Constructing family time in low income families. *Family Process, 44,* 77–91.

Turner, W. L., Wallace, B. R., Anderson, J. R., & Bird, C. B. (2004). The last mile of the way: Understanding caregiving in African American families at the end-of-life. *Journal of Marital and Family Therapy, 30,* 427–438.

Van Langenhove, L., & Harré, R. (1993). Positioning and autobiography: Telling your life. In N. Coupland & J. F. Nussbaum (Eds.), *Discourse and lifespan identity* (pp. 81–100). Newbury Park, CA: Sage.

Van Maanen, J. (1988). *Tales of the field: On writing ethnography.* Chicago: University of Chicago Press.

Van Maanen, J. (1990). *Researching lived experience: Human science for an action sensitive pedagogy.* London: Althouse.

Vidich, A. J., & Lyman, S. M. (2003). Qualitative methods: Their history in sociology and anthropology. In N. K. Denzin & Y. S. Lincoln (Eds.), *The landscape of qualitative research: Theories and issues* (pp. 55–129). Thousand Oaks, CA: Sage.

Vygotsky, L. S. (1962). *Thought and language.* Cambridge, MA: MIT Press.

Vygotsky, L. S. (1978). *Mind in society.* Cambridge, MA: Harvard University Press.

Warren, C. A. (2002). Qualitative interviewing. In J. Gubrium & J. Holstein (Eds.), *Handbook of interview research: Context and method* (pp. 83–101). Thousand Oaks, CA: Sage.

Wax, R. (1971). *Doing fieldwork: Warnings and advice.* Chicago: University of Chicago Press.

Weirsma, N. S. (2003). Partner awareness regarding the adult sequalae of childhood sexual abuse for primary and secondary survivors. *Journal of Marital and Family Therapy, 29,* 151–164.

Wenger, G. C. (2002). Interviewing older people. In J. Gubrium & J. Holstein (Eds.), *Handbook of interview research: Context and method* (pp. 259–298). Thousand Oaks, CA: Sage.

West, C., & Zimmerman, D. H. (1987). Doing gender. *Gender and Society, 1,* 125–151.

White, M., & Epston, D. (1990). *Narrative means to therapeutic ends.* New York: W. W. Norton.

Wight, D. (1994). Boys' thoughts and talk about sex in a working class locality of Glasgow. *Sociological Review, 42,* 702–737.

Wilkinson, S. (1988). The role of reflexivity in feminist psychology. *Women's Studies International Forum, 1,* 493–502.

Wilkinson, S. (2004). Focus group research. In D. Silverman (Ed.), *Qualitative research: Theory, method and practice* (pp. 177–199). London: Sage.

Wolff, K. H. (1964). Surrender and community study: The study of Loma. In A. J. Vidich, J. Bensman, & M. R. Stein (Eds.), *Reflections on community studies* (pp. 233–264). New York: John Wiley.

Wright, K. (2003). Relationships with death: The terminally ill talk about dying. *Journal of Marital and Family Therapy, 29,* 439–454.

Zvonkovic, A. M., Manoogian, M., & McGraw, L. A. (2001). The ebb and flow of family life: How families experience being together and apart. In K. J. Daly (Ed.), *Minding the time in family experience: Emerging perspectives and issues* (pp. 135–160). Stamford, CT: JAI.

Zvonkovic, A. M., Solomon, C. R., Humble, A. M., & Manoogian, M. (2005). Family work and relationships: Lessons from families of men whose jobs require travel. *Family Relations, 54,* 411–422.

Index

About the Author

Kerry J. Daly (PhD, Sociology, McMaster University) is a full professor in the Department of Family Relations and Applied Nutrition at the University of Guelph. In more than a decade of teaching a graduate course on qualitative methods, he has had students from his own interdisciplinary department as well as students from Psychology, Sociology, Nursing, and Nutrition, thus sensitizing him to the many different values and procedures that exist across the varied audiences and disciplines that contribute to family studies. With Jane Gilgun and Gerald Handel, he coedited the book *Qualitative Methods in Family Research* (Sage, 1992), and he has authored a number of articles focusing on qualitative methodology in journals such as *Qualitative Inquiry, The Journal of Contemporary Ethnography, Qualitative Sociology, Symbolic Interaction,* and *Journal of Marriage & Family.* He coauthored the chapter on qualitative research methods in Leon Kuczynski's *Handbook of Dynamics in Parent-Child Relations* (Sage, 2003). He was recipient of the Anselm Strauss Award for the best qualitative research article in 2001. He was a member of the Steering Committee for the Qualitative Family Research Network, then Chair for three years, and served for a period as Editor of the *Qualitative Family Research* newsletter. His teaching, research, and professional background combine to offer the perfect combination for undertaking this new text.